Language in Context in TESOL

Language in Context in TESOL

Joan Cutting

EDINBURGH
University Press

Edinburgh University Press Ltd
The Tun – Holyrood Road, 12(2f) Jackson's Entry, Edinburgh EH8 8PJ

www.euppublishing.com

Typeset in 10/12 Minion by
Servis Filmsetting Ltd, Stockport, Cheshire,
and printed and bound in Great Britain by
CPI Group (UK) Ltd, Croydon CR0 4YY

A CIP record for this book is available from the British Library

ISBN 978 0 7486 4282 3 (hardback)
ISBN 978 0 7486 9927 8 (webready PDF)
ISBN 978 0 7486 4281 6 (paperback)
ISBN 978 0 7486 9928 5 (epub)

CONTENTS

FIGURES AND TABLES

FIGURES

TABLES

ABBREVIATIONS

ACE	Asian Corpus of English
AL	Applied Linguistics
BNC	British National Corpus
CA	Conversation Analysis
CANCODE	Cambridge and Nottingham Corpus of Discourse in English
CIC Cambridge	International Corpus
CL Corpus	Linguistics
CLC Cambridge	Learner Corpus
COCA	Corpus of Contemporary American English
CP	Cooperative Principle
CS	code-switching
DDL	data-driven learning
EAP	English for Academic Purposes
EIL	English as an International Language
ELF	English as a Lingua Franca
ELFA	English as a Lingua Franca in Academic Settings
ELT	English Language Teaching
ENL	English as a Native Language
ESL	English as a Second Language
ET	Exchange Theory
FTA	face-threatening act
GE	Global Englishes
ICE	International Corpus of English
ICLE	International Corpus of Learner English
KWIC	key words in context
MICASE	Michigan Corpus of Academic Spoken English
NES	native English speaker
NNES	non-native English speaker
SAT	Speech Act Theory
SCOTS	Scottish Corpus of Texts and Speech
SELF	Studying in English as a Lingua Franca
SLA	second language acquisition
VOICE	Vienna–Oxford International Corpus of English
WE	World Englishes

TRANSCRIPTION SYMBOLS

//   **Interruption,** e.g.

        A   Hey, what are you do- //

        B   // I'm just checking my emails

        in which A is prevented from finishing her utterance by B's words

=   **Overlap,** e.g.

        A   Hey, what are you doing? =

        B   = I'm just checking my emails

        in which B's first words occur simultaneously with A's words but do not prevent A from finishing her utterance

(0.5)   **Pause,** expressed as number of seconds, e.g.

        A   Hey, what are you doing?

        B   I'm just (2) checking my emails

        in which B hesitates for two seconds while he thinks or is distracted by actually reading his emails as he speaks

[laughs]   **Non-verbal sounds or gestures,** e.g.

        A   Hey, what are you doing? [snaps her fingers]

        B   I'm just [sighs] checking my emails

        in which extraneous noises, meaningful or otherwise, are noted.

ACKNOWLEDGEMENTS

Many thanks to my colleagues for our many explanations, discussions and rewritings to get these chapters into shape. I offer thanks to Aled Owen for his editorial comments aimed at increasing the accessibility of the text. I am most grateful to Fiona Farr, co-editor of the *Edinburgh Textbooks in TESOL* series, for her invaluable and insightful suggestions. Thanks to the series Editorial Board for extending their experience to the development of the series.

Joan Cutting

SERIES EDITORS' PREFACE

Editors Joan Cutting, University of Edinburgh and Fiona Farr, University of Limerick

This series of textbooks addresses a range of topics taught within **TESOL programmes** around the world. Each volume is designed to match a taught 'core' or 'option' course (identified by a survey of TESOL programmes worldwide) and could be adopted as a prescribed text. Other series and books have been aimed at Applied Linguistics students or language teachers in general, but this aims more specifically at students of ELT (English Language Teaching – the process of enabling the learning of English), with or without teaching experience.

The series is intended primarily for college and university students at third or fourth year undergraduate level, and graduates (pre-service or in-service) studying TESOL on Masters programmes and possibly some TESOL EdDs or structured PhDs, all of whom need an introduction to the topics for their taught courses. It is also very suitable for new professionals and people starting out on a PhD, who could use the volumes for self-study. The **readership level** is **introductory** and the tone and approach of the volumes will appeal to both undergraduates and postgraduates.

This series answers a need for volumes with a special focus on **intercultural awareness**. It is aimed at programmes in countries where English is not the mother tongue, and in English-speaking countries where the majority of students come from countries where English is not the mother tongue, typical of TESOL programmes in the UK and Ireland, Canada and the US, Australia and New Zealand. This means that it takes into account physical and economic conditions in ELT classrooms round the world and a variety of socio-educational backgrounds. Each volume contains a number of tasks which include examples from classrooms around the world, encourage comparisons across cultures and address issues that apply to each student's home context. Closely related to the intercultural awareness focus is a minor theme that runs throughout the series, and that is language analysis and description, and its applications to ELT. Intercultural awareness is indeed a complex concept and we aim to address it in a number of different ways. Taking examples from different cultural contexts is one way of tackling the issue of intercultural awareness, but the volumes in the series also look at many other educationally relevant cultural dimensions such as sociolinguistic influences, gender issues, various learning traditions (e.g. collectivist vs individualistic), culturally determined language dimensions (e.g. politeness conventions).

TESOL students need **theory clearly related to practice**. This series is practical and is intended to be used in TESOL lectures and workshops, providing group tasks and independent activities. Students are invited to engage in critical thinking and to consider applications of concepts and issues to their own particular teaching contexts, adapting the tendencies and suggestions in the literature to their own countries' educational requirements. Each volume contains practical tasks to carry out individually, in small groups or in plenary in the classroom, as well as suggestions for practical tasks for the students to use in their own classrooms. All the concepts and issue encountered here will be translatable into the ELT classroom. It is hoped that this series will contribute to your improvement as a teacher.

The series presents ELT concepts and research issues **simply**. The volumes guide students from the basic concepts, through the issues and complexities, to a level that should make them alert to past and recent teaching and research developments in each field. This series makes the topics accessible to those unaccustomed to reading theoretical literature, and yet takes them to an exam and Master's standard, serving as a gateway into the various fields and an introduction to the more theoretical literature. We also acknowledge that technology is a major area within TESOL and this series is aware of the need for technology to feature prominently across its volumes. Issues of technological integration and implementation are addressed in some way in each of the volumes. The series is based on state-of-the-art research. The concepts and issues raised are intended to inspire students to undertake their own research and consider pursuing their interests in a PhD.

Editorial Advisory Board

As well as the two editors, the series has an Editorial Advisory Board, whose members are involved in decisions on commissioning and considering book proposals and reviewing book drafts. We would like to acknowledge and thank members of the Board for all of their work and guidance on the Textbooks in TESOL series:

- Prof. David Bloch, University of London, UK
- Dr Averil Coxhead, Victoria University of Wellington, New Zealand
- Prof. Donald Freeman, University of Michigan, USA
- Mr Peter Grundy, Northumbria University, UK
- Ms Annie Hughes, University of York, UK
- Prof. Mike McCarthy, University of Nottingham, UK
- Dr Liam Murray, University of Limerick, Ireland
- Dr Anne O'Keeffe, Mary Immaculate College, University of Limerick, Ireland
- Dr Jonathon Reinhardt, University of Arizona, USA
- Prof. Randi Reppen, North Arizona University, USA

- Assoc. Prof. Ali Shehadeh, UAE University, United Arab Emirates
- Assoc. Prof. Scott Thornbury, the New School, New York, USA
- Prof. Steve Walsh, Newcastle University, UK

AUTHOR AND CONTRIBUTOR BIOGRAPHIES

Joan Cutting (PhD Edinburgh) is a Senior Lecturer in TESOL at the University of Edinburgh, where she teaches courses on TESOL methodology, materials evaluation and design, curriculum development, and text and discourse for TESOL. She researches vague language, in-group code, English for Specific Purposes, Scottish English, cross-cultural differences and international students' interactions in UK Higher Education. She was meetings secretary of the British Association of Applied Linguistics 2004–06. She is author of *Analysing the Language of Discourse Communities* (2000) and *Pragmatics and Discourse* (2008), editor of *Vague Language Explored* (2007), and co-editor of the *Edinburgh Textbooks in TESOL* series.

Florence Bonacina-Pugh (PhD Edinburgh) is a Teaching Fellow in TESOL at the University of Edinburgh. Prior to 2012, she held an ESRC Post-Doctoral Research Fellowship there. She taught French as a foreign language for nine years, developing curriculum and teaching materials. She is a co-organiser of the Edinburgh TESOL and Applied Language research group and a collaborator in the Bilingualism Matters Project. Her research interests are discourse analysis, language policy and practice in multilingual settings and classroom code-switching. She has recently published in *The International Journal of Bilingual Education and Bilingualism*, *Language and Education* and *Language Policy*.

Kenneth Fordyce (PhD Lancaster) is a Lecturer in TESOL at the University of Edinburgh, where he teaches on language awareness and research methods courses. He previously taught at Hiroshima University, Japan for over ten years. His PhD thesis focused on the relative effects of explicit and implicit instruction on second-language development in the use of epistemic stance. His research interests cover interlanguage pragmatics, learner corpus research, academic literacies, the teaching of research methodology at postgraduate level and the internationalisation of higher education.

Nicola Galloway (PhD Southampton) has examined attitudes towards English and English language teaching in relation to English as a Lingua Franca in the Japanese university context. From 2005 to 2012, she worked at two Japanese universities where she taught courses on Global Englishes and incorporated the topic into English for Academic Purposes and English for Specific Purposes courses. Since 2012, she has worked as a Lecturer in Education (TESOL) at the University of Edinburgh, teaching courses on materials evaluation and design, individual differences and Global Englishes. She is currently working on several publications related to Global Englishes including *Introducing Global Englishes*.

Eleni Mariou (PhD Birmingham) is a Teaching Fellow in TESOL at the University of Edinburgh. She has previously taught English as a Foreign Language and ESP for a number of years in the UK and in Greece, and has also worked as an assessor in General Education teacher education programmes. Her research interests are situated in the areas of language and identity construction in multilingual contexts, language ideologies, discourse and the sociopolitics of education, cultural and political implications of English as an International language and ELT methodology. She is a co-organiser of the Edinburgh TESOL and Applied Language research group.

INTRODUCTION

INTRODUCTION

This volume is one of the first in the *Edinburgh Textbooks in TESOL* series, which is designed to match the content of the most common courses in TESOL programmes (third and fourth year undergraduate and Masters degrees) round the world. *Language in Context in TESOL* responds to the fact that 78 per cent of 15 TESOL Masters programmes surveyed in the UK and 12 TESOL Masters worldwide have core and/or option courses entitled variously 'Linguistic Analysis', 'Discourse, Pedagogy, Identity', 'Language in Context', 'Language in Society', 'Corpus Linguistics', 'Text and Discourse for TESOL' and 'Intercultural Communication and Language Teaching'. It is hoped that this volume will be useful for you if you are a student on courses such as these, or if you are a teacher of English as a Foreign, Second or Additional Language (EFL for the sake of argument) studying independently with a view to incorporating the social aspects of language into your English language classes.

The volume presents language analysis in a way that is practical and suggests applications in EFL classrooms. It is:

- **introductory,** aimed at people who are new to reading theoretical literature and who need to know about state-of-the-art research and its applications
- **intercultural,** taking into account the variation in physical and economic conditions in ELT classrooms worldwide, encouraging comparisons across cultures and guiding you in adapting the suggestions in the literature to your own educational requirements
- **practical,** providing tasks to be carried out in class individually, in small groups or in plenary, as well as outside the classroom independently

The volume is based on the general principle that an understanding of language contributes to teachers' development as reflective practitioners and researchers. This chapter explains how the volume can enable you to:

- answer general questions about language systems, functions, social and cultural dimensions that you might have or that the language learners that you teach might ask you

- understand theories about language and studies of it, and incorporate findings into your classes, in terms of materials, tasks and procedures

This chapter explains the structure of the volume:

- Chapter 2 introduces the main technique for data analysis.
- Chapters 3, 4 and 5 present the sociolinguistic and cultural dimensions of language in context, providing the background to the approaches to data analysis and hopefully challenging assumptions.
- Chapters 6, 7 and 8 cover techniques and approaches to data analysis for understanding language, relating them to the sociolinguistic and cultural dimensions, using new technologies.
- Chapter 9 points forward to directions that teaching and research might take.

1.1 RATIONALE AND AIM OF *LANGUAGE IN CONTEXT IN TESOL*

Learners of EFL need to know about the way that the language they are learning reflects society and how it functions in context, so that they can interact with people who consider themselves native speakers of English (from Australia, Canada, New Zealand, the UK or the USA) and other speakers of English (from the rest of the world) in a way that expresses effectively what they are trying to say and communicates their intention in a socially acceptable way. Learners need to know about the cultural background of the language they are learning, so that they can be sensitive about the general social norms of speakers of that language.

There are many reasons for learning, of course. If they plan to travel as tourists or carry out diplomatic or commercial negotiations with people from Australia, Canada, New Zealand, the UK and the USA, learners will most likely perceive knowing about cultural differences as a way of improving their holiday or their business. On the other hand, a large proportion of learners believe that they will never meet a native English speaker (NES) or any language other than their own: they are learning English either because they have to (it is on their school curriculum), in which case learning about social dimensions may add interest and motivate them, or they are learning English in order to increase their cultural knowledge of the world, in which case learning about social dimensions is exactly what they want.

As an EFL teacher or future EFL teacher, you might have found that in your context, learners are taught mainly grammar and rarely learn about social conventions or practise communicating their intention in a socially acceptable way. 'Micro-level grammatical accuracy is being prioritised at the expense of macro-level pragmatic appropriateness' (O'Keeffe et al. 2011: 139) due to the prevalence of examinations as indicators of success, and the fact that the classroom context is the only place in which learners use the target language and hence they have little opportunity for real communication, with all its social differences and conflicts, its negotiations, misunderstandings and reformulations. Bardovi-Harlig (2001: 25) believes that 'in general, textbooks cannot be counted on as a reliable source of pragmatic input for classroom language learners'. This is because what is in textbooks has mostly been based on native-speaker intuition and not so much on the findings of corpus linguistics, which is the study of naturally occurring language stored in electronic databases. Textbooks tend to contain little about politeness expressed through language, about the way that the purpose in communicating influences language choices (pragmatics). They rarely cover the effect of cultural background on the way we speak and write (sociolinguistics). Textbooks are beginning to take this into account; see, for example, *Exploring Spoken Language* (Carter and McCarthy 1997) and *Touchstone* (McCarthy et al. 2005).

Despite this, EFL teachers can teach sociolinguistic and pragmatic dimensions of language. Bardovi-Harlig and Mahan-Taylor (2003) propose that, in order to do so, teachers should use authentic language samples and then encourage learner production. They also understand that pragmatics can be taught at early levels of language learning. *Language in Context in TESOL* aims to enable language teachers and those who plan to become language teachers to understand something about English as it is used in real life by flesh-and-blood speakers, and to design classroom activities so that they can raise awareness in their learners of the sociocultural dimensions.

1.2 CONTENT OF *LANGUAGE IN CONTEXT IN TESOL*

This book is not about one particular variety of English and culture; it is about **English in use around the world**. It introduces you to World Englishes, or varieties of English in specific geographical regions (e.g. Singaporean English or African American English), and English as a Lingua Franca, or the way that English is used worldwide among speakers of different first languages to communicate with each other. The book examines communication between people with different cultural backgrounds and explores the way that second language learners develop cultural knowledge of the target language.

Language in Context in TESOL is not about words and structures in isolation as they might be presented in dictionaries, grammar books and course books; it is about **language in context**. It is about stretches of language and cohesion: how they are held together by the surrounding text, by grammatical (structural) and lexical (vocabulary) links, as in 'The blog was fun. It told a story. The entry set off a stream of other stories', and coherence links, or logical connections. It is about the way that the situational and contextual background gives meaning to language. Thus 'Have you got a spare sheet?' means one thing if asked by a student taking notes in a lecture, and another if asked by someone preparing a hotel room. This is the focus of discourse analysis.

The book is about understanding not only the surface features of language, such as grammar, vocabulary and phonetics; it is about understanding the **meaning underneath language,** the functions of utterances and the meaning implied. This is known as pragmatics, which can show that the implied meaning of words is often different from the words themselves (as in 'Lovely day!' shouted from under an umbrella in the pouring rain) and that forms can have more than one function ('It's seven o'clock' can mean 'I'm just telling you the time because you asked' or 'Get up – you're late!'). The book is about the way that particular people use language with particular people for specific purposes, such as showing a polite and friendly attitude (e.g. 'Hi – you're looking good today!') or exerting power ('Give me that report by five on Friday, or there'll be trouble').

Language in Context in TESOL introduces you to **theories of data analysis,** with a view to guiding you to understand how findings can be applied to English Language Teaching (ELT), either as cultural background knowledge or as the focus of classroom tasks. The theories covered are Conversation Analysis and Exchange Structure, which analyse the structure of stretches of discourse; Speech Act Theory and the Cooperative Principle, which analyse the functions and social maxims of interaction; and Politeness Theories, which analyse the social rules of face-saving. These ways of analysing naturally occurring language will be introduced through discussion of variation according to domains (situational contexts characterised by particular features of language, such as a hospital waiting room or a court room), and social variables of gender, age and social class. The theories also involve a consideration of culture as regards World Englishes and English as a Lingua Franca, comparing social rules and norms of other languages.

The book does not rely on specially devised language samples to back up assertions or illustrate findings; as often as possible, it uses **authentic language as it occurs in everyday life**. Similarly, all the theories of data analysis are presented here in conjunction with **Corpus Linguistics,** which is a tool for exploring language, using specialised software to find the most frequently occurring words and grammatical patterns in electronic databases of naturally occurring language.

The main emphasis of the volume is on the relevance of the theories of language analysis to TESOL and ELT. Thus, you will learn how to **evaluate ELT methodology, curriculum, course and materials** in terms of Global Englishes, functions and social maxims of interaction and face-saving. Importantly, you will consider ways of **teaching with these issues in mind,** and **designing tasks and lessons** with a sociological and cultural focus.

At the end of this book there is a **glossary,** which provides simple definitions of terms frequently used in this book to refer to quite complex concepts and issues. The glossary aims to enable easy access to the terms at any point as you read theough.

1.3 STRUCTURE OF EACH CHAPTER

The structure of the core chapters (that is to say, every chapter except Chapter 1 and Chapter 9) is as follows:

- **Introduction**
- **Three Input sections**
  Each one contains
  - An explanation of basic concepts and findings from research-based studies, with authentic texts to demonstrate points
  - Three tasks, to be used in class and outside as self study:
    - Applying the concept to teaching, evaluating how the issues covered can suit your own pedagogical purposes, and considering ways of applying the theories to your teaching methodology and course materials

- Trying out research, experimenting with the theories of analysis on language excerpts, and designing mini-projects involving English speakers and language learners
  - Using the internet, focusing on the internet and the language classroom, and discovering how to teach about the sociolinguistic and pragmatic features of English using online resources
- **Two Further Reading sections**
  Each one contains
  - A research-based article or chapter summary, with bite-size chunks from the article or chapter
  - Two tasks, to be used in class and outside as self study:
    - Applying the concept to teaching
    - Trying out research
- **Summary**
- **Additional reading,** with guiding comments

1.4 TOOLS AND SOCIOLINGUISTIC DIMENSIONS

Chapters 2 to 5 provide the important theoretical background that you will need in order to understand how TESOL is taught today and to proceed to the later chapters on approaches to linguistic analysis. Chapter 2 provides a series of techniques for analysing data. Chapters 3 to 5 introduce you to the sociolinguistic dimensions.

Chapter 2 – Corpus Linguistics is the first of the core chapters because it introduces you to corpora (electronic databases of naturally occurring language) and techniques for analysing them, which will be referred to in most of the chapters in this volume. This chapter describes a range of English corpora – spoken, written and multimodal, including communication with hand gestures, facial expression and body posture. The chapter describes software for carrying out analyses to produce concordances, making wordlists and searching for keywords. It also presents the techniques for building corpora. Importantly, it suggests how Corpus Linguistics can be used to study Global Englishes, social variables, social groups, context, register, intercultural and cross-cultural pragmatics, which are the subject of the remaining chapters. This chapter proposes ways of including findings from Corpus Linguistics in the ELT classroom, and ways to use corpora for teaching.

Chapter 3 – Global Englishes sets the scene of English in the world, and the world in English. It introduces you to the spread of Englishes in the world, the emergence of varieties of English, the native/non-native speaker dichotomy and the globalisation of English as an International Language. It then moves on to examine the World Englishes paradigm and explores the concept of 'Standard English' and its link with concepts of ownership, linguistic imperialism and learner/speaker identity. The chapter also introduces you to the English as a Lingua Franca paradigm and the pedagogical implications for English Language Teaching. Lastly, it encourages the analysis of these issues in ELT courses, coursebooks and methodology.

Chapter 4 – English across Cultures shows how users of different World Englishes, with different social variables and identities and in different social groups, communicate with each other. It starts with a description of bilingualism and multi-lingualism, and discusses issues relating to language choice and an ethos of mutual understanding. The second section focuses on cross-cultural pragmatics, which compares the way language is used in different contexts and cultures. This is followed by an introduction to intercultural pragmatics (communication between people with different cultural backgrounds) and interlanguage pragmatics (the development of pragmatic competence in a second language).

Chapter 5 – Context and Registers focuses on social groups, style and register. It begins with the distinction between co-text, situational context and background context, introducing you to grammatical and lexical cohesion and coherence. The following section begins by introducing communities of practice and in-group codes, before moving on to register and genres, in other words, the ways in which language is typically used and organised when it is used for different purposes. The third section of this chapter describes electronic communication registers and genres which have emerged in the past two decades. It gives a specific focus to emails, e-forum postings and text messaging, and looks at how they compare with more traditional spoken and written registers.

1.5 APPROACHES TO DATA ANALYSIS

Chapters 6 to 8 introduce you to five essential approaches to linguistic analysis. Chapter 9 moves on to applications and further research.

Chapter 6 – Exchange Theory and Conversation Analysis explores ways of analys-ing the structure of stretches of discourse. It looks at turn-taking (the rules around one person talking at a time), adjacency pairs, pre- and insert-sequences in English, as well as acts, moves, exchanges, transaction, initiation–response–follow-up. It examines the way that the sociolinguistic and cultural dimensions of English can be seen in the structure of stretches of discourse, showing how different varieties of English and different languages dictate different social expectations of turn-taking, adjacency pairs, and initiation–response–follow-up, and how this in turn affects intercultural communication. The implications for ELT are explored.

Chapter 7 – Speech Act Theory and the Cooperative Principle introduces you to the functions and social maxims of interaction. It explains the theory of direct and indirect speech acts, felicity conditions and the relation between speech acts and society. It relates this to conversational and interactional maxims, conversational implicature, the violating of cooperative maxims, and Relevance Theory. Speech Act Theory and the Cooperative Principle are taken in conjunction because they can both explain underlying meanings of English, in face-to-face and online interaction. Linguistic features discovered using Corpus Linguistics are seen in conjunction with their sociocultural variables in a way that explains cross-cultural communication and enables teachers of English to evaluate their TESOL methodology, curriculum, course and materials.

Chapter 8 – Politeness Theories takes an intercultural approach to face-saving, comparing positive and negative politeness strategies and politeness maxims across cultures within one country and from country to country. It covers research in the emergent field of impoliteness and transgressions of social rules. The chapter discusses findings about the social functions of face-saving in English and shows how new technologies bring new social rules and how Corpus Linguistics can enable systematic analysis of all these features. All of these concepts are set firmly in the cross-cultural pragmatics and interlanguage pragmatics context. You are encouraged to see teaching and learning in TESOL from this perspective and to think about ways of building face and politeness in curriculums, materials and tasks.

Chapter 9 – Conclusion brings all the theories and approaches together to consider where research is going next in all the fields described, and what EFL teachers can take away from this volume that will help them improve their lessons.

Finally, it should be noted that many of the themes dealt with in this volume are also mentioned in Spiro, *Changing Methodologies in TESOL* (2013), also in this series. Spiro touches briefly on developments in the fields of Corpus Linguistics, English as a Lingua Franca, Conversation Analysis, the Cooperative Principle and Politeness Theories, in order to explore the implications for teaching the skills of reading, writing, speaking and listening, as well as social and pragmatic competence.

CORPUS LINGUISTICS

INTRODUCTION

This chapter describes a technique that can be used to analyse the sociolinguistic dimensions of English in context, and combined with approaches to data analysis. Corpus Linguistics (henceforth CL) studies **corpora**, which are electronic databases of authentic texts selected according to defined research purposes and stored on computers. It studies them using specialised software, which provides lists of word frequencies and typical grammatical patterns contained within the corpus.

Corpora are widely used in the world of language teaching and research. Most dictionaries, grammar reference books, coursebooks and tests nowadays are based on them, for example *COBUILD Dictionaries*, *Longman Grammar of Spoken and Written English* (Biber et al. 1999), *Cambridge Grammar of English* (Carter and McCarthy 2006) and *Touchstone* (McCarthy et al. 2005).

Why would you as an English teacher want to study a corpus?

- You may be curious about how language is used in daily life, and muse along the lines of 'I wonder whether "raise" or "increase" occurs most with the noun "awareness"?'
- It could be that, in class, your learners ask you questions such as 'What's the difference between "think about" and "think of"?' You are not entirely sure how most English native speakers use 'think' grammatically, and you wonder if it depends on whether they are from the UK, Australia, New Zealand or the US.
- You may be interested in the language used in your classroom, and wonder about issues such as 'In pairwork, are the boys using the politeness expressions I just taught them as much as the girls are?'
- You may have a concern that the language in your EFL coursebook dialogues is not very realistic: 'Do people really say "Have you ever been to Paris?" in casual conversation, or is ellipsis as in "Ever been to Paris?" more common?' You wonder if it might depend on how old the speaker is or how well interlocutors know each other.

CL can help you to find answers to questions such as these.

This chapter describes how to make CL suit your purposes. The first input section describes types of already existing corpora and ways of building a corpus for yourself, and the second explains ways of analysing publicly available corpora. The third turns to the English language in context and society and ways of using CL in conjunction with other approaches to language analysis. All the way through, there is a focus on suggestions of ways to include findings in the English language classroom, and to use corpora for teaching English and take a data-driven approach, in which learners work with findings from corpus analysis in class.

2.1 TYPES OF CORPORA AND WAYS OF BUILDING THEM

Corpora come in all shapes and sizes. The majority are collections of authentic, naturally occurring language, that is to say, language not specifically devised for language-learning materials, and include the following:

- written language, such as novels, policy documents, notices, text messages, wikis, tweets, etc.
- transcriptions of spoken language, such as TV documentaries, telephone conversations, pop songs, classroom interaction, YouTube, internet pages, etc.
- multimodal corpora, with recordings (audio or video), transcription alongside and body language (head movements, hand gestures etc.) tracked simultaneously

In addition, there are corpora that are of special interest to language teachers:

- non-native-speaker corpora with texts in non-teaching settings, an example being the VOICE corpus (see the chapter in this volume on Global Englishes)
- language learner corpora, collections of data produced by learners, such as presentations, essays and exam scripts
- pedagogic corpora, which are collections of texts such as coursebooks or DVDs devised for language learners

Corpora can be any size. The larger ones tend to be general and contain a variety of text types; the smaller are more specialised, containing particular genres of text:

- a few thousand words, collected by individuals on small projects, for example transcriptions of a particular group of EFL learners on a speaking course
- one to four million words, for example the Hong Kong Corpus of Spoken English (one million) and the Cambridge Learner Corpus of ESOL, 180,000 exam scripts
- 10 to 30 million, for example the International Corpus of English (ICE) (15 million)
- several hundred million, for example the Bank of English http://www.collins.co.uk/books.aspx?group=153 (500 million)
- the internet can also serve as a corpus (WebCorp enables word searches on the web, http://www.webcorp.org.uk/live/)

Here are a number of corpora that are publicly available and free. Their sites are worth exploring in order to get an idea of what a corpus looks like and what can be done with it:

- Backbone (Pedagogic Corpora for Content and Language Integrated Learning): http://projects.ael.uni-tuebingen.de/backbone/moodle/
- Bank of English sampler: http://www.collins.co.uk/Corpus/CorpusSearch.aspx and http://web.quick.cz/jaedth/Introduction%20to%20CCS.htm
- British National Corpus (BNC): http://www.natcorp.ox.ac.uk/ (a simple word search can be carried out using http://sara.natcorp.ox.ac.uk/lookup.html)
- Business Letter Corpus: http://www.someya-net.com/concordancer/index.html;
- COCA Corpus: http://www.americancorpus.org/
- HCRC Maptask Corpus: http://hcrc.ed.ac.uk/maptask/interface/
- Lancaster Corpus of Children's Project Writing: http://www.lancs.ac.uk/fass/projects/lever/index.htm
- Michigan Corpus of Academic Spoken English: http://quod.lib.umich.edu/m/micase/
- SCOTS: Scottish Corpus of Texts and Speech: http://www.scottishcorpus.ac.uk/about/
- The Brigham Young corpus collection site: http://corpus.byu.edu/
- The Oxford Text Archive holds a large number of freely available specialised corpora: http://ota.ahds.ac.uk

Although there are many corpora available to work with, it is worth knowing how they are built, partly so that you can understand them better, but mainly so that you know where to start when you **build your own corpus** as a reflective practitioner, analysing your own teaching in order to improve it (see *Developing Practice in TESOL* by Fiona Farr in this series for a full discussion of the reflective practitioner).

If you feel that you are not at a stage in your research career where you would want to collect your own data for analysis, you could pass over the rest of this section and go straight to Section 2.2, Analysing Corpora. You could return later, when you are ready, to the rest of this current section on corpus design, techniques of data collection, and ways of labelling and annotating data.

When considering building your own corpus, the first thing to do is decide on a **corpus design** that reflects your overall rationale or research purpose, and provides a representative sample of a larger population, for example the variety or genre. This influences the number of text types and the number of texts within each type that you are going to collect. For example, you may want to get a cross-section of what goes on in lecturer–student interaction in your university, and so record across five departments 50 lectures, 50 workshops and 50 one-to-one tutorials.

As far as **data collection** is concerned, if you are researching written language, you simply scan the paper into your computer or download the electronic language, whereas if it is spoken language that you are interested in, you either audio or video-record it with a high-quality digital camcorder, and then transcribe it.

You can transcribe just by playing back the recording and typing the words. Note that one hour of recording takes about two working days to transcribe. You will probably write down literally every word uttered (for example 'So, I- I- I went to the – I'd been going to the library late at night') and you may want to represent how some words are pronounced (for example 'How-ja-do?' and 'Wassup?'). If it relates to your research or teaching purpose, you will also need to devise transcription conventions to indicate phonetic features (for example, stress, intonation), turn-taking (for example, pauses, overlaps) and paralinguistics (for example, laughter, coughing). On the other hand, you may prefer to use automatic transcription and speech recognition software such as *SpeechWare* or *DragonNaturally Speaking*.

There are **ethical considerations** to be taken into account: you should obtain written permission to use written data from those who produced it, and you need signed consent forms from the people that you recorded. Ethics also necessitates anonymisation, or the removal of names and other identifying details. Consent forms generally give participants the chance to withdraw their data from your corpus at any time. Keep a careful record of their consent if you eventually want your corpus to be publicly available.

If your data is in separate files, it is best to give each a label. **File labels** can indicate the date, genre (for example, novel), domain (for example, classroom), speech event (for example, student presentation), speakers' names and biodata (for example, gender, age, socio-economic group, ethnic group).

You can quite easily stop there, with a database that you can then analyse for general trends. If, on the other hand, your overall rationale is more detailed and focuses on specific words and structures, you will need to annotate elements of the data within each file. **Data annotation** implies tagging individual words or word clusters to indicate features of the lexis (for example, common or proper nouns) and grammar (for example, parts of speech, cohesion). Some people find it more appropriate to annotate the data manually, using Microsoft Word's 'Find' function and tagging every instance of the words in question. The example below is from the 26,000-word Applied Linguistics (AL) Common Room corpus (Cutting 2000) with 'thing' tagged with _GN for general noun:

AM   But things_GN like this linguistics as well. You know I don't mi-mind it.
CM   You still got enough time for that? (0.5)
AM   There's not a lot of things_GN they can ask.

Standard annotation can also be done electronically. If you want to make your corpus publicly available, you can, for example, convert the transcript files to xml and submit them to *WMatrix* (2007) for automatic part-of-speech and semantic-category tagging, so as to comply with the guidelines of the Text Encoding Initiative (TEI), which maintains a standard for specified encoding. Another popular annotation package is *ELAN*, which is freely downloadable.

If you aim to do more of a qualitative analysis of video data, with a focus on functional or interactional themes, you can label functions and interactions electronically with *Transana*, which lets you 'identify analytically interesting clips, assign keywords to clips, arrange and rearrange clips' and 'create complex collections of interrelated clips'. A slightly more sophisticated package is *NVivo*, which allows automatic classifying, sorting and arranging of information, and analysis of material straight from audio and video files.

Here are a few useful websites that will give more detail than is contained in this section. A visit to them might prepare you for the tasks that follow.

- Information on Corpus Building: http://www.corpus.bham.ac.uk/corpus-building shtml
- Introduction to Corpus Linguistics: http://www.engl.polyu.edu.hk/corpuslin guist/corpus.htm
- David Lee's website: http://devoted.to.corpora

Task 2.1 Applying the concept to teaching

You might be surprised how practical and indeed useful it is to teach your learners to build a mini-corpus and analyse it. Read the following account of a small project that I carried out with my English for Academic Purposes (EAP) students (Cutting 2006: 176–7), and think about whether you could do something similar with your learners.

> In order to test whether EAP students can be trained to recognise vague language and appreciate its function, Cutting (1999) organised a series of activities with authentic data in their normal class time, at the University of Sunderland. The students were told about the features of in-group code and were helped to find them in a sample dialogue from the MSc common room data. They were then asked to go with a cassette recorder and record any group of home students who appeared to have known each for some time and were talking informally. In the next class, they were trained to transcribe and they then analysed the dialogues to find features of in-group code in their dialogues. Their analyses were successful.
>
> A questionnaire showed that many students did not understand their dialogues but realised that the implicit reference was partly to blame. A significant proportion of the students agreed that implicitness was a marker of intimacy. One said, 'It is very often the case within my group of friends. I think we developed something like a group code which is probably difficult to understand for outsiders.' When asked if studying this language closely had helped them in their socialising with British students, some offered answers such as, 'If I don't understand a conversation between two persons that's because they have a closed talking.' The exercise itself had proved enjoyable: comments such as 'I found this project really thrilling since I had never done such a study on language' abounded. This suggests that students can be made aware of the function of in-group code, and that they can be reassured that it is not always their own language competence level that makes conversations difficult to understand.

This story demonstrates that you do not have to be an expert to collect and analyse data, and it shows that corpus studies of this sort need to be accompanied by other research tools such as questionnaires and interviews, so as to gain information of contextual, functional and evaluative nature.

In order to consider what you could do with your learners, discuss with colleagues the following questions. Note that for the moment, we are only talking about collecting the data, not analysing it:

- What would be the rationale for getting your learners to collect data?
- What would be your research question?
- How many words would you aim to collect in your corpus?
- How many words would you ask each of your learners to collect?
  - You might like to tell them about this in terms of minutes.
  - You would need to be guided by how much time they have got for transcription, taking into account that ten minutes of spoken language can take an hour and a half to transcribe.
- How would your learners collect the data?
  - In what location? Keep in mind your rationale and research question, and the practicalities of recording in a noisy place.
  - With what machines would they record it? Would they have to share or work in pairs?
  - How much detail would you expect them to transcribe? Would you need them to indicate repetitions, overlaps, interruptions, laughter, shouted words and body language such as nods and frowns?
  - Would you want to ask them to annotate the data somehow? Again keep in mind your rationale and research question.
- How do you think your learners might react to this exercise? Could you in some way relate it to their syllabus of knowledge and skills that their curriculum already contains?
- How would you encourage them to relate their findings to their own language?

Task 2.2 Trying out research

Do you think that a corpus of your own learners' written work could be useful for you to research? Discuss how it might help your understanding of your learners and consequently your teaching of them:

- What would be the rationale for collecting the data?
- What would be your research question?
- How many words would you aim to collect in your corpus?
- What written work would you want to collect? Exposition essays? Reports? Reflective journals? Written tests of descriptive or a narrative nature? Spelling tests?
- Would the work be handwritten and need to be copied into an electronic format, or would it already be in an electronic format?
- How would you label each piece of work, when putting them in the corpus?
- Would you annotate the data within each piece of work somehow? Again keep in mind your rationale and research question.

Task 2.3 Using the internet

- Do you think that WebCorp would be useful for your students? For what purpose?
- Think about how you would use it with your learners to raise their awareness of a certain linguistic feature in a way that fits in with their existing syllabus.
- What sort of productive exercise would you do with them?

- Design one that ensures that the learners practise the linguistic feature that you chose in a way that is productive, free, fluent, creative and interactive.

2.2 ANALYSING CORPORA

Whether you are analysing a ready-made or home-made corpus, you can use software such as *Wordsmith*, *MonoConc Pro* and *Antconc*, which contain a variety of tools. Check these out on the internet before reading any further.

A common tool is the **concordance**, which lists key words in context (KWIC) as in the example with 'thing' below, and shows

- the **collocation**, or words frequently co-occurring with the word, e.g. 'first thing' and 'difficult thing'
- the **colligation**, or the grammar that usually surrounds the word, e.g. 'the thing to remember about X is Y', as in 'The thing to remember about mountains is that the weather is unpredictable.'

Some corpora which are open to the public and free of charge contain in-built searching resources. Examples are the Corpus of Contemporary American English (COCA) and the Bank of English. Below are the first ten lines (out of 1,319) of a concordance for the word 'thing' in the British National Corpus Sampler (BNC), which contains spoken and written language, using the concordance package *Sara*:

Arne from next door comes in first	thing	and last thing and fills the hob
It is the most beautiful	thing	I have had in my whole life
Haircare of the 90s means one	thing	– physical wear and tear
This demand may become a	thing	of the past if club management
'This	thing	's heavier than I thought' puffed
The only	thing	to remember about telling jokes
The most difficult	thing	is to know when to stop
Erm yes it's, it's funny	thing	I haven't sent things to the
But there was a group er previous	thing	but I think that there was
It is one	thing	to determine that better use

The full 1,319-line concordance would let you determine how 'thing' is used. However, just these ten lines show that to the left of 'thing' there tends to be an adjective ('first', 'beautiful', 'this', 'only', 'difficult', 'funny', 'previous', 'one'), and to the right an infinitive, for example 'to remember', 'to know', 'to determine'. The pattern 'adjective + thing + infinitive' is already emerging.

The concordance tool can re-order the lines with **Left Sorting** (putting the words to the left of the word in alphabetical order) and **Right Sorting** (putting the words to the right in alphabetical order). This can be demonstrated with a 6,000-word corpus of blogs from a group of lecturers discussing research (Cutting 2008b), and using *Wordsmith* to find concordances of 'research'. Left sorting shows that the most frequent words preceding are 'of' and 'my'; here is a selection:

before has the frustration and anguish	of research	had such an
cher ones, and pushing up the quality	of research	dissemination
to go for it. And this huge issue	of research	questions and the
– yes, yes. My concept	of research	is changing as I
nding so to speak. (I see us as a sort	of research	collective).
ime will tell. Maybe the video will be	my research	disciplinarian. Now
uancy or classroom organisation, but	my research	motivation in all
from among other things – I guess if	my 'research	time' had that
ra benefit is that it means I don't feel	my research	has to save the
o expect that this will be accepted as	my research	for this past week

Even this demonstrates the emotion surrounding research ('frustration and anguish', 'huge issue') and the fact that although the lecturers work collaboratively, their research is an individual event ('my research' as opposed to 'our research'). Right sorting shows that 'research' is mostly a pre-head modifier, as demonstrated by this selection:

might be tempted to feel that my	'research topic'	should be of super-
among other things – I guess if my	'research time'	had that kind of
lots of beer, consideration of	research spaces	and thoughtful
he expectation that I had to find a	'research question'	of my own. Until such
hen why not work with teachers as	research partners	and explore the natu
or classroom organisation, but my	research motivation	in all cases was
instrumental (the need to bring in	research money).	Real interest was
What has been happening in your	research lives?	Tuesday, 2 October
The reality of our existence in a	research driven	community is that
quest for the holy grail	research direction	is less important than

Sometimes it is not possible to understand how the word is being used just by looking at the words to the left or to the right of the word concerned. Some software, such as *Wordsmith*, allows researchers to expand the concordance and bring up on the screen the line before each line with the word and the line after (thus each concordance is three lines wide); if that still does not allow an understanding of the function or interactional features, researchers can click on 'grow' and see yet another line before and after (thus each concordance is five lines wide).

Concordances can be carried out by **selecting social and textual variables** that narrow the search. For example, it is possible to run a concordance for the word 'thing' in the Scottish Corpus of Texts and Speech (SCOTS Project), clicking on one box that indicates the gender of interest, and clicking on another to indicate whether one wants to focus on spoken or written texts. This allows the researcher to discover the following instances:

	Female	Male
Spoken	1,174	833
Written	154	745

This in itself does not reveal much about the usage of the word 'thing' by male and female speakers and writers. The researcher should take into account what the proportion of texts spoken and written by women and by men is, throughout the whole corpus, before deciding whether 'thing' is a female spoken phenomenon.

Closely related to the concordance is the **collocate cloud**. This is simply a graphic way of representing the words that collocate with the word being studied. The following figure is a cloud for 'thing' in the SCOTS Project; size reflects frequency of usage (large = more frequent), i.e. how often the collocate occurs five words before or after the node ('thing') (http://www.scottishcorpus.ac.uk/corpus/search/collocate-cloud.php?word=thing). A quick glance at this cloud shows you that 'the' and 'that', which frequent words generally, are also the most frequent words that co-occur with 'thing', as in 'the thing' and 'that thing'. A more careful look at the cloud suggests that 'thing' lives among informal words such as 'like', 'sort' and 'yeah', and may occur on transition points between clauses: note 'and' and 'but'. For a more reliable survey of how the word is used, one would certainly have to carry out a concordance:

Software programmes can also calculate the number of occurrences of words and

---

thing

a about ae ah all an and another are as at aye be been big but can d dae did do eh er erm f963: first for good got had have he his I if in [inaudible] is it just kind know [laugh] like ll m me mean mm mmhm my nae no not o of oh on one only or other re right S said same say see she so sort t tae that the there they thing think this ti to up ve was we wee well what when whole wi wis with would ye yeah you your

---

list them in order of frequency, producing **wordlists** in alphabetical or frequency order. Table 2.1 shows the twenty most frequent words of the Research Blog corpus, found with *Wordsmith*. The first eleven words are unexceptional: 'the', 'to', 'I', 'and', 'of', 'a' and 'in' are in the top ten of Cambridge International Corpus (CIC) samples (Carter and McCarthy 2006). What is distinctive and predictable is 'research' in 12th position. The Research Blog corpus is about group formation, hence 'we' and 'with' marking togetherness, and 'this' pointing to the shared here and now.

Software programmes also produce **keyword** lists, which are comparisons of the wordlist from smaller, more specialised corpora and against the wordlist from a larger reference corpus, showing the words that are most different in frequency terms in the two corpora. Many corpora and software include this tool, for example:

the user can click on compare frequency list to perform a comparison of the frequency list for their corpus against another larger normative corpus such as the BNC sampler, or against another of their own texts. (http://ucrel.lancs.ac.uk/wmatrix/)

Table 2.1   The twenty most frequent words in the Research Blog corpus

N	Word	Freq.	%
1	THE	250	4.12
2	TO	203	3.34
3	I	199	3.28
4	AND	170	2.80
5	OF	151	2.49
6	A	144	2.37
7	IN	98	1.61
8	#	90	1.48
9	THAT	88	1.45
10	IT	87	1.43
11	IS	81	1.33
12	RESEARCH	78	1.29
13	WE	73	1.20
14	FOR	64	1.05
15	HAVE	58	0.96
16	ON	58	0.96
17	THIS	57	0.94
18	BE	49	0.81
19	WAS	47	0.77
20	WITH	46	0.76

Table 2.2 shows an example of a list comparing the Research Blog corpus with the larger AL Common Room corpus. Interestingly, now 'research' tops the list, scoring a massive 225.48 in keyness; it is the word that makes the two corpora most different. This can be explained by the fact that the AL students discussed courses and assignments but not projects. 'Blog' is second because the AL Common Room corpus was collected before the blog era. 'Presentation' refers to conference papers that the researchers worked on together, not part of AL students' lives. 'We' is still significantly more frequent in the Research Blog; 'our' has joined it.

Within the concordance tool is the **cluster** tool, which displays words that regularly recur in patterns. Table 2.3 shows an example from the Cambridge and Nottingham Corpus of Discourse in English (CANCODE) spoken corpus which lists the top ten six-word chunks, indicating the frequency of occurrence (O'Keeffe et al. 2007). You will recognise 'do you know what I mean' and 'at the end of the day' as fillers and hedges related to informal sociable talk. The expressions 'and all the rest of it', 'and all that sort of thing', and 'and this that and the other' are general extenders, or end-of-utterance fillers possibly pointing to shared knowledge.

Here are some tools for analysing corpora. The sites are worth a visit.

- Simple concordancing programme: http://www.textworld.com/scp/
- ConcApp concordancer: http://www.edict.com.hk/PUB/concapp/
- AntConc: http://www.antlab.sci.waseda.ac.jp/antconc_index.html

- Online concordancer for the Corpus of Contemporary American English, BNC, TIME corpus of American English, Oxford English Dictionary, Corpus del Español, Corpus do Português: http://corpus.byu.edu

The question now is how does this relate to **English Language Teaching**? Teachers need to learn how to use information from corpora to help inform pedagogy, and

Table 2.2   The Research Blog corpus compared with the AL Common Room corpus

N	Word	Research Blog		AL Common Room		Keyness
		Freq.	%	Freq.	%	
1	RESEARCH	78	1.29	6	0.02	225.48
2	BLOG	21	0.35	0		71.54
3	OF	151	2.49	236	1.20	50.53
4	TO	203	3.34	479	1.83	49.23
5	HEATHER	14	0.23	0		47.68
6	GHENT	12	0.20	0		40.86
7	WILL	19	0.31	6	0.02	39.58
8	NEIL	11	0.18	0		37.46
9	PRESENTATION	11	0.18	0		37.46
10	HAS	25	0.41	16	0.06	36.75
11	OUR	18	0.30	6	0.02	36.73
12	FROM	29	0.48	26	0.10	33.17
13	WE	73	1.20	136	0.50	33.03
14	MY	44	0.72	60	0.22	32.35
15	ME	35	0.58	40	0.15	31.69
16	BOB	9	0.15	0		30.64
17	UMEA	9	0.15	0		30.64
18	WITH	46	0.76	73	0.27	27.29
19	IS	81	1.33	174	0.64	27.21
20	THE	250	4.12	768	2.82	26.10

Table 2.3   The top ten six-word chunks from the Cambridge and Nottingham Corpus of Discourse in English (CANCODE) spoken corpus

Position	Six-word chunk	Frequency of occurrence
1	do you know what I mean	236
2	at the end of the day	222
3	and all the rest of it	64
4	and all that sort of thing	41
5	I don't know what it is	38
6	but at the end of the	35
7	and this that and the other	33
8	from the point of view of	33
9	A hell of a lot of	29
10	in the middle of the night	29

how to effectively involve learners in hands-on learning with corpora (Reppen 2009). McEnery and Wilson (1996: 120) say that corpus examples in language classes expose learners to 'the kinds of sentences and vocabulary that they will encounter in reading genuine texts or in using the language in real communicative situations'. Asking learners to interpret concordance lines and keyword lists engages them in active 'consciousness-raising' activities.

Carter and McCarthy (1995) advocate a corpus-based, exploratory approach to language pedagogy, called the 'three Is': illustration–interaction–induction, in which 'illustration' is observing real data in concordances, 'interaction' is discussing and sharing opinions, and 'induction' is making one's own rule for a particular feature, classifying it, refining it and generalising it. With data-driven learning (DDL), the learner is the researcher, sometimes teacher-led and sometimes autonomous.

Here is an example of a DDL exercise:

> Look at this selection from the concordance for 'laugh' from the Bank of English, and answer these questions:
> – Is 'laugh' used as a noun or as a verb?
> – What verbs come before 'laugh'? What structure relates the two verbs?

way to encourage an audience to	laugh	at your show! It is a much better
is guaranteed which will make you	laugh,	make you cry, make you want to
swipe at the guest, and waiting to	laugh	at all his jokes rather than the guest
whether to make an audience	laugh	or draw them into a character's
some Displeasure, and to have	laugh	'd and shook their Heads, as they

Task 2.4 Applying the concept to teaching
Think of a specific reason to use a concordance in your class. In relation to this purpose, discuss with your colleagues:

- How many lines would it be? Would the number of lines depend on the level of your class and the objective of the task?
- Would you select the lines to give to your learners or just give them all the lines as they appeared?
- Would you show them the concordance list and ask them to think what patterns emerge or would you give them some sort of guidance?

Discuss whether you would prefer your learners to use online corpora and

- get them to use concordancing packages in the online corpora to research particular collocations, colligations and frequencies, such as *Text World*, *ConcApp Concordance* and *AntConc*; or
- ask them to search the internet using *Webcorp* as a resource, to find how words that they want to use in essays function?

Task 2.5 Trying out research

At the beginning of this chapter, we mentioned that CL can give you answers to questions such as these:

- You may be curious about how language is used in daily life, and muse along the lines of 'I wonder whether "raise" or "increase" collocates most with "awareness"?'
- It could be that, in class, your learners ask you questions such as 'What's the difference between "think about" and "think of"?' You are not entirely sure how most English native speakers use 'think' grammatically, and you wonder if it depends on whether they are from the UK, Australia, New Zealand or the US.
- You may have a concern that the language in your EFL coursebook dialogues is not very realistic: 'Do people really say "Have you ever been to Paris?" in casual conversation, or is ellipsis as in "Ever been to Paris?" more common?' You wonder if it might depend on how old the speaker is or how much interlocutors know each other.

Make a list of four or five questions such as these that you find yourself wondering about either in class or in your daily life. Choose an online corpus that is publicly available and free, and search for the answers to your questions. Discuss the answers that you find with your peers or colleagues. Exchange experiences with them as to how easy it was to find answers to your questions.

Task 2.6 Using the internet

Take a look at this excerpt from *AOL Teens message boards*. Let us imagine that you wanted to collect 500,000 words from this website, in order to find the most frequent words and five-word clusters, and the collocations of the ten most frequent words and clusters, so that you could teach your learners how to write in this genre and take part.

- What problems would you come across?
- How would you get round these problems?

LIKE SCHOOL?

Jamieharding123

I hate the work in school, but when i think bout it, im glad i have to go to school so i can see my mates and chat 2 them, cos sum live far away, so school is da only chance i get to talk 2 'em. My sister hated school, but now shes left shes missin it. I'm joinin da army next year (I'll b 16) so thats da year I'll be leavin. I wont miss school,but I'll miss talkin 2 all ma m8s.
    Any1 else Agree?

Malibu105

well most people at my school are horible 2 me. so i dont like it. works is ok. but in my opinion its the people that make me hate going into school.

Rosiepattis

I tell every1 dat i h8 school but ur right, school is alright. Most lessons r crap but sum r alright n u get 2 see all ur m8s.

Jones1gareth

i quite like school, there's only 500 there so everyone knows everyone and it's gr8. U should really just enjoy it. the only thing is our school gives SO MUCH homework, it's really bad . . . But because it's ridiulous that there's so much no1 takes it seriously so thats OK.

Meadow Jono

And another good thing is that if anyone didn't go to school we wouldn't be using computers like we are now

2.3 SOCIAL VARIABLES AND INTERACTION

CL can be used in conjunction with sociolinguistics, stylistics, variation studies, psycholinguistics and cultural studies.

World Englishes (see Chapter 3) can be explored easily with CL because there are so many corpora of **varieties of English**. In the SCOTS Project, if you search 'wee' meaning 'small', you will get 2,613 occurrences, the first three of which are:

> . . . Issa Look oot, ye fyreflies! Ye'l mebbe clour yeir wee heids on that whunstane. Issa Closer an closer nou ti . . .
> . . . That was till last Thursday, when I went and said Some wee slur on his Ma. And then he turns red, Comes at me, a . . .
> . . . lands them, like me, a right sock on the jaw. That's the wee tale of wir class's new chiel As we took for an angel, and . . .

The International Corpus of English (http://ice-corpora.net/ice/index.htm) introduces itself thus:

> The International Corpus of English (ICE) began in 1990 with the primary aim of collecting material for comparative studies of English worldwide. Twenty-four research teams around the world are preparing electronic corpora of their own national or regional variety of English. Each ICE corpus consists of one million words of spoken and written English produced after 1989. For most participating countries, the ICE project is stimulating the first systematic investigation of the national variety.

ICE lists the following corpora (the ones marked * may be downloaded under licence from the site): Canada*, East Africa*, Great Britain, Hong Kong*, India*, Ireland,

Jamaica*, New Zealand, the Philippines*, Singapore*, Sri Lanka (written) and USA (written)*. The site contains sample sound files that merit exploration from the following varieties: Australia, East Africa (Kenya and Tanzania), Great Britain, Hong Kong, India, Jamaica and the Philippines.

There are two notable corpora of English as a Lingua Franca (ELF): the Vienna–Oxford International Corpus of English (VOICE) and English as a Lingua Franca in Academic Settings (ELFA), which involve non-native English speakers (NNES). Then there are learner corpora, which are a very interesting resource for teachers of English. An example is the Cambridge Learner Corpus (CLC), which is a collection of exam scripts written by learners of English built with Cambridge ESOL, containing scripts from over 180,000 students from around 200 countries, speaking 138 different first languages. Another example is the International Corpus of Learner English (ICLE), which contains:

> argumentative essays written by higher intermediate to advanced learners of English from several mother tongue backgrounds (Bulgarian, Chinese, Czech, Dutch, Finnish, French, German, Italian, Japanese, Norwegian, Polish, Russian, Spanish, Swedish, Tswana, Turkish). (http://www.uclouvain.be/en-cecl-icle.html)

There is a certain amount of controversy about the difference between an ELF corpus and a learner corpus; the legitimacy of each depends on the ideology and theoretical framework of the researcher and teacher (see Chapter 3 for an in-depth discussion of this issue).

Some corpora allow an examination of **social variables**. Many publicly available corpora can be explored by comparing sub-corpora within the corpus, which contain particular **social variables**. To take an example, the SCOTS Project allows an advanced search using selection criteria such as 'participant details' ('gender', 'decade of birth', 'educational attainment'), 'setting' ('business/commerce', 'education', 'leisure/entertainment') and 'speaker relationships' ('family members or other close relationships', 'friend', 'acquaintance'). A search along these lines would give the following result for the number of spoken documents with female participants:

	Business/commerce	Education	Leisure/entertainment
Family/close	0	5	59
Friend	0	14	0
Acquaintance	0	4	0

Although these numbers in themselves say a lot about female speakers, further analysis can take place within each document with the criteria selected to find how language is used in each document type.

The Michigan Corpus of Academic Spoken English (MICASE) contains almost two million words of university lectures, seminars and tutorials, and allows researchers to call up lines with variables of gender, age, academic role and first language. If you were to search for the word 'really' used by female 24–30-year-old junior graduate student NNES, you would get these three lines:

and i did the, um, non-native speakers surveys, but um, and, it was after a class,
and they were <u>really</u> into it and they, they wanted, all of them to finish so i could
say what was the purpose of it, they view
language learners still, have problems with pragmatic concepts so we would like
to, see how they are <u>really</u> different any questions?
't write anything but he was the last one to turn it in so it was not even lack of
interest, he was, <u>really</u> into it, so (xx) yeah?

A limited number of corpora focus on the variable of age. Examples are COLT, the
Bergen Corpus of London Teenage Language, which contains transcripts of spoken
language of London teenagers, and POW – Polytechnic of Wales Corpus, which
offers researchers transcripts of spoken language of children.

Some corpora invite a study of **genres** and **registers** (see Chapter 4 for a full discussion of these terms). The Corpus of Contemporary American English (COCA)
allows researchers to choose whether to search in the categories 'spoken', 'fiction',
'magazine', 'newspaper' or 'academic'. Within these macro-categories, there are sub-
categories such as 'spoken ABC', 'spoken NBC' and 'spoken CBS', all of which are
television channels. There is a further temporal dimension: researchers can narrow
their search to four-year periods from 1990 to 2012. The Brigham Young University
Corpus of Global Web-Based English (GloWbE) is another corpus with a variety of
genres and registers and a historical dimension. It is also accessible, free of charge and
easy to work with. With both of these, researchers can compare the use of particular
words or clusters of words across genres and time.

There have been many studies of genres and registers in corpora. We describe two
here, to illustrate this. Carter and McCarthy (2006) analysed the Cambridge and
Nottingham Corpus of Discourse in English (CANCODE), which is described as
'casual conversation, people working together, people shopping, people finding out
information, discussions', and proposed a spoken grammar of these more informal
genres. Features include (examples taken from AL Common Room corpus):

- Repeating: 'She just couldn't remember if we were on the – the right track.'
- Pauses: 'It was in em – where was it (1) in em'
- Recasting: 'actually – in it – and one guy – there was three guys on the stage.'
- Vague language: 'sort of', 'or something'
- Interactional clusters: 'know what I mean?'
- Discourse markers: 'right', 'anyway'

Biber (2006: 91) examined the TOEFL 2000 Spoken and Written Academic Language
(T2K-SWAL) project corpus, which contains university genres: lectures, seminars
and tutorials. He looked at lexical, grammatical and paralinguistic features used to
indicate stance (value-judgements, assessments, feelings and attitudes), and found
that the most frequent devices are grammatical words such as 'unfortunately', phrases
such as 'in all probability' and clauses such as 'as we all know'.

CL can combine with other approaches to language analysis, taking into account
social and interactional features of language. You will meet these in Chapters 6, 7 and
8 of this volume. Here is a taster:

- **Exchange Structure Theory** (Coulthard 1977) focuses on classroom interaction; the type of questions are 'In class, who initiates, responds and follows up – the teacher or learners?' and 'How does the teacher elicit learners' responses?'
- **Conversation Analysis** (Ochs et al. 1996) looks at the structure of conversation and addresses questions such as 'What response are you expected to give after an offer/order/apology?' and 'How to prepare the hearer for what you are going to say next.'
- **Speech Act Theory** (Austin 1962; Searle 1969) looks at the function of language, and answers questions such as 'What functions do words express?' and 'How do you say things indirectly?'
- **Cooperative Principle** (Grice 1975) is about keeping conversation going smoothly, and answers questions such as 'How do you indicate you are giving the right information, being sincere, relevant and clear?' and 'What is the implied meaning?'
- **Politeness Theory** (Brown and Levinson 1987) is about saving face, and addresses issues such as 'How do you save your face and avoid offending?' and 'What strategies do you use to respect space and show closeness?'

Adolphs (2008: 2–4) explored the combination of CL and speech acts, focusing on suggestions in reported speech in CANCODE (Adolphs 2008: 56–9), and found, for example, that 'just' as a downtowner occurred so often to the right of 'why don't you' that it was part of the collocational pattern. Witness:

't like C and A. Or you know	why don't you just	go down to the market an
$2>	Why don't you just	wait.
Why don't you just t= </$>	Why don't you just	try one off hand Jean
<$1>	Why don't you just	put loads and loads a
Garage in <$G2> And I said	"Why don't you just	erm phone a garage in
Don't need to work on it so	why don't you just	

Combining CL with Conversation Analysis, Carter and Adolphs (2007) analysed a multimodal corpus and discovered that supervisors demonstrated active listenership by head-nods and backchannels, and that there were five types of head-nod, each combining with linguistic features; for example, small nods of short duration co-occurred with information receipt, and intense nods with short duration co-occurred with a verbal signal classified as 'continuer' or 'convergence'.

Again, how does this relate to **English Language Teaching**? CL studies findings have influenced some EFL coursebooks, and yet, as McEnery and Wilson (1996: 120) say, 'There exist considerable differences between what textbooks are teaching and how native speakers actually use language as evidenced in the corpora.' Take this dialogue from *Headway Intermediate* (Soars and Soars 1986: 18):

Man 'I'm dying of thirst. Would you make me a cup of tea?'
Boy 'OK. I'll put the kettle on.'
Man 'And could you bring some biscuits?'
Boy 'Yes, I'll open the new packet.'

As a classroom exercise, the teacher could ask learners to add features of spoken grammar discovered in CANCODE studies, such as ellipsis, recasting, vague language and discourse markers, to show politeness and save face,

> Man 'Dying of thirst. I want – would you make me a cup of tea or
>   something?'
> Boy 'OK. I'll put the thingy on.'
> Man 'And something to eat?'
> Boy 'Right, the new packet of biscuits.'

CL findings can also be built into fluency practice. For example, learners could do a role play of two old friends meeting at a bus stop, and use high-frequency word clusters such as 'do you know what I mean?' and 'and all the rest of it'.

Task 2.7 Applying the concept to teaching
Discuss with colleagues:

- What tasks could you do with your learners, putting into practice findings from CL studies, taking into account social variables and interaction theories?
- Discuss three ways in which you could make them aware of World Englishes.
- How could you make these tasks fit into the existing coursebook that your students use?

Task 2.8 Trying out research
Go to the MICASE corpus site and limit your word search to one of these social dimensions: gender, age or academic position / role. Search for words and expressions that you associate with one gender, or one age-group, or one position / role, depending on the social dimension that you chose. Compare results with the other gender, another age-group, another position / role. See whether your assumptions were right.

To take an example, you could compare the language of females with that of males. If you do a search for 'gosh' for females, there are 30 matches, mostly in the cluster 'oh my gosh'. For males, there are nine matches, and not mainly in 'oh my gosh' clusters. You might find that the function is different too. Share your results with your colleagues.

Task 2.9 Using the internet
Look on the internet to find corpus linguistics studies and social dimensions. You will get the best results if you search 'corpus linguistics and gender', rather than just 'women and language'. Or you could search 'corpus linguistics and age' or 'corpus linguistics and power'. Prepare a short Powerpoint presentation on a brief survey of the findings that you could give to peers and colleagues. Prepare a list of questions and issues that you would like them to debate. Discuss how useful CL has been in the studies and say whether you consider the findings more reliable than other ways of analysing language usage.

2.4 FURTHER READING ONE

Lee, D., and J. Swales (2006), 'A corpus-based EAP course for NNS doctoral students: moving from available specialized corpora to self-compiled corpora', *English for Specific Purposes*, 25: 56–75.

This paper describes a way that CL can be used in the language classroom. It outlines a study carried out with six PhD students (a Russian, a Pakistani and four mainland Chinese) from pharmacology, biostatistics and educational technology on a 13-week English for Academic Purposes (EAP) course entitled 'Exploring your own discourse world'.

The students were given access to specialised corpora of academic writing and speaking and introduced to the corpus way of investigating language using *Wordsmith Tools* (Scott 1996). The syllabus was this:

Wk 1:   Corpora, concordancing, and exploratory self-learning
Wk 2:   Using *Wordsmith* to explore language patterns
Wk 3:   Using concordances to examine common errors and raise awareness of lexico-grammar and discourse conventions
Wk 4:   Using concordances to examine collective nouns and using BNCweb's 'Distribution' and 'Subcorpus' features to examine distributional patterns in language
Wk 5:   Subjunctives: Using BNCweb's 'Thin' and 'Delete hits' features to examine distributional patterns
Wk 6:   Corpus, usage patterns and subtle nuances
Wk 7:   Grammar (for + V-ing structures); semantic prosody
Wk 8:   Worksheet on ISSUE/FACTOR/CONCEPT + Grammar (Active/Passive Voice)
Wk 9:   Grammar: Adj premodification and [Bare participles + ing/ed]
Wk 10: Grammar: Count and non-count nouns
Wk 11
and 12: Project preparation
Wk 13: Oral presentations

Each student compiled two written corpora: one of their own writing (term papers, dissertation drafts, unedited journal drafts) and one of 'expert' writing, taken from electronic versions of published papers in their own field or subfield. They compared the two corpora from the point of view of discourse and language, and gave a presentation on their findings at the end of the course.

The first excerpt evaluates the content of the course:

> Some of our activities were particularly successful. We have already mentioned the V-ing patterns in Week Seven. Another example was the class exploration of the usage of subjunctives (Week Five). Here we found a difference in frequency between the natural and social sciences on the one hand (subjunctives not commonly used), and the arts, humanities, politics, law and education on the

other (subjunctives more frequent, especially in law). From the Hyland corpus data, we concluded that the subjunctive is still quite common after REQUIRE THAT (e.g. 'requires that a detailed energy audit be conducted') but rarely used after SUGGEST. In academic speech (MICASE) there was no clear pattern, but it appeared that for strong modal lexical verbs such as INSIST, REQUIRE, RECOMMEND, the subjunctive is still sometimes used. In Week Six, where our participants brought in their own pairs of near-synonymous words, the exercise also proved enlightening, as we were able to show how corpus data could be used to help tease apart the differences. One prepared example we used also caught the participants' interest: Using BNCweb, we showed that for instance is used a lot more frequently in the social sciences and humanities (where it often introduces casual, non-essential exemplifications of points, mainly for emphasis or color), whereas in the natural sciences for example is clearly favored (being used to illuminate and clarify a difficult or complex point through the exemplification). (Lee and Swales 2006: 64)

The second excerpt discusses the implications of the study:

Our aim was to introduce students to the corpus approach to language, where the authority for language standards is decentered, and where learners, given some guidance and structured help, can take a more active role in their own learning. We believe the corpus approach is 'decentering' because: (i) it allows non-native speakers a chance to make their own discoveries about what is 'done' in the language, instead of relying on native-speaker intuitions or grammar/style books; (ii) it typically involves texts from a variety of different writers/speakers (not all of whom are necessarily native speakers), instead of just one native-speaker teacher standing at the front of the classroom. In other words, it is decentered away from the native-speaker and away from any one individual person or grammar book or stylistic convention. The feedback we received from the participants seemed to bear out this claim, as the following points which emerged from the post-course interviews reveal:

- Our participants found the use of corpora confidence-building and empowering, as they discovered they do not now always need access to a native-speaker to check up on certain linguistic issues.
- Some felt that having access to corpora was better than using reference books or grammar books. Not only was access possible any time, all the time ('24/7'), it also allowed for variation across writers/speakers and across disciplines. This access to disciplinary differences is important for some linguistic structures. Overall, they felt that the exemplification was often much closer to their contextual and textual circumstances.

The proof of the pudding here is that by the middle of the semester, most of the participants had actually already bought their own personal copies of the *Wordsmith* concordancing program, so that they could continue their concordancing activities outside the classroom, on their own (laptop) computers, on their own time, and, by implication, far into the future. Relevant here is a quotation from Starfield (2004): 'An approach, which may at first sight appear overly technicist, can become a strategy that is empowering for students' (p. 158). (Lee and Swales 2006: 70–1)

Task 2.10 Applying the concept to teaching
Discuss with colleagues:

- In what way could this technique be adapted to your own teaching context?
- If you would have to make changes, explain why.
- What problems do you envisage?
- How would you get round them?

Task 2.11 Trying out research
Discuss whether there is an aspect of the study described in this article that you would like to look into further, and outline a small research project that you would like to carry out.

2.5 FURTHER READING TWO

O'Keeffe, A., M. McCarthy and R. Carter (2007), *From Corpus to Classroom: Language Use and Language Teaching*, Cambridge: Cambridge University Press, Chapter 11, 'Exploring teacher corpora', pp. 220–45.

This chapter describes corpora of classroom interactions, focusing on teacher talk, and recommends 'the development of corpora and corpus skills as a tool for reflective practice within pre-service teacher education and on-going in-career development' (O'Keeffe et al. 2007: 220). The chapter suggests that a corpus of teacher interactions can be developmental, in that it evolves over the teacher's career (the teacher analyses his or herself) and it contributes to their development: 'small corpora are created by teachers and analysed so as to reflect on, better understand and enhance their own professional practice' (2007: 220).

The authors demonstrate how Exchange Structure Theory and Conversation Analysis can be used with CL, by focusing on a discussion of teacher questions in the classroom. They describe a study done by Farr (2002) on a corpus of classroom interactions of pre-service language teachers, examining yes–no questions ('Have you done your homework?'), wh-questions ('What's the past simple of "begin"?'), alternative questions ('Is this an adjective or a pronoun?'), declarative questions ('You've understood that?'), tag questions ('This sounds more formal, doesn't it?'), and echo questions ('I didn't knew' – 'You didn't what?'). Farr discovered the relation between the type of question and the length of learner response: declarative questions produced the longest answers in learners (the average number of words per answer was 18.33) and yes–no questions produced the shortest (the average number was 7.36). She also compared referential questions, 'genuine questions to which the teacher does not already know the answer' (O'Keeffe et al. 2007: 239) ('So what book did you use last year?'); narrow display questions, or questions with only one possible response which the teacher knows ('One child; two what?'); and broad display questions, with a range of possible answers which the teacher knows ('How do pupils come to school? Some on foot. And the rest?'). She discovered that referential questions provoked the longest answers (17.92 words per reply) and narrow display the shortest (3.34).

The excerpt is about corpora of interactions outside the classroom, in teacher education discussion after observations, and in teacher staff meetings.

> As noted by Sarangi (2002: 106), the primary focus of classroom-based teacher–pupil interaction is at the expense of looking at what happens outside the classroom. Corpora are beginning to have applications to teacher talk outside of the classroom, particularly in the broadening model of teacher observation. Two corpora have been independently developed to focus on this type of interaction and to learn from it (see Farr 2003, 2005; Vásquez and Reppen 2004; Vásquez 2004, 2005). Farr, working with the Post Observation Teacher Training Interactions (POTTI) corpus of over 80,000 words, looks at the interaction of trainers and trainees on an Irish postgraduate teacher education programme (see also chapter 6). Her work gives many insights into the post-observation interaction, including the role of relational strategies such as inclusive pronoun use when advising, so as to draw on professional solidarity, the use of first name vocatives, hedged directives, shared socio-cultural references as well as engaged listenership (responses, overlaps, interruptions) and small talk. Extract (11.10) is an example from Farr (2005: 214), where at the beginning of a post-observation session small talk is used as a relational strategy by the trainer to mitigate forthcoming criticism (the trainee had made a major organizational mistake in her teaching practice by preparing the wrong lesson). The small talk extends for 19 turns in all:
>
> (11.10)
> Trainer: . . . are you feeling okay now cos you weren't feeling great earlier you said?
> Trainee: Em not any better I can tell you actually+
> Trainer: Really?
> Trainee: +I'm very tired and em I think I've an ear infection or something every time I talk I can it's like major feedback in my ear+
> Trainer: Oh
> Trainee: +yeah I I'll need to get to the doctor or something
> Trainer: You need to be careful with that. (Farr 2005: 214)

Vásquez and Reppen's work draws on a corpus of language teachers and their mentors in a longitudinal, action research study in an American university intensive English programme. Post-observation meetings between mentors and teachers were recorded and transcribed over a period of two years. The authors were involved as mentors in these interactions and their initial findings showed that they were responsible for the majority of the talk in the meetings and that teachers tended to be passive. Based on things, changes were made to their practice with the goal of eliciting more talk from teachers. Focusing primarily on interactional data from four teacher–mentor pairs collected over two semesters, Vásquez and Reppen (in press) describe how this study enabled mentors to become aware of the linguistic and interactional subtleties of their existing practices. They illustrate how mentors were able to successfully change the meeting dynamics from mentor-centred to more teacher-centred through changes in the distribution of talk among participants. Important changes came about, for example, as a result of the ways that teachers were positioned by mentors in the openings of meetings. As in Farr's work, Vásquez and Reppen have created their own corpus to look at their own professional practices in context.

Vaughan (in press) looks at a corpus of English language teacher meetings in which she participated. She applies Goffman's (1959) dramaturgical metaphor of frontstage and backstage to teacher discourse. The contrasts the teachers' highly regulated and formalized frontstage talk in the classroom with their less organized backstage identity. Somewhere between this highly regulated and formalized frontstage and less organized backstage lies the area of mediated interaction which has as its goal the facilitation of professional development (e.g. Edge 1992, 2002) and reflective practice (e.g. Walsh 2002, 2003). Vaughan argues that, while the frontstage interaction has been considered the most significant type of discourse that teachers engage in, interaction outside the classroom, the teacher's backstage (teacher to teacher) discourse, is equally significant and has not thus far received as much attention as it merits. Vaughan, working with a corpus of over 40,000 words of teacher staff meetings, looks at how characteristics of this Community of Practice (after Lave and Wenger 1991; Wenger 1998) may be realized in linguistic features, and how these features together comprise a 'badge of identity'. She finds, for example, that the type of vague language used by the teachers is specific to their practices and that humour is key to the establishment of a shared communicative space. She also highlights the creation of this space through the construction of in- and out-groups. (O'Keeffe et al. 2007: 241–2)

Task 2.12 Applying the concept to teaching
Discuss:

- What aspect of pre-service teacher education in your context would be enhanced by a corpus study?
- How would you go about convincing colleagues that it should be included in initial teacher education?

Task 2.13 Trying out research
Explore in groups:

- What out-of-classroom backstage teacher discourse (teacher-to-teacher talk, e.g. in staff meetings, emails, informal nights out) would it be useful for you personally to study?

- What features would you like to look at specifically in it and why?
- How would you record it?
- What might be the drawbacks of doing this?

2.6 SUMMARY

This chapter has helped you to:

- think about building your own corpus and know the basics about data collection and transcription, about labelling files and annotating data
- try out analysing corpora, producing concordances, wordlists and keyword lists
- think about the ways that CL can be used in conjunction with studies of World Englishes, social variables, registers and genres, and other approaches to language analysis that take into account interactional features

As regards using CL to improve your EFL teaching, you have considered how to:

- analyse your own classroom interaction and reflect on your teaching practices
- incorporate findings into the classroom input
- use CL to help you answer learner questions
- design DDL tasks for your learners to learn from concordances and wordlists
- adapt your EFL coursebook and materials by designing realistic texts

Finally, let it be said that CL has spread to ELT round the world. There is a burgeoning of books on the topic (see Additional Readings below), claiming that 'Corpus-aided language pedagogy is one of the central application areas of corpus methodologies, and a test bed for theories of language and learning' (Aston, Bernardini and Stewart 2004); finding that 'corpus work provides students with a useful source of information about ESP language features' and 'the process of "search-and-discovery" implied in the method of corpus analysis may facilitate language learning and promote autonomy in learning language use' (Gavioli 2005); and offering advice on 'how to cope with teachers' queries about language, what corpora to use including learner corpora and spoken corpora and how to handle the variability of language' (Sinclair 2004) (quotes from Benjamins Publishers website).

Conferences are another example of the wide-reaching impact. At the 8th Teaching and Language Corpora Conference (2008), Tono talked about the creation of the world's first corpus-based TV English conversation program:

> The program ran from 2003 to 2006, a hundred units featuring 100 keywords selected based on BNC. Each unit focuses on useful collocation patterns of the keywords, with model skits videotaped in UK, USA and Australia, and ample exercises. A special CG character called 'Mr Corpus' introduced the corpus ranking.
>
> The impact of the program was significant. More than a million people watched the program and the word 'corpus' became a familiar term. Various

corpus-based teaching materials have been published since then. There is also a growing demand among English teachers to know more about corpora and corpus-based ELT. (Tono 2008)

2.7 ADDITIONAL READINGS

Below are five texts that relate CL to language teaching. They suggest practical applications of the theory and may provide ideas that you could use in your classroom.

Aijmer, K. (2009), *Corpora and Language Teaching*, London: Continuum.

Campoy, M., B. Belles-Fortuno and M. Gea-Valor (2010), *Corpus-Based Approaches to English Language Teaching*, London: Continuum.

Cheng, W. (2012), *Exploring Corpus Linguistics: Language in Action*, London: Routledge.

Reppen, R. (2010), *Using Corpora in the Language Classroom*, Cambridge: Cambridge University Press.

Sinclair, J. (2004), *How to Use Corpora in Language Teaching*, London: Continuum.

3

GLOBAL ENGLISHES

Nicola Galloway and Eleni Mariou

INTRODUCTION

The English language no longer has traditional assumed linguistic boundaries: it is used by speakers all over the world from diverse lingua-cultural backgrounds. This unprecedented diversification of the language on a global scale makes English unlike other lingua francas. This chapter sets the scene of English in the world. It begins with a look at the spread of English and the way that people from different parts of the globe use English in a wide variety of settings. It explores how English is used by people from different linguistic and cultural backgrounds.

A large number of terms have been used to describe the worldwide spread of English including 'English as a Global Language' (Crystal 2003), 'English as a World Language' (Mair 2003), 'International English' (McKay 2002), 'Global English' (Crystal 2003), 'English as a Medium of Intercultural Communication' (Meierkord 1996) and 'English as an International Language' (Holliday 2005; Sharifian 2009; Alsagoff et al. 2012). This volume uses the term **World Englishes** (WE) and the **English as a Lingua Franca** (ELF) research paradigm, which form part of a larger research paradigm, **Global Englishes** (GE).

The volume defines GE as a research paradigm and a theoretical approach for exploring the worldwide spread of English, and the way that English is now used by people from different language backgrounds for a wide range of purposes and in a wide range of contexts. GE is an inclusive paradigm that incorporates WE and ELF and, therefore, the English spoken in the Inner Circle, Outer Circle and Expanding Circle, as well as the use of English between and across these 'circles' (see Section 3.1 for an explanation of these terms).

The GE approach also involves practice, and emphasises the relevance of WE and ELF to ELT. In this chapter you are introduced to the pedagogical implications of such research for English Language Teaching (ELT). Despite changes in the use of English worldwide and the fact that non-native English speakers (NNESs) now outnumber native English speakers (NESs), the native English model still dominates in ELT.

The internationalisation of English is relevant to you as an English teacher if you are:

- interested in the demographics of English
- curious about who speaks English today and for what purposes

- interested in how to best categorise English speakers today
- interested in finding out about the native-speaker model and its relevance for those who uses ELF
- interested in recent examinations of ELT in relation to the spread of English and the proposals that have been suggested for change

This chapter examines perspectives on how English can be viewed and taught.

3.1 ENGLISH IN A GLOBAL WORLD

English is without a doubt a global language. Its global significance is understood through its use in the fields of technology, science, trade, the media, diplomacy etc. It is an international language for communication among people from various countries and cultural contexts. As more and more people are involved in English-language learning, and educational policies around the world emphasise the need for ELT, it becomes apparent that the field of education plays a major role in the promotion of the English language. Due to the expansion of English, it is not surprising that TESOL programmes around the globe include GE in both teacher education and language instruction programmes, in an attempt to familiarise teachers and learners with the diversity of the English language.

The spread of English, which suggests 'adaptation and non-conformity' (Widdowson 1997: 140) and relates to the notion of varieties discussed in the next section, can be explained through three 'diasporic' movements, a term which refers to the metaphorical 'migration of English'. The first movement includes the varieties which developed in countries such as Canada, the USA and Australia, and it was marked by the first 'English attempt at settlement in North America' (Graddol et al. 1996: 194). These also constitute the so-called 'native' varieties. The second includes the 'Englishes that have emerged out of colonial enterprise' (Saxena and Omoniyi 2010: 4–5), and are used in former British colonies such as India, Kenya and Hong Kong, and former colonies of the United States such as the Philippines. The third diasporic movement includes those countries where English has spread as a result of globalisation, such as China and Japan, where English assumes an important position due to the increasing demands of international communication in several domains. However, this diaspora model is problematic, and categorising the spread of English is a difficult task (for criticisms see Galloway and Rose 2015).

English language speakers are commonly categorised using 'a tripartite model [which] has been . . . adopted by English language professionals' and its 'categories have become systematised as **English as a Native Language** (ENL), **English as a Second Language** (ESL) and **English as a Foreign Language** (EFL)' (McArthur 1998: 43). Although the three categories do not fully account for the bilinguality/multilinguality of speakers in these territories, and are largely based on the notion of monolinguality, as will be discussed later, they broadly reflect how the English language is distributed around the world. Based on this model, it is estimated (Graddol 1997, 2006; Crystal 2003) that there are:

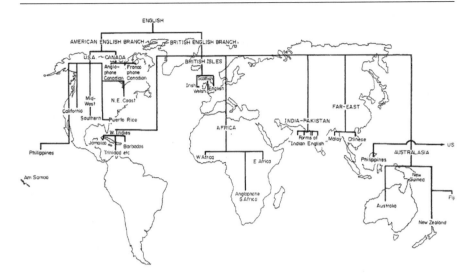

Figure 3.1   Strevens's World map of English (Strevens 1980: 86)

- between 320 and 380 million people who speak English as a first language
- 300–500 million people who are ESL speakers
- nearly one billion who speak EFL

It is difficult to calculate the exact numbers, but it is clear that in the future, non-native speakers will be the norm, as they already outnumber native speakers (Kachru et al. 2009).

Due to the diversity of English speakers around the world, there have been several attempts to categorise them. The oldest model is Strevens's (1980: 86) **world map of English**. Figure 3.1 shows a world map shown on a 'family tree' diagram and displays the spread of English and the various branches, and how every form of English is seen to align itself with either British or American English.

Figure 3.2 shows McArthur's (1987) circle, which places '**World Standard English**' in the centre, despite the fact that it is now commonly accepted that this does not exist. It also shows regional varieties, including both standard and other forms, and then eight regions represented by various spokes, which McArthur (1998: 95) calls sub-varieties.

Perhaps the most widely known model is Kachru's (1992a) **three-circle model** (Figure 3.3). Here, WE are divided into three circles: the Inner Circle (IC), the Outer Circle (OC) and the Expanding Circle (EC), corresponding to ENL, ESL and EFL as discussed earlier. The IC refers to countries where English is used as the main language, including Australia, the US and the UK. The OC, where English also plays an important role as an additional, official language, includes former IC colonies, such as Singapore and India. The EC includes countries such as China and France, which were not colonised by IC countries, and where English has few intra-national users and is often considered to be a foreign language.

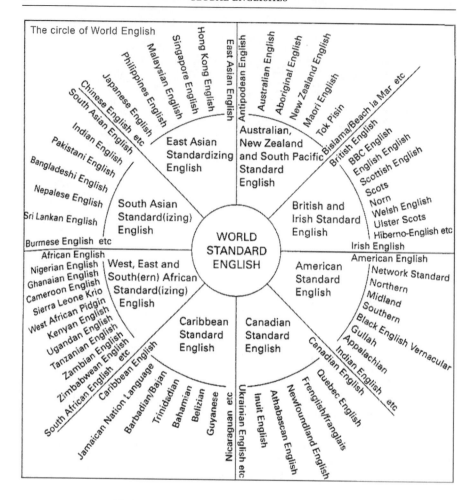

The circle of World English

WORLD STANDARD ENGLISH

Figure 3.2   McArthur's (1987) Circle of World English

Kachru's model has been very influential in raising awareness of the existence of varieties of English, but it has come under criticism for its focus on geography and history rather than the sociolinguistic uses of English. Many OC speakers, for example, speak English as a first language and many grow up bilingual or multilingual. An increasing number of EC speakers also use English on an everyday basis and as a consequence the role of English is changing. In the Gulf Corporation Council (Saudi Arabia, Kuwait, Bahrain, Qatar, the United Arab Emirates and the Sultanate of Oman), the official language is Arabic but English is widely spoken because of the presence of large expatriate communities and the importance of English as the language of business (Ali 2009: 35). In addition, in Japan, several companies have also adopted English as their official working language. Phillipson (2003) notes that the trend in transnational corporations throughout Europe is to shift to English as the

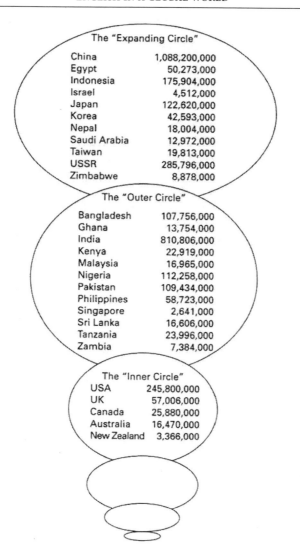

The "Expanding Circle"

China	1,088,200,000
Egypt	50,273,000
Indonesia	175,904,000
Israel	4,512,000
Japan	122,620,000
Korea	42,593,000
Nepal	18,004,000
Saudi Arabia	12,972,000
Taiwan	19,813,000
USSR	285,796,000
Zimbabwe	8,878,000

The "Outer Circle"

Bangladesh	107,756,000
Ghana	13,754,000
India	810,806,000
Kenya	22,919,000
Malaysia	16,965,000
Nigeria	112,258,000
Pakistan	109,434,000
Philippines	58,723,000
Singapore	2,641,000
Sri Lanka	16,606,000
Tanzania	23,996,000
Zambia	7,384,000

The "Inner Circle"

USA	245,800,000
UK	57,006,000
Canada	25,880,000
Australia	16,470,000
New Zealand	3,366,000

Figure 3.3   Kachru's three-circle model of World Englishes
(Kachru 1992: 356)

in-house corporate language. Thus, English clearly has a changing role in the EC. In addition, being an IC speaker does not imply better proficiency, nor is the number of IC speakers smaller than EC speakers as represented by the size of the circles (for criticisms see Canagarajah 1999; Yano 2001, 2009; Bruthiaux 2003; Jenkins 2009; Pennycook 2009).

Shifting away from a strict categorisation based on the native/non-native speaker spectrum, Modiano's (1999a) model (Figure 3.4) prioritises the use of English as an international language and focuses on international intelligibility,

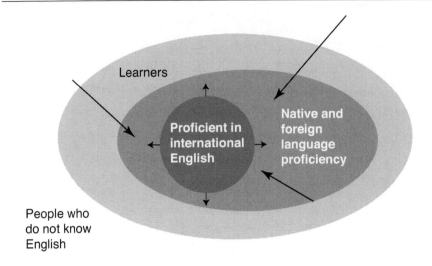

Fig. 3.4   Modiano's centripetal circles of international English (1999a)

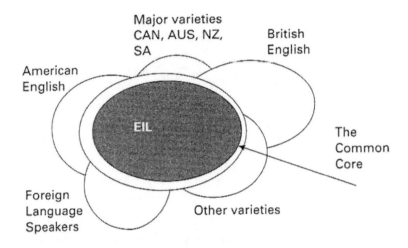

Fig. 3.5   Modiano's English as an international language (EIL) (1999b)

not native-speaker proficiency. Proficient users of 'international English' are at the centre and are defined as those who can function in cross-communication and have no 'strong' regional accent or dialect regardless of whether or not they are a 'native' speaker. Next are those with first or second language English proficiency who function well in the language; and the third group consists of learners of English.

Modiano's (1999b) second model (Figure 3.5) focused on a common core (comprehensible features of English common to all varieties), a second circle (features which may become internationally common) and an outer area (unintelligible context-specific features). However, the distinction between core and non-core varieties and the use of the term 'major varieties' is questionable, as it may lead some to assume that 'major' means superior, or even 'standard'.

These models highlight the problem of categorising speakers as 'native' and 'non-native' and of deciding whether proficiency or expertise is more relevant today than the region that people are from. Traditionally, theories about language learning have typically posited the native English speaker as the 'ultimate goal'. NESs dominate ELT materials, examinations and major ELT periodicals. This prejudice is also evident in hiring practices, where NESs are normally favoured. Davies (2006: 435) sustains six criteria for NES status, including childhood L1, grammatical intuition, capacity for fluent spontaneous discourse and creative communicative range. However, it is questionable whether these are necessary or present in all NESs. The terms have also been criticised for labelling people as a 'non' something, which can reduce confidence, while unrealistic goals, such as achieving the debated notion of 'native competence', can cause people to see themselves as failed NESs as opposed to competent users of more than one language. Seidlhofer (2003: 183) points out that the terms imply homogeneity, although most NESs do not speak a 'standardised' version. In addition, monolingualism is no longer the norm and the concepts 'native speaker' and 'mother tongue speaker' make little sense in multilingual societies where it may be difficult to single out someone's mother tongue (Kirkpatrick 2007: 9).

Many have argued that it is time for a critical evaluation of how English is taught around the world. As Leung and Street (2012: 88) point out, 'the unquestioned assumption that the language norms and practices associated with native-speaker varieties should be regarded as automatically relevant and legitimate has been considerably lessened'. The prevalence of NES norms has also been challenged within the WE paradigm and the ELF paradigm, each of which are discussed in the next section.

Task 3.1 Applying the concept to teaching

Read the following excerpt taken from Kirkpatrick (2007: 8–9):

Claire was born in Sicily and migrated to Australia when she was eight. As a child she learned Sicilian as her first language/mother tongue and standard Italian as a second language. When she arrived in Australia she started to learn English. She is now 40 and has been in Australia for more than 30 years. The language that she learned third, from the age of eight, is the language that she is now best at. Her second-best language is Standard Italian and her third is Sicilian. In other words, what was her first language and mother tongue is now a language that she does not speak as well as the other languages she speaks. She is a so-called native speaker of Sicilian but one who does not speak it well. She is a so-called non-native speaker of English, but speaks it fluently. The language she speaks best is a language that she only started to learn once she was eight. Claire is by no means an unusual example. There are many people who have what I shall call a 'shifting L1'. Indeed in immigrant communities it is common. It is also common in multilingual societies.

Discuss in groups answers to the following questions:

- What does the author mean by a 'shifting L1'?
- Which of Kachru's three circles would you place Claire in?
- Would you be happy if Claire was your English teacher, if you were studying English?
- Which of the three circles would you place your learners in?
- What perceptions does this extract raise in terms of the native/non-native dichotomy?

Task 3.2 Trying out research
Sifakis and Sougari (2003) outline the need to raise learners' awareness of what they term 'EIL-related matters', including the 'need' for an international language today, the reasons for the spread of English, the relationship between English and their mother tongue and information on the possible detrimental effects of English on their mother tongue or local dialect.

In your own context, research the impact of the globalisation of English. Use the following questions to guide an interview with a speaker from a different country to you:

- For which purposes is English used in a context you are familiar with today?
- How has this use changed over the years?
- Has English been adapted to the local context?
- Is English a crucial component of the country's policies to engage in globalisation?
- Has English become an integral part of the national identity of this country?

Once you have finished, compile the results and report them to a small group in the form of a presentation.

Task 3.3 Using the internet
'NNS English countries emerge as places where NSs of English go to teach, NS countries as places that NNSs go to learn, and where experts and authoritative publications originate' (Jenkins 2007: 48). This prejudice is also evident in hiring practices. Print out some common job recruitment websites for English teachers in a context familiar to you and tell your colleagues about the answers to the following questions:

- What qualifications are required?
- What skills are required?
- Are there any restrictions in terms of nationality?
- What skills and qualifications do you think are important for English teachers in your context?

- As a student English teacher, how do these advertisements make you feel?
- Are references to 'native' 'addressing a hypothetical preference by L2 learners for NESTs' (Moussu and Llurda 2008: 316), NESTs being native English-speaking teachers, and how do you feel about such labels?

3.2 VARIETIES AND WORLD ENGLISHES

WE and ELF are part of the larger paradigm of GE. This section discusses WE, paying particular attention to varieties of English that have emerged through the spread of English in postcolonial times.

The spread of English has resulted in the formation of different varieties. As Widdowson (1997: 140) notes, in the process of its spread, English 'gets adapted . . . [and] becomes subject to local constraints and controls'. A **variety** is a 'set of linguistic items with similar distribution' (Hudson 1996: 22), and can be 'a language, a dialect, an idiolect or an accent' (Bolton 2009: 290). These terms can be explained as follows: German is a language and Bavarian is a dialect of German; an idiolect is a personal style of language use (individual way of pronouncing certain words, choice of vocabulary or grammatical patterns); accents are differences in the way words are pronounced and are either regionally or socially defined: for example, Irish or American English speakers tend pronounce the /r/ (in words such as 'farm', 'car') whereas English speakers from England generally tend not to (an exception being people from the West Country). In this sense, WE comprises a vast array of varieties which are mainly **geographically** or **politically** defined, as denoted by the plural form 'Englishes'. Kachru's (1992a) model (Figure 3.3) highlights the heterogeneous nature of English, and WE scholars have concentrated on the investigation and description of various national varieties, often labelled as **nativised** or **indigenised** (Kirkpatrick 2007), due to local linguistic and cultural influences. A lot of research has been conducted in this area (e.g. Kachru et al. 2009), particularly in the OC, and scholars have described these varieties in terms of phonology, lexicon, syntax, pragmatics and discourse, as well as literary creativity, in order to identify characteristics of these national varieties as distinct from native or **'standard'**, that is 'accepted', norms. Such attempts at **codification**, that is to say formal recording of a variety (Jenkins 2003; Kachru et al. 2009; Mullany and Stockwell 2010), legitimise WE varieties. Some examples are outlined below:

- In Indian English some words take on a different semantic meaning from the so-called 'standard varieties': *'Shift'* = *move* (especially house or office) (Sailaja 2009: 68).
- In African American English the verb 'to be' is usually omitted: *They walking to school* (Mufwene et al. 1998: 38).
- In terms of phonology, Malaysian, Sri Lankan and Singaporean as well as some African English speakers tend to use the sounds /tθ/ and /dð/ instead of /t/ and /ð/ in the words 'thin' and 'this', so they sound like 't-thin' and 'd-this' (Jenkins 2003: 23).

The existence of such varieties raises the issue of the **ownership** of English (Widdowson 1994), in that English is no longer 'owned' by NESs in IC countries: it has been adapted by speakers around the globe. This challenges the view that 'Standard British English' and 'Standard American English' are norms (Bolton and Kachru 2006), showing that they are merely varieties themselves.

However, scholars who see the spread of English as **linguistic imperialism** (Phillipson 1992, 2002; Pennycook 1998) claim that the persistence of British or American English varieties (IC) in ELT materials perpetuates the notion of a 'standard language'. Despite attempts at codifying WE varieties, they are still classed as illegitimate or viewed as 'deficient' or 'fossilised' versions, and NES varieties tend to be regarded as the 'legitimate' offspring because of the mistaken belief that they have evolved from old English without 'contamination' (Mufwene 2001).

As the study of WE highlights the contextual nature of varieties, where social, linguistic and cultural influences exist, the notion of **identity**, and what is more **learner identity**, has recently received recognition in the field of WE (Kachru et al. 2009; Kachru and Smith 2008; Saxena and Omoniyi 2010). WE scholars argue that mutual intelligibility, that is to say the ability to understand each other through a common language, is more important than attempting to imitate NES accents. They believe that language learners should not feel compelled to abandon the accent which derives from their own first language in favour of approximating their accent to British or American English. This approach respects learners' identities and indeed their varieties of English. Identity cannot be defined without paying attention to a speaker's cultural background. In Australia, for example, Aboriginal Australians speak Aboriginal English, which in itself marks a distinct identity due to the influences of their own 'mother tongue' (Bodba 2010: 172).

The concepts discussed have a major impact on the ELT profession globally; WE research has highlighted the need to critically examine ELT practices (Matsuda 2012: 5). WE scholars advocate the incorporation of WE in TESOL education programmes in IC, EC and OC countries, for both NES teachers and NNES teachers. Teacher awareness of different varieties can pave the way to acceptance of other varieties, challenging the status quo of 'Standard English' as the norm, and promoting tolerance of 'norm-deviant' varieties. Awareness of cultural differences can enhance intercultural communication.

Proponents of the WE paradigm suggest that in the ELT language classroom, learners' awareness of phonological, lexical and pragmatic features of different varieties should be raised. Matsuda (2003) and Jenkins (2006) suggest that teaching activities and materials could reflect more speakers from the OC and EC, while assessment could focus on testing communicative competence, rather than insisting on adherence to 'standard' varieties of British English or American English. The use of the internet can play a decisive role in familiarising learners with a range of varieties of English. There are websites which include samples of spoken language that can be used in the classroom, such as IDEA (http://web.ku.edu/~idea) and the Speech Accent Archive (http://accent.gmu.edu/). Speech samples of varieties from radio or news broadcasts are also a useful resource. In addition, videos can enable learners to notice gestures and other paralinguistic features typical of speakers of a variety X (Baik and Shim 2002). Moreover, literature (Kachru and Smith 2008) helps learners appreciate stylistic differences. If, for example, teachers use short stories or extracts from literary works by authors from different countries, learners can be helped to notice differences in terms of grammar and vocabulary, as well as the sociocultural context of regional varieties. It is not, of course, suggested that teachers introduce every variety that exists; they should always consider the needs of their learners and what varieties are salient to the particular learning context.

Task 3.4 Applying the concept to teaching

Despite the recognition of different varieties of English, most English language instruction still continues to focus on NES norms, which may indirectly impose on learners the idea that these are the only legitimate varieties, and that English presents no significant variation in the IC countries where it is spoken, while ignoring the fact that English is widely spoken in other regions.

Discuss whether it would be possible to carry out the following plan with your learners/people in your class:

- Introduce them to the idea of varieties of English spoken in IC, OC and EC countries by presenting them with a world map and Kachru's model (Figure 3.3).
- Collect examples of English language spoken in IC, OC and EC countries. These may have to do with the use of vocabulary, use of grammar or regional cultural features which are apparent in discourse.
- Ask learners/classmates about their attitudes towards these utterances.
- Analyse language features and highlight the difference in varieties of English.
- Ask your learners/classmates to do a small-scale research project on the internet and prepare a short presentation on a variety of English in either an IC or OC country and present it in class.

You may also want to ask classmates to design a lesson plan based on these activities, try it out, and reflect on it afterwards.

Task 3.5 Trying out research

Due to the spread of English, the concepts of 'speaker' and 'learner identity' have become more complex. In the case of English speakers from IC countries, their identity may be influenced by the specific variety they speak and their region of origin. For speakers from OC and EC countries, identity positioning can be understood through the concept of bi-/multilingualism and thus the merging of two or more languages and/or cultures (the latter either through direct or indirect exposure).

Considering the above, design a small-scale research project and interview one or two speakers from an IC, OC and EC country, for example NES or NNES from your own teaching context or other colleagues on your course. Then discuss the following:

- How do these speakers define their identity as an English speaker/learner?
- To what extent is their English identity influenced by the contexts in which they function, for example school, work environment?
- How do their views relate to the concept of 'ownership' of English?
- You may also wish to extend this by researching 'teacher identity' and focus on investigating the perceptions of both 'native' and 'non-native' teachers concerning a possible 'identity shift' in the work environment.
- How does the work environment shape the identity of these teachers and vice-versa?
- What are the differences and similarities you can notice through their accounts?

Task 3.6 Using the internet
Visit either IDEA or the Speech Accent Archive and select some listening samples from speakers (IC and OC countries) of varieties salient to your learners. After you have selected 3–4 samples and downloaded them, listen and transcribe orthographically the first 30–50 seconds of each. Bring the sound samples and transcripts to class and design an activity for English language learners which highlights pronunciation differences in the varieties of English spoken. You may wish to focus on specific vowel or consonant sounds and contrast these with 'Standard English'. Discuss the answers to the following questions:

- How would you incorporate this activity in a lesson in order to raise learners' awareness of WE?
- Does this task challenge your own views about what constitutes a 'proper English accent'?
- What debates emerge from this activity regarding linguistic imperialism and mutual intelligibility? Discuss this with your peers, both in terms of the needs and perceptions of English language learners, as well as in terms of your views as student teachers.

3.3 ENGLISH AS A LINGUA FRANCA

As a result of globalisation and the resulting increased mobility and interconnectedness, people from different countries and linguistic backgrounds commonly use English to communicate. ELF can be defined as 'any use of English among speakers of different first languages for whom English is the communicative medium of choice, and often the only option' (Seidlhofer 2011: 7). ELF researchers are interested in examining what happens to the language when it is used among such speakers in diverse and changing contexts.

Early ELF research focused on the identification of surface-level features, or rather what ELF might look like. For instance, Seildhofer (2004: 220) lists common lexis and grammatical features:

- 'Dropping' the third person present tense –*s*
- 'Confusing' the relative pronouns *who* and *which*

- 'Omitting' definite and indefinite articles where they are obligatory in ENL, and inserting them where they do not occur in ENL
- 'Failing' to use correct forms in tag questions (e.g., *isn't it?* or *no?* instead of *shouldn't they?*)
- Inserting 'redundant' prepositions, as in *We have to study about . . .*
- 'Overusing' certain types of verbs of high semantic generality, such as *do, have, make, put, take*
- 'Replacing' infinitive constructions with *that*-clauses, as in *I want that . . .*
- 'Overdoing' explicitness (e.g., *black colour* rather than just *black*)

While many people, English teachers included, may regard such features as mistakes or as non-standard usage of English, ELF research shows how such features are common in many ELF situations. It highlights that such features should not be treated simply as errors, that ELF is a usage in its own right, and that IC English is not superior or something to be modelled.

ELF communication takes place in **multilingual settings**. Most of the work of ELF scholars focuses on how and why ELF functions in these settings. The settings can be short-term, fleeting exchanges, for example a conversation between a Japanese tourist and a Swedish tour conductor on a sightseeing bus in Stockholm, or a service encounter between a Spanish tourist and a Turkish market-stall holder in Istanbul; or they can be more long-term, for example daily conversations between a French and a Chinese international student sharing a flat on a one-year study-abroad programme, or ongoing meetings between Greek and German business partners.

While WE research focuses on the identification of varieties of English in specific geographical regions (see Seidlhofer 2009 and Cogo and Dewey 2012 for an overview of the main differences between WE and ELF), ELF research examines how English is used worldwide among speakers from all three of Kachru`s circles across physical and linguistic boundaries, in **communities of practice** (Lave and Wenger 1991; Seidlhofer 2007, 2009; Wenger 1998), which are groups of people with common interests, purposes and in-group linguistic practices. ELF is not tied to 'fixed' geographical settings, therefore: it changes according to the nation, the location and the community of practice (Cogo and Dewey 2012). For example, an ELF business negotiation between French and Korean colleagues in Paris may look rather different from one between Thai, Japanese and Indian colleagues in Bangkok, and different again if the Thai colleagues were absent in the latter scenario.

ELF research involves an examination of the **strategies** used by ELF speakers, focusing on the ways that people use the language to negotiate meanings and achieve successful communication. An example of such work is Cogo's (2009), which highlights how ELF speakers make use of **accommodation**, by which they adapt their language to accommodate to their interlocutors. ELF users' accommodation strategies (e.g. translation, paraphrasing, elaboration, repetition, clarification, code-switching) 'allow their exchanges to be more intelligible than if they had referred to "standard native-speakers" norms' (Cogo 2009: 257). Studies show that ELF users can be particularly accomplished at negotiating meaning through the collaborative sharing of their multilingual repertoires, and that misunderstanding is rare among competent ELF users. Of course, monolinguals have a linguistic repertoire which allows them to negotiate and co-construct meaning. The difference is that ELF users exploit their additional language. The communication can be a creative process, as can be seen in the example below, in which a German, French and Italian speaker discuss honeymoon photos:

18   JEAN: no it's nice yeah . . . yeah they have picture of them
19   KAREN: =eh?
20   JEAN: =they have pictures of them you know . . . in
21   Australia, [in Katmandu, in Tibet, like
22   KAREN: [(laughing)
23   ANNA: they sent pictures . . . [on the internet/
24   JEAN: [it's nice but it's **a bit**
25   ANNA: =**too much** eh?
26   JEAN: =**cheesy**
27   KAREN: [YE::AH
28   ANNA: [YE::AH
29   KAREN: yeah **a bit too much** I think (laughing)
30   JEAN: so . . . **blue flower** we say, . . . **fleur bleue/**
31   ANNA: why . . . [to say that it's cheesy?
32   JEAN: [fleur-yeah . . . fleur bleue means . . . you
33   know when you have these pictures with little
34   angels of
35   KAREN: a:::h [yeah
36   ANNA: [yeah
37   JEAN: fleur bleu
38   KAREN: **kitsch- [kitschig]**
39   JEAN: [kitschig yeah (laughter) . . . (Cogo and Dewey 2006: 67)

In this example, the French speaker uses the French expression *fleur bleue* to para-phrase the English *cheesy*. The German and Italian speakers clearly know the term *cheesy* so this use is interesting to them. The French speaker then elaborates (*when you have these pictures with little angels*) to explain the meaning of the French expres-sion, and the German translates the idiom into the German *kitschig*. This is evidence of accommodation and co-construction of meaning to enhance communication. Another way that ELF speakers adapt their multilingual resources is **code-switching**, a communication strategy in which speakers slip between two languages as they talk, which has a range of functions, including specifying addressees, asking for help, introducing ideas and signalling culture and identity.

ELF research has met with criticism (Modiano 2009). Some opponents see ELF descriptive work as an attempt to codify a variety of English. Saraceni (2008: 22) states that the concept of ELF attempts to 'replace one model with another' with a 'one-size-fits-all model of English', and that ELF research does not involve a representative sample of speakers. The focus of ELF research is not on establishing a variety, but on describing forms that commonly emerge in ELF interactions. In addition, this work also takes into account those NESs who feature in exchanges with ELF users. As Cogo explains, 'ELF is not monolithic or a single variety because cultural and linguistic resources are inevitably transformed as they are locally appropriated' (2012: 98).

Since Jenkins's (2000) and Seidlhofer's (2001) seminal pieces, ELF research has flourished despite this opposition. There has been an increase in corpora, including the English as a Lingua Franca in Academic Settings (ELFA) corpus (Mauranen 2003), the Studying in English as a Lingua Franca (SELF) project, the Vienna–Oxford International Corpus of English (VOICE) (Seidlhofer 2004) and the Asian Corpus of English (ACE) (Kirkpatrick 2011). Many of these corpora are accessible for public use, as we saw in Chapter 2.

This work has important ramifications for **English Language Teaching**. Like WE, ELF challenges the traditional emphasis on teaching based on the 'Inner Circle Model' (Kubota 2012: 57). Research findings in ELF 'have major implications for a multitude of common beliefs and assumptions about what is sanctioned as good practice by the profession' (Jenkins et al. 2011: 305). The ELF paradigm challenges assumptions about norms in ELT. In many countries, textbooks still adhere to NES norms: for example, Matsuda's (2002) study of textbooks in Japan from 1997 to 2001 reveals an over-representation and almost exclusive representation of American English. A GE approach to ELT does not focus on the norms of a minority of English users. It places all users of English on an equal footing, aiming to prepare learners for using English in a globalised world.

ELF usage changes as ELF users adapt the language in different contexts. Canagarajah (2005) states that English learners are not learning English to join a single language community, but are '**shuttling between communities**' where a variety of norms and a repertoire of codes are needed. ELF researchers believe that the aim of English learners should be to achieve mutual understanding in a wide range of contexts and communities, and that English classes should help learners 'shuttle' (move) between these contexts. This approach represents a departure from the 'hierarchical approach', with a focus on NES norms, and an adoption of a more 'levelled approach' (see Table 3.1).

Table 3.1 Shifts in pedagogical practice

From hierarchical approach. . .	to levelled approach
'Target language'	Repertoire
Text and language as homogeneous	Text and language as hybrid
Joining a community	Shuttling between communities
Focus on rules and conventions	Focus on strategies
Correctness	Negotiation
Language and discourse as static	Language and discourse as changing
Language as context-bound	Language as context-transforming
Mastery of grammar rules	Metalinguistic awareness
Text and language as transparent and instrumental	Text and language as representational
L1 or C1 as problem	L1 or C1 as resource

In order to make the transition to the levelled approach suggested in Table 3.1, towards what Galloway and Rose (2015) term Global Englishes Language Teaching (GELT), teachers can make **needs analysis** an integral part of their curriculum building. They can investigate the purposes for which the language is needed, the communities of practice that learners will find themselves in, and the types of communication that will be used (written, spoken, formal, informal). Brown (1995) notes that needs analysis should include questions about problems experienced when using English with NESs, but ELF scholars advocate adding questions about problems experienced when using English with other ELF speakers.

Nevertheless, it may be the case that due to the dominance of the NES episteme in ELT, learners may feel that it is necessary to use an NES model in the classroom. They may also perceive their future interlocutors to be NESs, and teachers may find themselves having to 'convince' learners that this is not necessarily the case. 'Needs analysis thus includes the study of perceived and present needs as well as potential and unrecognized needs' (Richards 2001: 53). It is these unrecognised needs that ELF researchers feel have to be stressed to learners.

ELF listening materials are also vital to allow the transition to the levelled approach. English teachers can create a bank of materials which include different contexts, such as those described in the VOICE and ELFA corpora. Using in ELT classes recordings that include expert ELF users means that learners are exposed to the various strategies employed to achieve successful communication, such as repetition, paraphrasing, clarification and code-switching, and that they can gain some insight into how mutual understanding is co-constructed among the interlocutors in a variety of settings around the world. Classroom tasks based on VOICE and ELFA corpora may raise learners' confidence by showing them that proficient ELF speakers do not merely attempt to use one particular variety of English such as 'standard' British or 'standard' American, but that they exploit the language in a flexible and resourceful way to enable communication and signal solidarity to fellow ELF users.

Learners can also be given opportunities to interact with other ELF users and practise communicating with people from different linguistic backgrounds: this is seen as key to learning how to develop communicative strategies for ELF situations. Online resources can be exploited; skype exchanges and social networking exchanges with schools around the world can expose learners to ELF and encourage them to reflect on their interactions. Interacting with other ELF users can also raise learners' confidence.

The idea of changing in this way may be rather daunting to some teachers. Teachers may be obliged to use ELT materials that focus on NES norms. They may be preparing learners for large-scale examinations which continue to have an NES focus, such as the Test of English for International Communication (TOEIC), the Test of English as a Foreign Language (TOEFL), the International English Language Testing System (IELTS) and the Certificate of Proficiency in English (CPE). Teachers may have limited knowledge of GE-related concepts, and of how to introduce a GE perspective into their classrooms. Teacher education about GE can be very useful in this respect. However, as Jenkins (2012) notes, ELT practitioners must make their own informed decisions about whether to include GE or not. Of course, teachers are not the only barriers to implementing change (see Galloway and Rose 2015).

Task 3.7 Applying the concept to teaching

As Kirkpatrick (2007: 195) points out, English language teachers who wish to work in outer and expanding circle countries should 'be able to evaluate ELT materials critically to ensure that tests do not, either explicitly or implicitly, promote a particular variety of English or culture at the expense of others'. In relation to your teaching context(s), discuss the following questions:

- Which variety of English, or ELF contexts are my learners familiar with (and why)?
- Which English varieties or ELF contexts are relevant for my learners?

Analyse a textbook from your teaching context using the following questions:

- Which variety of English is the textbook based on? Is it appropriate for my learners? Are other varieties or ELF contexts included?
- What cultures are included in the textbook and are they relevant?
- Does the textbook promote stereotypical images of 'English-speaking' cultures?
- Does the textbook raise awareness of Global Englishes (e.g. diversity)?
- To what extent are mutual intelligibility and native English competence stressed in your context?

Task 3.8 Trying out research

Most people are aware that they have an attitude towards the concept of standard language ideology, as well as towards the variety of English spoken in their own country. Compose a questionnaire and/or interview that investigates the attitudes of people in your context towards English and the reasons behind these attitudes. Include questions about:

- Attitudes towards English and ELT
- Attitudes towards own language/variety of English
- Attractive varieties of English
- Attractive varieties of English for ELT
- Perceived future use of English
- Language learning goals

Discuss how you think people in your context would answer.

Task 3.9 Using the internet

It is vital for teachers to raise awareness of how ELF speakers make use of strategies such as repetition, paraphrasing and code-switching and that 'successful ELF communication relies on crucial adaptive accommodation skills along with appreciation and acceptance of diversity' (Cogo 2009: 270). Research suggests that proficient ELF speakers are very skilled users of English. They do not merely use one particular variety of English (e.g. in an attempt to model 'standard' British or 'standard' American), but they exploit the language in more flexible and resourceful ways. Proficient ELF speakers respond to the demands of the particular situation rather than relying on one rigid code. Discuss answers to these questions

- How do you think they exploit the language?
- How do you think these speakers respond to the demands of the situation?

Look at the VOICE corpus online (www.univie.ac.at/voice/). Discuss examples of things that help the speakers achieve successful communication, and consider whether communication would have been easier if all speakers were using NE, and what is wrong with relying on a single, rigid code.

3.4 FURTHER READING ONE

Kubota, R. (2001), 'Teaching World Englishes to native speakers of English in the USA', *World Englishes*, 20(1): 47–64.
The article analyses and discusses the implications of raising native English-speaking learners' awareness towards WE through a pilot project implemented in an English high school class in North Carolina, USA. The project involved a series of instructional sessions on WE. The author argues that due to the global spread of English, native and non-native speakers often encounter situations where they need to interact with each other for various purposes. However, native speakers are not always encouraged to develop the skills and knowledge necessary in order to participate in intercultural communication. This mainly stems from the fact that native speakers are found in a position of power, often seeing themselves as 'owners' of the language, and therefore do not feel the need to become involved in familiar-ising themselves with other cultures and thus other varieties of English. Based on this, the article highlights issues around ethnicity, stereotypes and racist attitudes, which tend to be generalised and thus prevent native speakers from changing their views with regard to the fact that non-native speakers also speak different varieties of English.

The study analyses the effects of the instructional unit on learners' attitudes and views towards WE and foregrounds important concerns about the need for the development of intercultural communication and an awareness of linguistic and cultural diversity, which would eventually help to limit instances of xenophobia and racist attitudes, which all link to a wider ideological discourse of unequal rela-tions of power. It thus stresses the need for critical pedagogy, especially in language education.

The results of the study which, apart from the instructional part, included ques-tionnaires and interviews, revealed that generally there was significant improve-ment in learners' understanding of the difficulty of second language acquisition and perceived understanding of speech samples. Despite the fact that results were positive, other areas, such as perceived personal traits of WE speakers and the ability to communicate, were not improved. It also needs to be mentioned that individual differences, such as background, exposure to other cultures, learning of a second language and either existence or lack of cross-cultural encounters, affected the responses of learners. For example, learners whose attitudes were initially less positive did not alter their views and did not feel they benefited from the pilot project.

Based on these observations, the author thus outlines five pedagogical implications of the study: '1) the difficulty of critically examining the global spread of English; 2) the need for creating classroom interaction that is conducive to critical examination of the issue; 3) the need to use more experiential approaches when exploring cross-cultural communication strategies; 4) the need for earlier interventions for promoting cultural/linguistic diversities; and 5) the need for more emphasis on cross-cultural/linguistic awareness in foreign language learning' (Kubota 2001: 60).

The pilot project which was implemented and presented in this study is outlined in the extract below.

> This project was conducted in an English IV class at a public high school in North Carolina (see more detailed descriptions about the class later). The lesson unit on WE consisted of a total of eight sessions (55 minutes each) which were taught during eight weeks (generally, one session a week) in the fall semester of 1998. The overall goals of the unit were: (1) to understand that there are many varieties of English used in the United States and in the world, (2) to understand a brief history of English, (3) to understand the difficulty of acquiring native-like proficiency in a second language, (4) to explore ways to communicate effectively with WE speakers, and (5) to critically investigate implications of the global spread of English. The instructor of this unit was a female who was not the regular teacher of the class but was certified to teach English and had formerly taught at the same school. This instructor and I created lesson plans together prior to the project. The instructional objectives, materials and approaches were further modified as the instruction proceeded. The instruction included mini-lectures, visual aids, whole class discussion, group work, videos, free writing, and guest speakers. The intended pedagogical principles derived from critical pedagogy (cf. Frederickson, 1998; Freire, 1970/1993, 1998) and efforts were made to make the instruction dialogic, inquiry-oriented and collaborative. However, because of some uncontrollable factors described later, the pedagogical approach tended to be teacher-directed.
>
> Day 1
> The objectives of this class were (1) to become aware of the existence of American Tongues, (2) to examine one's own perceptions about American Tongues, and (3) to reflect on one's own experiences interacting with speakers of American Tongues.
>
> Activities included: short writing on existing knowledge of regional/ethnic varieties of English; discussion; a video segment on American Tongues; subsequent discussion and writing on what students learned.

Day 2

This session focused on international varieties of English and had the following objectives: (1) to understand different types of WE, and (2) to reflect on students' experiences of interacting with WE speakers and their perceptions about WE.

Activities included: student written countries where English is spoken; introduction of three concentric circles of WE and immigrant populations in America; discussion; videos of fiction/non-fiction movies; identification of speakers on world map; written account of what they learned.

Day 3

The objectives of this class were (1) to discuss why it is necessary to communicate effectively with speakers of WE, and (2) to discuss why it is necessary to think critically about the global spread of English.

Activities included: facts of minority populations, linguistic diversity; presentation of World Map with Inner, Outer and Expanding Circle/ representation of population in each; pair work on summarizing how to meet the language needs of immigrants from newspaper articles; discussion.

Day 4

This session moved to the topic of the historical development of English and the status of English in various countries. The objectives were (1) to understand a brief history of the English language, and (2) to further understand the global stratification of English.

Activities included: historical development of the English Language; group work to study linguistic situation in one region (inner, outer or expanding circle) through the use of a map and Ethnologue website.

Day 5

Since the class did not finish the group project in the previous session, each group continued their work from Day 4, and the class discussed their findings.

Day 6

This session consisted of presentations given by two university professors: a male from India and a female from Mexico. The objectives were (1) to listen to and interact with WE speakers, and (2) to understand some of the social and cultural issues related to English in these countries.

Activities included: listening to WE speakers' talks on the influences of American culture and English on Indian music, the attitude of Mexicans towards English, as well as linguistics and demographic facts about Spanish-speaking people in the US. After listening to the guest speakers, students asked them questions and wrote down what they learned.

Day 7

The last two sessions focused on topics related to communicating with WE speakers. One topic left from Day 5 was also addressed. The objectives of Day 7 were (1) to understand the impact of the global spread of English on other languages, (2) to understand some facts about second language acquisition, and (3) to explore ways to communicate effectively with WE speakers.

Activities included: reading a news article and discussing question on the power of language, introduction of examples about the length of time it takes for immigrant children to learn academic English skills and the age factor present in the likelihood of acquiring native-like pronunciation were introduced with concrete examples. To underscore the influence of English on other languages and linguistic diversity in the world, newspapers in various languages were shown to the class, and students worked in small groups to study how much English is used in articles or advertisements.

Day 8
The objectives of this final class were (1) to review the topics discussed in the unit, and (2) to explore strategies for cross-cultural communication with WE speakers. After reviewing the topics and contents introduced in previous sessions, the same movie segments that the class had viewed on Day 2 were played again. Then, the class watched part of a video titled *The World of Diversity*, analyzed the miscommunication that happened in the episode, and discussed how to make the situation better. Students finally reflected on the entire unit in writing. (adapted from Kubota 2001: 50–3)

Task 3.12 Applying the concept to teaching
Discuss whether you would use a similar pilot project with your learners in your own context, and if so, how you would adapt and modify the one above in order to raise non-native learners awareness of WE (and also ELF), what other activities could you add and whether there would be any limitations in terms of its implementation.

Task 3.13 Trying out research
Discuss what other aspects of the study intrigued you which you would like to investigate further, and outline a small research project that you would like to carry out.

3.5 FURTHER READING TWO

Jenkins, J., A. Cogo and M. Dewey (2011), 'Review of developments in research into English as a Lingua Franca', *Language Teaching*, 44(3): 281–315.
This paper describes the beginnings of the ELF research paradigm. It then outlines research in the areas of lexicogrammar, phonology and pragmatics. It also presents a discussion of recent research in the linguistic fluidity of ELF. In addition, there is a focus on ELF in business English and academic English. The article ends with the implications of ELF research for ELT.

The paper begins with a brief description of some of the most influential ELF research. These include the following:

- Jenkins's (2000) study of ELF pronunciation
- Seidlhofer's (2001) conceptual piece of research describing and explaining ELF
- The compilation of the first ELF corpus, the Vienna–Oxford International Corpus of English (VOICE), launched at the University of Vienna
- A definition of ELF as 'an additionally acquired language system which serves as a common means of communication for speakers of different first languages'.
- The differences between the WE and the ELF paradigms
- ELF research in the areas of lexis, lexicogrammar, pronunciation and pragmatics
- ELF research in business and academic English

The first excerpt describes the implications of ELF research for ELT:

ELF empirical work and theoretical discussions have raised profound questions about current PRINCIPLES and PRACTICE in ELT (Widdowson 2004). Research findings in ELF have major implications for a multitude of common beliefs and assumptions about what is sanctioned as good practice by the profession. The PEDAGOGIC IMPLICATIONS of ELF include the following key areas in particular: the nature of the LANGUAGE SYLLABUS, TEACHING MATERIALS, APPROACHES and METHODS, LANGUAGE ASSESSMENT and ultimately the KNOWLEDGE BASE of language teachers. All this has, of course, far reaching implications for language teacher education.

Debate surrounding the global presence of English has gradually become more commonplace at ELT conferences and publications. A number of teacher education manuals now incorporate sections that deal with the spread of English in the world. In Harmer (2007), for example, the opening chapter includes a section on developments in World Englishes and a passing mention of 'the newly-observed phenomenon that is sometimes called ELF' (2007: 10). Yet, while texts of this kind are an important first step in raising awareness of ELF among novice teachers, much more detailed discussions are needed if there is to be proper engagement with ELF in practice. So far there has been little detailed discussion of how different varieties of English, or how the dynamic variability of ELF, might impact on language teaching MODELS or METHODOLOGY. In Harmer (2007) for instance, the conclusions arrived at are somewhat conservative: after a brief discussion of English varieties, Harmer observes that learners' and teachers' options largely amount to a choice between British English or American English. In other words, practically no consideration is given to empirical work on nativized Englishes or the expanding body of ELF research.

Several texts have also begun to address the internationalization of English in relation to ELT more extensively (e.g. McKay 2002; Holliday 2005). But apart from Walker (2010), a handbook for teachers who wish to use an ELF approach to teach pronunciation, there has been little discussion of what an ELF-oriented PEDAGOGY might actually look like, and little consideration of what teachers might do in order to incorporate an ELF perspective, the extensive discussion occupying the final chapter of Seidlhofer (2011) being a rare exception. (Jenkins, Cogo and Dewey 2011: 304–5)

The second excerpt also discusses the implications of ELF research for ELT:

Thus, a fundamental initial consequence of ELF research is the need to raise awareness of the relationship between language models (which are necessarily abstractions) and the variable nature of language in interaction. From this perspective, developing an ELF perspective in pedagogy entails above all, at least for now, the generating of an understanding among learners and teachers of the inherent variability (even instability) of human language in general and English more specifically.

ELF research, then, is not about determining what should or should not be taught in the language classroom. Rather, ELF researchers feel their responsibility is to make current research findings accessible in a way that enables teachers to reconsider their beliefs and practices and make informed decisions about the significance of ELF for their own individual teaching contexts. Canagarajah (2005) describes a less 'hierarchical', more 'leveled approach' to language education, in which teaching models, materials and methods are developed at a local level. Although addressing the impact of World Englishes on pedagogy without discussing ELF in particular, Canagarajah's recommendation that a more PLURICENTRIC approach should be adopted is directly relevant to the pedagogic implications of ELF research. The same is true of Pennycook's (2009) PLURILITHIC ENGLISHES. And Kirkpatrick (2007) presents similar arguments in favour of adopting a pluralistic approach. Of most significance vis-à-vis ELF is his discussion not only of the need for learners and teachers to be exposed to a range of Englishes, but also the need to focus less on language norms and more on the communicative practices and strategies of effective speakers.

Baker (2011, forthcoming) has begun to explore what some of these communicative practices and strategies might be, and how they can be translated to the ELT classroom. He utilizes previous work on intercultural competence, but in keeping with ELF perspectives, adopts a more fluid approach to the 'norms' of communicative practices than the nation–culture–language correlations typically regarded as forming part of intercultural competence. This has resulted in the formulation of a range of attitudes, knowledge and skills associated with successful multilingual and multicultural ELF users that Baker terms 'intercultural awareness' (ibid.). Crucially, these are not based on the communicative practices of any one particular community and certainly not a native-speaker 'target community'. Instead the emphasis is on the ability to adapt, negotiate and mediate communication in dynamic and context-sensitive ways, which both recognizes that communication may be influenced by the norms of specific communities, but, equally, that in ELF it may not. Furthermore, suggestions for developing this awareness or competence within the classroom both in general (Baker forthcoming) and in specific settings (Baker 2011) are provided. However, this work remains exploratory and further research within ELT classrooms is much needed. (Jenkins, Cogo and Dewey 2011: 306)

Task 3.10 Applying the concept to teaching
Discuss in what ways ELF research makes you question the language syllabus, teaching materials, approaches and methods, language assessment and the knowledge base of language teachers in your context.

Task 3.11 Trying out research
Discuss what problems you envisage (if any) with incorporating a more ELF-based perspective into your teaching context, and design a simple interview to find out how teachers feel about this.

3.6 SUMMARY

This chapter has introduced you to the spread of English in the world and you have considered:

- Different models which depict the categorisation of English speakers in the world, as well as relevant criticisms
- Global Englishes (GE), which includes two major research paradigms: World Englishes (WE) and English as a Lingua Franca (ELF)
- The main differences between WE and ELF
- The problems associated with fact that the terms 'native' and 'non-native' speaker are subject to criticism, mainly due to the fact that this dichotomy alludes to English being associated with Inner Circle speakers, while this no longer seems to be the case in multilingual societies
- The relevance of research in the area of GE to ELT

This chapter has also helped you to:

- Raise your awareness and critically reflect on the different concepts which are foregrounded through the discussion on WE and ELF
- Understand the relevance of the two paradigms in ELT
- Reflect on the impact of research on WE and ELF on ELT
- Consider ways of applying WE and ELF in your teaching context

Research on GE not only describes how English is used in the world, but it stresses the pedagogical implications.

3.7 ADDITIONAL READINGS

Alsagoff, L., S.L. McKay, G.W. Hu and W. Renandya (eds) (2012), *Principles and Practices for Teaching English as an International Language*, New York: Routledge.
(This book focuses on the pedagogical implications of the continuing spread of English and its role as an international language, highlighting the importance of socially sensitive pedagogy in contexts outside inner circle English-speaking countries.)
Kachru, B.B., and C.L. Nelson (2006), *World Englishes in Asian Contexts*, Hong Kong: Hong Kong University Press.

(This mainly focuses on the theory of World Englishes and the use and profile of varieties of English in Asian countries.)

McKay, S.L. (2002), *Teaching English as an International Language: Rethinking Goals and Approaches*, Oxford: Oxford University Press.

(This book discusses the spread of English and the cultural assumptions underlying English teaching, and makes suggestions for ELT based on the requirements of an international language).

4

ENGLISH ACROSS CULTURES
Kenneth Fordyce and Florence Bonacina-Pugh

INTRODUCTION

In Chapter 3, we saw how English speakers in a globalised world use different Englishes in different social groups to communicate with each other. In this chapter, we examine more closely what happens when English is used across different cultures, alongside other languages.

Three different types of interactional encounters are examined

- Communication in bilingual or multilingual contexts where speakers use English as well as one or more other languages; for instance, communication between two Indian learners working together on an English task in a college in India.
- Communication among first language speakers; for instance, exchanges between a doctor and a patient who share English as a first language, and how this compares to, for example, doctor–patient communication by first language speakers of German or Japanese.
- Communication among speakers of English as a second language or among native and non-native speakers of English; for instance, a meeting conducted in English between American and Japanese business people.

The analysis of these three types of communication will serve as an introduction to three key research fields, which are respectively:

- The study of **language choice** in bilingual or multilingual contexts; for instance, what language(s) would the two Indian learners mentioned above use in this task and why?
- The study of **cross-cultural pragmatics;** for instance, in what ways does doctor–patient interaction in English in Britain differ from doctor–patient interaction in Arabic in Saudi Arabia?
- The study of **intercultural pragmatics;** for instance, how would the Japanese business people speak in English to the American business people in that meeting and how might the American business people react?

In this chapter, key terms and recent theoretical perspectives from these research fields will be presented and related to the teaching of English. We believe that these can shed light on English language teaching issues such as:

- Are my learners' first language(s) and culture(s) a problem or a resource for learning English?
- How can I teach English in a multicultural and multilingual context while also acknowledging my learners' first language(s) and culture(s)?
- Should I allow my learners to use languages other than English in my classroom?
- What do I need to teach my learners about how communication is carried out differently in specific English-speaking contexts?
- How can I prepare my learners to be able to use English appropriately and effectively when they are travelling or studying abroad?
- Do I need to teach learners about the pragmatics of English, or will they just pick that up as they go along if they know enough vocabulary and grammar?

The discussion in this chapter is based on research on interaction occurring in culturally and linguistically heterogeneous contexts. In this sense, this chapter shows the importance and usefulness of the analysis of communication to anyone attempting to embark on the complex task of understanding English language use in a globalised world. It also gives a foretaste of Chapters 5 to 8 of this book where different approaches to the analysis of interaction are introduced.

4.1 ENGLISH LANGUAGE TEACHING IN BILINGUAL AND MULTILINGUAL CONTEXTS

In most parts of the world, using two or more languages on a daily basis is the norm. This is the case for instance in Luxembourg (Europe) where French, German and Luxembourgish are official languages. People who use two languages on a daily basis (even if at various degrees of proficiency) are said to be **bilingual**, while people who can only use one language are said to be **monolingual**. In communities where more than two languages are used, speakers are said to be **multilingual**.

English language learners (and sometimes teachers) bring one or more languages to the English language classroom. As a consequence, English language classrooms are complex bilingual or multilingual contexts. For instance, learners may not share a common language apart from the target language, English; this is the case in classes where English is taught as an additional language to newly arrived immigrant children in the UK. Alternatively, learners may share a first and/or second language(s) in addition to English; this is the case in English classrooms in Malaysia, where learners may share Malay as well as another local language. As a teacher, you may share a language other than English with your learners – or you may not. The point is that English language teaching usually takes place in bi/multilingual classrooms where multiple sets of linguistic repertoires are available. This is the reason why understanding issues related to bilingualism and multilingualism is crucial in English language teaching. Some of the main issues are introduced in this section.

One of the main challenges consists of understanding what language(s) classroom participants use in a bi/multilingual educational context. Observation of different English language teaching contexts shows that, in practice, it is quite common for bi/multilingual classroom participants (whether teachers or learners) to switch between

English and their other language(s). This phenomenon is usually referred to as the **alternation** between a first language (L1) and a second language (L2). These language alternation practices may occur in verbal or written communication, in peer interaction as well as teacher-led interaction – that is, if the teacher shares a language other than English with their learners. In fact, language alternation is not specific to the English language classroom and is a common practice in other language classrooms (see, for instance, language alternation practices between French and English in a French school in Scotland in Bonacina and Gafaranga 2011) as well as content-based classrooms (see, for instance, language alternation practices between Maltese and English in a secondary classroom in Malta in Camilleri 1996). Language alternation is also and perhaps even most frequently observed *outside* the classroom, at the level of bi/multilingual communities (see, for instance, language alternation practices in a Chinese community in Britain in Wei and Milroy 1995). An umbrella term used to refer to language alternation practices within as well as outside the classroom is 'code-switching'. The fields of code-switching and classroom code-switching research have been flourishing in the past four decades and a variety of frameworks have been proposed to describe different types of practices (for a detailed review see, for instance, Lin 2008). As a result, many other terms such as 'code-mixing' (Muysken 2000), 'polylingual languaging' (e.g. Jørgensen 2008) and, more recently, 'translanguaging' (García 2007; Canagarajah 2011) can be found in the literature in addition to – or instead of – 'code-switching'.

Since code-switching can take place in the bi/multilingual language classroom, you may wonder whether your learners' bi/multilingual repertoire is to be considered as a problem or as a resource for the teaching and learning of English. In this regard, Ruiz's (1984) comments are still of relevance today. For him, the answer to this question depends on whether one views linguistic diversity as a problem, a right or a resource. Many language policymakers, for instance, tend to see linguistic diversity in the classroom as a problem and argue for monolingual language-in-education policies to be put into place. Their argument is usually grounded in a variety of pedagogical and/or sociopolitical reasons such as the belief that the target language is better learned through the use of that language only or the belief that only powerful languages such as English should be used at school if learners' aim is socio-economic mobility. This often results in the use of a single medium of instruction (usually the L2) in classrooms where learners – and sometimes teachers – are not fluent in that language (see, for instance, a review of the English-only movement in the ESL classroom in Auerbach 1993). Similarly, many language teachers are found to hold negative attitudes towards the use of learners' first language(s) in the language classroom (Macaro 2001).

However, a large body of research shows that classroom code-switching in the language classroom, the content-based classroom as well as in non-educational contexts is a **communicative resource** (Martin-Jones and Saxena 2003). More specifically, researchers have convincingly shown across a variety of linguistic and cultural contexts that code-switching can be functional. A wide range of **functions of code-switching** have thus been reported. Generally speaking, code-switching in the classroom is used for facilitating curriculum access or transmitting knowledge, classroom management discourse, and for building interpersonal relations (Ferguson 2003, 2009). A good example of code-switching for **facilitating access to the curriculum** can be found in Martin's (2003) study of code-switching in a primary classroom in Negara Brunei Darussalam (South-east Asia). In the following extract, he shows how the classroom participants' L1 (Malay) is used to unpack the meaning of a text found in their English monolingual textbook:

Normal font is used to transcribe talk uttered in English while underlined font is used to transcribe talk uttered in Malay. The English translation is provided in italics in between < >.

67   T: OK. sit down . . . next . . . 'Living things need food to live'.
68   ah. 'We need food to grow up healthily'. semua benda-benda .
69   <*all things*> semua benda hidup memerlukan makanan ah. <*all*
70   *living things need food*> untuk membesar dengan sihat. <*to grow*
71   *healthily*> makanan juga memerlukan bagi kita supaya kita dapat
72   berfikir dengan baik <*food is also necessary for us so that we*
73   *can think clearly*> ah. kalau kita tidak makan. <*if we don't*
74   *eat*> lemah. <*weak*> lapar. <*hungry*> ah. belajar pun . tidak.
75   sempat. <*we won't even be able to learn*> baik. <*good*> (Martin 2003: 193)

Examples of **code-switching used for classroom management** can be found for instance in Rashka et al.'s (2009) study of language choice in a Taiwanese EFL classroom. Consider the extract below where the teacher and the learners are engaged in an English reading activity. The L2 (English) is used until a learner arrives late. The teacher then switches to the L1 (Mandarin) to discipline the learner:

The translation of talk uttered in Chinese is given in square brackets.

1   T: you do your laundry at home
2   Ss: you do your laundry at home
3   {a student just arrived in class}
4   T: 迟到 [you are late]
5   S: 我找不到教室，教室换了哦 [I couldn't find the classroom,
6   the classroom had been changed] (Rashka et al. 2009: 168)

Examples of **code-switching used to build interpersonal relations** can be found in Lin's (1996) study of five English-medium secondary schools in Hong Kong. In the following extract, the teacher uses the classroom participants' shared L1 (Cantonese) to praise his learners' science projects and then switches to English to resume the pedagogic task and to re-establish distance with his learners:

Normal font is used to transcribe talk uttered in English while underlined font is used to transcribe talk uttered in Cantonese. The English translation is given in brackets.

94 T: <u>waahkje neih ho yih jeung tiuh sin cheun hei keuih diu hai neih go fong</u> **douh**; <u>hou leng ge. Mh hou saai jo keuih; ho yih jih gei lo faan laak.</u> (or you can put a thread through it and hang it up in your room; very beautiful. Don't waste it; you can get it back yourself.)

95 Now you take out your note book. We come back to Mathematics. Turn to Exercise Eleven C. We look at the problems. (Lin 1996: 67)

According to Lin, for praise to be taken seriously by the learners Cantonese had to be used because it establishes a warm and friendly atmosphere between the teacher and the learners. If the teacher had uttered the same praise in English, the learners would have still seen him 'as a Cantonese hiding behind the mask of an English-speaking teacher who remained socially distanced from them' (Lin 1996: 67).

Lastly, if code-switching is functional, you may wonder *how* your learners' first language(s) can be efficiently used in your classroom. There is no straightforward answer to this question since, as we know, teaching practices are context-sensitive. Consequently, it would be difficult (or even inappropriate) to draw general principles of when and how to use other languages in the English language classroom when each classroom context is different. This said, some scholars have recently tried to encourage the constructive use of classroom participants' bi/multilingual linguistic repertoire in teaching and learning practices. Of particular interest is Creese and Blackledge's proposed notion of what they call a '**flexible bilingual pedagogy**', whereby multiple languages are used fluidly and flexibly to teach and learn content and/or language in bi/multilingual educational contexts (Creese and Blackledge 2010; Creese et al. 2011).

Task 4.1 Applying the concepts to teaching

Suppose you are to plan a lesson on renewable energies. Find a text online explaining the different sources of renewable energies. Imagine the following two scenarios: 1) one group in which you and your learners share Spanish as a first language and 2) one group in which your learners share Chinese as a first language, which you do not understand. Discuss what language(s) you would like to use, when and for what purpose(s) in both groups. Discuss what language(s) you would like your learners to use when and for what purpose(s) in both groups.

Task 4.2 Trying out research

Attitudes towards the different languages available in the language classroom influence the way these languages will – or will not – be used in teaching and learning practices. We have also mentioned that many language policymakers and language teachers tend to view linguistic diversity in the classroom as a problem to overcome as opposed to a resource to draw upon. We invite you now to turn to a third body of agents in the language classroom: namely, learners. Find out what language learners' attitudes are regarding the use of L1 and L2 in their classroom:

- Do they think they use their L1 in classroom talk?
- If so, why and when?
- How do they feel about using their L1 or about peers using their L1?

In a class that you have easy access to (either as a teacher or as a learner), where there are at least a few bi/multilingual speakers, conduct audio-recorded interviews with a few of these learners. Then identify common themes in the learners' responses to get a sense of what learners' attitudes towards L1 use in their classroom are, and discuss your findings with your colleagues.

You may also want, at a later stage, to compare these attitudes with the teacher's attitudes as these may not always match. You may also want to compare your findings with those in Liang (2006).

Task 4.3 Using the internet

Chatterbox is an English nursery and primary school based in Sardinia (Italy) open to local Sardinian children. Have a look at its website (www.chatterboxenglishschool.co.uk/), especially at the pages entitled 'Why Chatterbox?' and 'Methodology'. Try to identify what language policy is adopted in this school (monolingual? bilingual?). Is linguistic diversity seen here as a problem or a resource (remember Ruiz 1984 mentioned in section 4.1 above)? Discuss how this policy might be put into practice in the Sardinian classroom and what challenges may arise.

4.2 CROSS-CULTURAL PRAGMATICS

Many ordinary aspects of daily life can be carried out quite differently according to the cultural context; for example:

- In Japan, parents would never explicitly boast about their children's achievements. In fact they may put them down by saying that they do not work hard enough. This does not mean that they actually think this is the case; in fact in most cases they will be extremely proud of their children and their achievements. In other cultures it is quite usual to speak highly of your children.
- In China, when people meet acquaintances on the street they may ask, 'Where are you going?' This does not mean they are being nosey and they may not expect an explicit answer to the question (Spencer-Oatey 2008: 1). It simply functions as a greeting. Likewise, in the United States, people will often use 'How are you doing?' as a greeting like 'Hi!' rather than as a question soliciting information about somebody's health and well-being.
- In Germany, if you are offered a piece of cake it is generally a good idea to say yes the first time and not wait for a second chance. By comparison, in Ireland, it is more polite to say no the first time and then to 'allow yourself to be persuaded' when asked a second time (see Barron 2001).

Cross-cultural pragmatics involves comparisons of the way language is used in different contexts, as demonstrated by the examples above. It focuses on contexts in which people are talking in their L1 to other speakers of their L1, and it involves research which contrasts the language of two or more different groups by collecting comparable data on language used in specific situations (for example, what guests say to hosts after receiving a meal; how business meetings are opened and closed; how a student addresses a professor in an email).

Two key terms to remember when investigating differences in cross-cultural pragmatics are **pragmalinguistics** and **sociopragmatics** (Leech 1983; Thomas 1983). The former refers to the words and expressions used in a specific situation, and what those words and expressions mean in that specific context. For example, the expression 'It's a bit chilly in here' could be used for any of these functions depending on the context:

- Simple observation upon entering an ice rink.
- A suggestion to leave somewhere because it is too cold.
- A request to somebody to close a window.
- A request to somebody to switch on a heater.
- An ironic comment upon entering a steaming sauna.

In all these cases the words used and the intended meaning are dependent upon the context, and it is also very likely that the speaker will use intonation and/or stress and/or body language to make the intended meaning clearer.

As regards pragmalinguistics and cross-cultural pragmatics, not all interpretations of a specific utterance will work in all contexts; in the case above, the use of irony as in the steaming sauna example may not work in some contexts. Another example which is relevant to teaching is the use of mitigated forms when giving feedback on learners' work. In the UK context, for example, teachers will often hedge their suggestions by using expressions such as 'it might be a good idea to' or 'I think you'd be well advised to'. In other cultural contexts, feedback to learners may be given without this hedging: e.g., 'you need to', 'you should'.

Sociopragmatics is concerned more with what people typically do in specific situations; in other words, rules and tendencies of behaviour in specific contexts and cultures. For example, in some cultures it is considered more polite to decline a compliment ('Oh, don't be so silly!') whereas in others compliments are typically accepted ('Thank you very much!'). Another example is the degree to which shop assistants greet customers. In Japanese convenience stores it is almost always the case that any customer who comes through the door will be welcomed into the shop by one or more shop assistants; in the British context, it is much less likely that a shop assistant will actually express a greeting to a customer (they may smile at the customer or they may just ignore them). A considerable amount of research on cross-cultural pragmatics has focused on speech acts, politeness principles and the concept of 'face'. These are all discussed in greater depth in Chapters 7 and 8.

After reading the examples above, you may be feeling a sense of irritation with the generalisations that are being made about linguistic and cultural behaviour in certain contexts (for example, 'my dissertation supervisor, who was British, was always being really rude about my spelling and punctuation'). This leads on to one of the most complex and controversial issues when making cross-cultural comparisons, which concerns the danger of stereotyping. While patterns and tendencies in behaviour can be identified within cultural groups, it is always essential to be clear that these tendencies cannot be applied uncritically to any individual within that group. For example, the use of irony may not be as frequent in, say, Austria, as it is in the United Kingdom, but that does not mean that you will not be able to find an Austrian who uses irony. In fact, one of the most ironic people the author of this section has ever come across happens to be an Austrian.

Research into cross-cultural pragmatics is essential because it can look under the surface of perceived tendencies (see the reading on apologising in Japanese and English in Section 4.5), and it can also provide valuable and precise information about other cultures for individuals who are going to spend time within another cultural context, for example, as a tourist or when studying or working abroad. In some circumstances, individuals can be provided with cross-cultural education in order that they will be able to operate more effectively in the new cultural context and avoid pragmatic failures. This leads us into the field of **intercultural pragmatics**, which investigates what happens when people with different systems meet and communicate; this is the subject of the next section.

Task 4.4 Applying the concept to teaching
Discuss the answers to these questions with your colleagues:

- Do the textbooks that you use in your teaching present information about cross-cultural differences?
- Do you think this information is a fair reflection of the culture that is described?
- What are some of the potential problems of introducing this information on cross-cultural differences in textbooks?
- How might you go about introducing cross-cultural elements which are not currently included in the textbooks you use?
- With what level of learners would you introduce this information?

Task 4.5 Trying out research
Imagine that you are going to carry out some cross-cultural research comparing your country with one other country. Discuss with your colleagues:

- What country would you choose?
- What would you focus your attention on?
- What would your research question(s) be?
- How would you go about collecting information to answer your research questions?

Task 4.6 Using the internet
Being invited to a dinner party at somebody's house may not seem very complicated but, in fact, the pragmalinguistics and sociopragmatics of this situation can vary quite extensively between cultures. Using the internet, find information to answer the following questions for your own country and two other countries in different parts of the world:

- The invitation states 7 pm – what time should I actually arrive?
- What should I wear (formal, semi-formal, informal)?
- Should I bring a gift for the host? If so, what kind of gift is appropriate?

- What should I say when I arrive? Are there any specific expressions that are used in this context or can I just say, 'Hello'?
- How will I know when it is appropriate to leave? What should I say when I leave?

Now use the information that you have gathered and develop a plan for a 50-minute language class in which you introduce this knowledge. Discuss with colleagues.

4.3 INTERCULTURAL PRAGMATICS

Communicating across cultures can be the cause of confusion, irritation and amusement; for example:

- In Japan, as you get to know people better it is not that uncommon to be told 'itsuka asobi ni kite kudasai', which literally means 'come over to our place some time'. However, it is typically not a serious invitation. This can lead to confusion and embarrassment when a newcomer to Japan who is keen to make friends asks, 'itsu?' ('When?')
- In her book *Understanding the English*, Fox (2004) provides a humorous and immensely detailed description of the various 'rules' involved in ordering a drink in a British pub (this actually involves a lot of non-verbal communication). Unwitting visitors to the UK who walk up to the bar and ask for a drink without being aware of the various sociopragmatic conventions involved can unintentionally cause irritation to the customers in the 'invisible' queue (see Task 4.8 in this section for the list of rules)

In intercultural communication, each individual brings pragmatic knowledge from their own language and culture. This involves what is called **pragmatic transfer**. For example, when the British author of this chapter was working at a Japanese university, he sometimes heard students whispering outside his office, trying to decide what they should say when they knocked on his door. In Japanese, it is usually the case that students will say 'Shitsurei shimasu' in this situation. However, this does not work in direct translation (it would literally mean something like 'I do rude'), and as a result, students were left flummoxed about how to negotiate the superficially simple task of knocking on a door! The problem was that they were trying to use a Japanese pragmalinguistic form in English communication, and they were not aware of the English version, which would typically involve simply knocking on the door, saying nothing and waiting for an answer. If they had translated the Japanese expression, it could have been considered as a case of **negative pragmatic transfer** because the L1 pragmatic knowledge would not function effectively in the L2 context.

While this example demonstrates a certain degree of communication failure, it should be pointed out that negative pragmatic transfer does not always result in miscommunication (Žegarac and Pennington 2008: 144). For example, if somebody with an L1 in which it is typical to react modestly to compliments ('Oh, you are too kind') uses this approach in an L2 in which compliments are typically accepted, it is unlikely to hinder communication in any way.

On other occasions pragmatic transfer can be **positive**: Hill (1997; see also Kasper and Rose 2002: 154) reports on advanced Japanese learners of English who were able to use the English expression 'If you don't mind . . .' in the production of requests because they were able to translate Japanese conditionals such as 'moshi yokattara' ('if it's okay') into English.

Successful communication between speakers with different cultures and languages often requires one or both speakers to adapt the way they communicate in order to help communication run more smoothly. **Accommodation Theory** (Giles et al. 1987; Coupland 1995; Ylänne 2008) was originally developed in relation to the way speakers change their accent either to make it easier for hearers (for example, a teacher who speaks in a more standardised way in order to make a lesson more inclusive to learners) or, alternatively, in a case of non-accommodation, to assert their cultural identity. More recently, this theory has been applied to the use of pragmatics in intercultural communication contexts.

Broadly speaking, three different processes relating to (non-)accommodation have been identified: **convergence**, **maintenance** and **divergence** (Ylänne 2008). Convergence involves a speaker trying to fit her communication style with that of the hearer in a spirit of cooperation and/or with the wish to be approved of. For example, it is quite normal in Japan for a Japanese business person to greet a non-Japanese business person with a handshake even though bowing is the norm in the Japanese context. Convergence to local norms can also have an entirely selfish motivation. The British author of this chapter realised that the only way to get a drink at a crowded Austrian bar involved assertively shouting his order at the barman. Adopting the British 'invisible queue rule' (Fox 2004) would have left him very thirsty.

Sometimes convergence can go too far and result in what has been described as **foreigner talk**. In other words, the speaker adopts an excessively simplified form of communication because they mistakenly underestimate the hearer's communication skills. While foreigner talk may in fact be well meant by the speaker, the hearer will often feel patronised and irritated. In other words, successful intercultural communication requires an appropriate degree of convergence.

While maintenance involves 'communicating as usual' and not making any adaptations with regard to the addressees, divergence describes situations in which a speaker chooses to exacerbate features of their own communication system in order to maintain distance from the hearer. This might happen, for example, in situations in which a minority group wishes to maintain their identity by reinforcing key pragmalinguistic forms or sociopragmatic conventions of their L1 system.

Intercultural encounters typically involve a situation in which one or both speakers are using a second language; in turn, effective intercultural communication can involve the ability to use a second language with pragmatic appropriacy. This is the focus of **interlanguage pragmatics**, which 'is a branch of study in second language acquisition (SLA) that focuses on second language learners' knowledge, use and development of performance in sociocultural functions in context' (Taguchi 2012: 1). A large body of research has shown quite convincingly that a high level of grammatical competence in a second language does not guarantee that a learner will also have a comparable level of pragmatic competence (Bardovi-Harlig and Dörnyei 1998;

Schauer 2009). An example of this situation would be an international student at a UK university who has an upper-intermediate or advanced level of English as measured by international tests such as IELTS or TOEFL, but who sends a draft chapter to her supervisor and writes, 'Please check it for me'. While her sentence is grammatically correct it is likely to annoy her supervisor due to its pragmatic inappropriacy.

Considering the importance of second language pragmatic competence in intercultural communication, it is surprising to find that classroom instruction on L2 pragmatics tends to remain marginal in many textbooks and curricula for the teaching of English as a Foreign Language. In spite of the fact that instruction on L2 pragmatics has been shown to be more effective than simple exposure to the second language (Takahashi 2001; Jeon and Kaya 2006; Fordyce 2013), it remains a common assumption that this knowledge can be acquired *in situ* when you are working or studying abroad.

Task 4.7 Applying the concept to teaching
Imagine that you are responsible for teaching a 'homestay preparation class' to learners who are about to spend one month with a family in your culture, and who do not know much about this culture. Plan a 50-minute class aimed at raising awareness of ways in which the learners can minimise possible intercultural communication problems during their homestay experience. Discuss with colleagues.

Task 4.8 Trying out research
The description below of how to order a drink in an English pub (the same rules would also typically apply in other parts of the UK and Ireland) is adapted from the description in *Watching the English* (Fox 2004: 91–3). Fox wrote down these rules

---

THE INVISIBLE QUEUE RULE

1. you should stand somewhere near the bar counter
2. you should be aware of your position in the invisible queue
3. you should NOT make any attempt to get served out of turn
4. you should make sure that the bar staff know that you need to be served
5. you should do (4) without speaking and without using any obvious gestures
6. you can achieve (4) by making eye-contact with the barman
7. you should NOT snap your fingers or wave at the barman
8. you can also achieve (4) by holding money or an empty glass in your hand
9. you may tilt the empty glass or slowly turn it in a circular motion
10. you should NOT raise your arm or wave money or an empty glass
11. you should NOT look too contented or the bar staff may think you are already being served
12. you should keep your eyes on the bar staff at all times
13. when you make eye-contact you should let the bar staff know that you are waiting with a quick lift of the eyebrows
14. the bar staff will respond to your signal with a smile or a nod, a raised finger or hand, and perhaps a similar eyebrow-lift.

after spending a considerable amount of time observing customer and bartender behaviour in pubs.

Spend some time thinking about a 'process' in your own culture which involves many unwritten rules, and which is likely to be very difficult to understand for people who are new to your culture. Carry out a series of observations and take notes on this process, so that you can divide it into constituent parts (as in the example) and then write this up as information which could be used in an intercultural communication awareness-raising programme, and circulate it to colleagues for discussion.

Task 4.9 Using the internet

Go to www.youtube.com and carry out a search under 'intercultural communication' and/or 'intercultural pragmatics'. Choose some videos to watch (some may be academic lectures, others may be homemade videos providing advice). Make some notes to address these questions:

- What kind of information did you get? What cultures? What rules?
- Do you trust the information you heard? Why/why not?
- Do you think this kind of intercultural information is helpful and important, or do you think it stereotypes and simplifies situations?
- If you were going to make a video to explain aspects of your own culture, what would you do to make the video informative, educational and interesting?

Having collected this information, design a 50-minute ELT class in which you use this information and the internet sources in order to get learners to: 1) learn about aspects of intercultural pragmatics and 2) consider and discuss issues relating to the 'tricky balance' between cultural tendencies on the one hand, and stereotyping on the other hand. Present it to colleagues.

4.4 FURTHER READING ONE

Üstünel, E., and P. Seedhouse (2005), 'Why that, in that language, right now? Code-switching and pedagogical focus', *International Journal of Applied Linguistics*, 15(3): 302–25.

This article explores the relationship between pedagogical focus and language choice in EFL classrooms at a Turkish university. The authors focus on six beginner-level English classrooms where code-switching is mainly teacher-initiated. Using Conversation Analysis (CA) to analyse the corpus of interactional data they collected, Üstünel and Seedhouse aim to understand why certain teaching practices are conducted in the first language (L1) while others are conducted in the second language (L2). They start by reviewing the status of English in Turkey and its educational system and then move on to reviewing the literature on a variety of topics: L1 and L2 use in the language classroom, code-switching at the community level, the functions of classroom code-switching, some key principles of CA (for more information on CA see also Chapter 6 of this volume) and the interactional architecture of the language classroom.

Of particular interest is their review of the two opposite standpoints held among scholars regarding the use of the L1 in the L2 classroom. They mention that, on the one hand, there are researchers who advocate the sole use of the L2 in the L2 classroom on the basis that it increases exposure to the target language and allows learners 'to experience unpredictability' (2005: 305). On the other hand, there are researchers who support the use of the L1 in the L2 classroom on the basis that drawing on learners' L1 can be a helpful tool for L2 teaching and learning, that it saves time and that it avoids L2 ethnocentricity. Interestingly, Üstünel and Seedhouse depart from this debate, as their aim is not to discuss whether the L1 should or should not be used in the L2 classroom but rather to understand how L1 use is *organised* in the L2 classroom and how it is related to pedagogical focus.

> Whereas much of the pedagogical literature debates the pros and cons of L1 use in isolation from its interactional implementation, this study suggests that language choice is embedded in the interactional architecture of the language classroom and is inextricably entwined with the evolution of sequence and pedagogical focus. Code-switching in L2 classrooms should be seen as one interactional resource among the many used by both teachers and learners to carry out the institutional business of teaching and learning an L2 in a complex, fluid and dynamic interactional environment. (2005: 322)

It should be emphasised that this study is the first to adopt CA to the study of code-switching (CS) in the foreign language classroom. In the following excerpt, the authors explain why CA is used in the study of CS in non-institutional contexts (referred to as 'conversational CS') and why it can also be useful in the study of L1 and L2 use in the language classroom.

> In recent years, an increasing amount of research into conversational CS has been carried out, focusing on the pragmatic and expressive meanings carried by switches. Stroud (1998) divides the bulk of this research into two main approaches. The principal characteristic of the first group (exemplified by Gumperz 1982) is that 'the social meanings of conversational code-switches are carried by a set of social categories metaphorically symbolized by particular languages' (McConvell 1988). [. . .] Researchers in the second group (e.g. Wei 1994; Moerman 1988), who apply conversation analysis (CA),
>
> > question the primacy of macrostructural or societal contributions to the social meanings of CS . . . and see the meanings of CS as emerging out of the sequential and negotiated development of conversational interaction . . . in the actual context in which they occur. (Stroud 1998: 322)
>
> Wei suggests that for those who are interested in the meaning of CS, the CA approach has at least two advantages.
>
> 1) It gives priority to what Auer (1984: 6) calls the 'sequential implicativeness of language choice in conversation', i.e., the effect of a

participant's choice of language at a particular point in the conversation
on subsequent language choices by the same and other participants.

2) It limits the external analyst's interpretational leeway because it relates his
or her interpretation back to the members' mutual understanding of their
utterances as manifest in their behaviour. (Wei 2002: 164)

Thus, the CA approach to CS was developed against the background of an
overwhelming tendency in bilingualism research to explain CS behaviour by
attributing specific meanings to the switches, and by assuming that speakers
intend these meanings to be perceived by their listeners. It is obvious that the CA
approach to bilingual interaction is very different from other sociolinguistic
models that have been proposed. The differences are that

> CA does not describe structures of CS in quantitative terms and divorced
> from its natural site of occurrence (conversation), or explain meanings of CS
> by invoking interaction-external concepts such as speakers' rights and
> obligations. Instead, the CA approach focuses on collaborative achievements
> of the conversation participants, especially the methods and procedures they
> deploy in achieving understanding. (Wei 2002: 177)

This CA methodological approach to CS also informs our analysis of the extracts
below. Essentially, we employ a synthesis of the CA approach to L2 classroom
interaction and to bilingual interactions which focuses on the sequential
implicativeness of language choice in relation to the evolving pedagogical focus.
(2005: 307)

The second excerpt gives an example of code-switching from English to Turkish and
how this switch is related to pedagogical focus. CA is used to analyse the extract.

Extract 1. Teacher-initiated CS dealing with a lack of response in the L2

1. T: okay (.) hh on Tuesday night?
2. (0.5)
3. on New Year's night?
4. (1.0)
5. on Tuesday (.) last Tuesday?
6. (2.0)
7. Salı günü? [tr: on Tuesday]
8. S4: (0.5)
9. er-
10. T: =YýlbaTý gecesi?
11. [tr: on New Year's Eve]
12. S4: I (2.0) study (0.5) English

Extract 1 is taken from a longer teacher–learner dialogue in which the teacher
asks the learner what she did on New Year's Eve. In line 1, T directs a question to

S4 in English but does not receive a reply after a pause of 0.5 seconds. In line 3, T rephrases the question and waits for a slightly longer time (1.0 seconds) for a reply. As the learner still does not answer, T repeats the initial question with minor changes in line 5. After a further pause of 2 seconds without a reply, T code-switches to Turkish and repeats the two phrasings of the question in lines 7 and 10. This pattern is found elsewhere in the data, revealing that T code-switches into L1 to repeat a question after a pause of more than 1 second. The repetition of a question signals trouble in the interaction that prevents the institutional business from proceeding. We can observe the pauses lengthening in lines 2, 4 and 6, after which the CS occurs. [. . .]

We want to understand why the teacher code-switches to the L1 after a lack of response and a lengthy pause and why the learner responds in the L2 to the teacher's question in the L1. In order to do this, we need to refer both to sequential issues (preference organisation) and institutional issues (the organisation of L2 classroom interaction). In the institutional L2 classroom setting, the teacher's question introduces a pedagogical focus, which in this case is that learners will produce an appropriate answer in the L2. For this institutional business to be carried out, it is essential that the learner understand the question, and thus the pedagogical focus. When the teacher does not obtain an answer, s/he modifies the linguistic forms in the L2 to clarify the question and pedagogical focus. When this still does not produce the required response, the teacher code-switches in order to present the question and the pedagogical focus in the L1, which is easier for the learner to understand. Thus, the CS is one further (but more radical) way of modifying and simplifying the linguistic forms. (2005: 314–15)

Task 4.10 Applying the concepts to teaching

Have a look at one of your ESL/EFL textbooks for beginners and find out what language(s) are used in different parts of the book. Then choose one unit. If you were to use this unit to teach a group of beginners with whom you share another language, what language(s) might you use in different parts of the unit? What other communicative strategies (e.g. gestures, gaze) might you use in addition to – or in combination with – the use of a particular language? Explain to colleagues.

Task 4.11 Trying out research

As you may have noticed, most studies on classroom code-switching use interactional data that the authors have audio-recorded (or video-recorded) and then transcribed. In this task, you will try and collect bilingual or multilingual interaction yourself. To do this, use a digital audio-recorder.

Audio-record a 10-minute conversation among a few bi/multilingual speakers, preferably in a classroom environment (where you are either a learner or a teacher). You may choose to focus on teacher-led interaction or peer-group interaction. If you do not have access to a classroom context, you may also audio-record a conversation between yourself and your friends (if you are yourself a bi/multilingual speaker). If you are not bi/multilingual yourself, ask a friend who is part of a bi/multilingual community to record a 10-minute conversation with their friends or family members. Whatever situation you choose to record, remember to seek consent prior to recording your participants. Then transcribe the audio-recorded interactions.

Now discuss your transcriptions with colleagues to find answers to the following questions:

- What language(s) is/are used in interaction?
- What functions do these language(s) serve? Are these functions similar to – or different from – the ones Ferguson (2003) talks about, as mentioned in Section 4.1 above?

4.5 FURTHER READING TWO

Tanaka, N., H. Spencer-Oatey and E. Cray (2008), 'Apologies in Japanese and English', in H. Spencer-Oatey (ed.), *Culturally Speaking: Culture, Communication and Politeness Theory*, London: Continuum, pp. 73–94

This chapter looks at apologising in Japanese, British English and Canadian English. The authors discuss the issue of preconceptions about apologising in Japan and North America which can be reinforced by media reports. As they state, 'To find out how people actually apologise, we need to turn to linguistic studies' (2008: 76). They briefly review several studies which involved the collection of empirical data on how Americans and Japanese apologise in various situations. These studies generally found that Americans would tend to explain failure rather than apologise for it, while Japanese would avoid explanations and simply say sorry for their actions. In the light of perceived weaknesses in the research methodologies of some of these studies, the authors decided to conduct their own research focusing on 'personal fault' in order to investigate when Japanese, British and Canadian respondents considered it necessary to take responsibility for a situation by apologising.

For each of eight scenarios, respondents from the three groups were asked to provide judgements on each of the scenarios in terms of how annoying they were for the person who was complaining; how responsible they considered themselves to be for what happened in each scenario; and the degree of importance they attached to placating the person who was complaining. They were then asked to write down what they would say in each of the situations. Data was collected from 131 Japanese students, 165 British students, and 96 Canadian students.

Overall, the findings found only minor differences in the way in which the different student groupings responded in each of the scenarios. The most surprising finding was that the Japanese respondents apologised less than the British and Canadian cohorts in the situation in which the person who was complaining was actually at fault. This finding contradicted the stereotype that Japanese tend to apologise even when they are not at fault for something. The extracts below (2008: 85–6) give two possible reasons for this finding:

'Sumimasen' versus 'I'm sorry'
One possibility is that people's stereotypical conceptions of the apologizing behaviour of Japanese compared with that of English speakers are inaccurate.

English speakers might think that Japanese apologize more frequently than they really do because 'sumimasen' is used so frequently. Sumimasen can be translated as 'I'm sorry' and be used for an apology; however, it can also be used for various other purposes. Ide (1998), for example, identifies seven different functions of sumimasen, after observing how it was used authentically in a clinic in Tokyo. She found that in addition to it being used to convey sincere apologies, sumimasen was also used to express thanks, to convey a mixture of thanks and apologies, as a preliminary to a request, as an attention-getter, as a leave-taking device and more ritualistically (i.e. with little semantic content) as a device to confirm what someone has said or simply to acknowledge it. Ide (1998: 510) argues that sumimasen thus 'functions in both a "remedial" and a "supportive" manner in discourse, carrying pragmatic and ritualistic functions that extend beyond conveying the semantic meaning of regret or gratitude in actual discourse.' One possibility, therefore, is that people with only a superficial knowledge of Japanese and English think that sumimasen and 'I'm sorry' are equivalent. So when they hear the Japanese use sumimasen much more frequently than they hear English speakers use 'I'm sorry', they interpret this as indicating that Japanese apologize more frequently than English speakers do.

The effect of situation
Another possible explanation for the findings is that people's conceptions of Japanese and English apologizing behaviour are accurate for certain types of situations, but not for others. For example, it could be that IFIDs[1] are used more routinely in Japan than in Britain and Canada, and/or are used more frequently in situations where the person apologizing is personally at fault and the offence is more substantive. Such types of contexts were not included in this study, so it is possible that a different set of results would have emerged with scenarios that manipulated a different set of contextual features. Even in this study, there was a certain amount of variation from scenario to scenario. For instance, the Japanese respondents used IFIDs more frequently than the British and Canadian respondents did (86.72 per cent compared with 68.84 per cent and 65.63 per cent respectively) when responding to Scenario 7, where the customer complains and external circumstances are to blame. And they used them much less frequently than the British and Canadian respondents did (12.31 per cent compared with 59.84 per cent and 61.46 per cent respectively) when responding to Scenario 5, where the lecturer complains but is in fact responsible for the misunderstanding. So it is clearly possible that a different set of scenarios might have yielded a different set of results. Nevertheless, this cannot explain why the variable 'source of responsibility' should have had a consistently much greater effect on the

---

[1] IFID = Illocutionary Force Indicating Device. This is defined by Spencer-Oatey (2008: 331) as follows: 'This is the utterance, or part of an utterance, that conveys the speaker's communicative intention. It is often formulaic and routinized. For example, if someone says "I'm sorry I'm late. The traffic was very heavy", the phrase "I'm sorry I'm late" is the IFID and indicates that the communicative intention of the utterance is an apology.' In Chapter 7 you will read more about illocutionary force in speech acts.

Japanese responses than on the British and Canadian responses, when according to the stereotype (that Japanese apologize more frequently than English-speakers do even when they are not personally at fault) the opposite should have emerged.

It is further suggested that the group of respondents in the study (Japanese university students) may not represent Japanese people in general, or that norms for apologising in Japan are changing among younger generations. It is also mentioned that the data collected (written responses) may not reflect what people would actually *say* in these situations.

Task 4.12 Applying the concepts to teaching

Ask your language learners to note down three stereotypes that they have about the behaviour of another cultural group. Next to the stereotype, learners should note down the source of evidence (e.g., something they read in a newspaper, a movie scene, somebody they met, their intuition) that they have for their stereotype. Finally, for each stereotype, learners should make some notes on how they think they could investigate this stereotype more carefully in order to find out more about how true or untrue it actually is. The learners should get together in groups to discuss their notes. If you do not have access to learners, discuss with colleagues what you think their reaction might be.

Task 4.13 Trying out research

In the study described above, the researcher found out what respondents would 'say' in specific situations by asking them to fill in a written discourse completion test. This meant that they *wrote down* what they would say in each of the situations. Discuss:

- What are the advantages and disadvantages of using this method of data collection in research on cross-cultural pragmatics?
- How could the researchers have collected authentic *spoken* responses?
- What would be the advantages and disadvantages of collecting spoken data?

4.6 SUMMARY

This chapter has helped you to:

- understand the potential of language choice in bilingual and multilingual contexts, with a particular focus on issues related to the use of two or more languages in classroom contexts
- develop your understanding of the field of cross-cultural pragmatics by looking at different ways in which meanings are expressed in different languages and cultures
- consider issues which arise when people from different linguistic and cultural contexts interact

As regards applications to second language teaching, this chapter has enabled you to:

- consider how the L1 can be used as a resource for specific pedagogical and communicative purposes (e.g., for classroom management and building interpersonal relationships)
- develop awareness of the fact that there are no hard and fast rules for L1 use in second language classrooms because each teaching context has its own dynamic
- consider how the same words used in different contexts can have different intended meanings
- investigate similarities and differences in the way people carry out communicative acts in different languages and cultures (for example, in your L1 you may typically reject compliments whereas in the L2 you are learning it may be more usual to accept them)
- develop your awareness of the extremely important role that second language classrooms can play in preparing learners to be able to use words, expressions and grammar effectively in L2 contexts in ways which mitigate the potential for misunderstandings, irritation and embarrassment.

This chapter has demonstrated the importance of conducting research on how language is used in authentic contexts in order to be able to move understanding beyond simplistic black-and-white conceptualisations (e.g., 'the L1 should not be used in the L2 classroom'). Detailed analysis of instances of communication through discourse analysis and/or conversation analysis has led to an increasingly precise and nuanced understanding of how bilingual resources can be effectively mobilised, how language functions in different contexts, and how language is used in intercultural encounters. It is to be hoped that the findings from these burgeoning areas of research will feed into the development of teaching materials (e.g., textbooks), language assessment instruments and the knowledge-base of second language teachers. In turn, increased focus on these elements should lead to improved levels of intercultural awareness and understanding.

4.7 ADDITIONAL READINGS

Baker, C. (2007), *A Parents' and Teachers' Guide to Bilingualism*, Bristol: Multilingual Matters. (A practical introduction to bilingualism at home and in educational contexts.)

Ferguson, G. (2003), 'Classroom codeswitching in post-colonial contexts: Functions, attitudes and policies', *AILA Review*, 16(1): 38–51.

(This article provides a detailed review of previous studies on the functions of code-switching in both the language and the content classroom.)

Kasper, G., and K.R. Rose (2002), *Pragmatic Development in a Second Language*, Oxford: Blackwell.

(This remains the best single-volume overview of interlanguage pragmatics, in our opinion. It has excellent sections on the relationship between grammatical and pragmatic competence, on learning pragmatics both inside and outside classroom contexts, and on individual differences in L2 pragmatic development.)

Phillipson, R. (2009), 'The tension between linguistic diversity and dominant English', in A. Mohanty, M. Panda, R. Phillipson and T. Skutnabb-Kangas (eds), *Social Justice through Multilingual Education*, Bristol: Multilingual Matters, pp. 85–102.
(This chapter is a good introduction to the potential consequences of the globalisation of English language teaching on learners' bi/multilingual linguistic repertoire.)
Rashka, C., P. Sercombe and H. Chi-Ling (2009), 'Conflicts and tensions in codeswitching in a Taiwanese EFL classroom', *International Journal of Bilingual Education and Bilingualism*, 12(2): 157–71.
(This article illustrates some of the current issues related to language alternation practices in EFL classrooms. It is published in a Special Issue where many other seminal articles on this topic can also be found.)
Spencer-Oatey, H. (ed.) (2008), *Culturally Speaking: Culture, Communication and Politeness Theory*, 2nd edn, London: Continuum.
(This collection provides an excellent introduction to both cross-cultural and intercultural pragmatics. It contains a well-balanced mix of theoretical explanations and empirical studies.)
Taguchi, N. (2012), *Context, Individual Differences and Pragmatic Competence*, Bristol: Multilingual Matters.
(This research monograph provides a wealth of insights into the development of intercultural communication skills among Japanese learners of English at an international university in Japan where English is routinely spoken on campus.)
Üstünel, E., and P. Seedhouse (2005), 'Why that, in that language, right now? Code-switching and pedagogical focus', *International Journal of Applied Linguistics*, 15(3): 302–25.
(This article describes the relationship between pedagogical focus and language choice in the EFL teaching/learning environment at a Turkish university and shows how to use interactional data to study bi/multilingualism in the EFL classroom.)

5

CONTEXT AND REGISTERS
Kenneth Fordyce

INTRODUCTION

The previous chapter focused on the ways in which language is used in different cultures, and the ways in which language is adapted in order to achieve effective intercultural communication. In this chapter we focus more closely on the way English is used in different contexts to achieve different communicative purposes. We will provide answers to questions such as the following:

- How are spoken and written texts connected together to make them accessible to listeners or readers?
- In what ways is spoken language (e.g. that of university lectures) different from written language (e.g. that of textbooks), and why is language used so differently in these two modes?
- Is language being used differently in new registers such as texting, email or online chat? And if so, what language features distinguish these new registers?
- Are mobile texts and emails more like spoken or written language?

The chapter begins by looking at the nuts and bolts of texts; in other words, the language tools that speakers and writers use to make their language **cohesive** (the term 'cohesion' refers to the way in which grammatical and lexical elements link a text together to make it meaningful, e.g. 'I bought an i-Pad yesterday – it's great!') and **coherent** (the term 'coherence' means the degree to which a text or unit of discourse makes sense as a whole). We will describe the use of lexical and grammatical markers of cohesion, and discuss how the presentation and structuring of information can help to create coherence. The second section looks at the patterning of language used for different purposes. It explains the terms **register** ('a variety associated with a particular situation of use'; Biber and Conrad 2009: 6) and **genre markers** (specific linguistic features which are used to structure complete texts; Biber and Conrad 2009: 16). The section looks at sources of variation in registers, gives examples of how registers differ in terms of linguistic features, and also describes genre markers as 'expected' components of particular registers (see Section 5.2). The last section of the chapter provides insights into electronic registers (for example, emails, online forums and texting) which have developed in line with the communicative revolution that has followed in the wake of technological advances in recent decades.

Through reading this chapter and carrying out some of the tasks provided at the end of each section you will be able to develop answers to the following questions which relate these issues to second language teaching:

- Does the textbook I am using provide sufficient focus on teaching learners to produce cohesive and coherent texts? If not, what can I do to supplement the text-book materials in this respect?
- Do the spoken dialogues presented in the textbook and the listening materials contain authentic features of spoken language?
- How can I introduce different registers to learners? Which are the most important or useful registers for my learners to learn about?
- Should I teach learners features of electronic communication such as abbreviated forms (e.g., 'How r u?') and emoticons?

Many of the findings presented in this chapter have been based on the analysis of existing texts by using **corpus analysis**, which is described in detail in Chapter 2. The exercises in this chapter will demonstrate some of the ways in which corpora can be utilised by language teachers, and also point the way towards developing your own corpora of specific registers which are relevant to your language teaching context.

5.1 CONTEXT, COHESION AND COHERENCE

This section focuses on the elements of language which make links between a text and the context in which it is situated; between different parts of a text (e.g., between paragraphs or between different speakers in a conversation); and between the topics, ideas and concepts which make up a text. The first part focuses on the role played by the **context** in communication; the second part describes the linguistic features which make texts **cohesive**; and the final part takes a look at the broader concept of textual **coherence**.

Every communicative event has a context: Cutting (2008a: 5) provides a neat distinction between three kinds of context:

- the **situational context**, what speakers know about what they can see around them
- the **background knowledge context**, what they know about each other and the world
- the **co-textual context**, what they know about what they have been saying

When the fisherman holds his arms out wide and says, 'it was this big, honest!', we need to see how far apart his hands are in order to know how large he is claiming that the fish was. This is an example of situational context: elements of the physical situation in which an interaction is taking place which are used to support communication, but which make understanding difficult for somebody who does not share that time and place.

Background knowledge context can be both cultural and interpersonal. The following example from *Harry Potter and the Philosopher's Stone* (Rowling 1997: 107) demonstrates cultural background knowledge [emphasis added]: 'Harry had caught Ron prodding Dean's poster of *West Ham football team*, trying to make the players move.' For those who do not know English football particularly well, the reference to 'West Ham football team' will not be clear; this may explain why it merits its own page in an online guide to the Harry Potter books (http://harrypotter.wikia.com/wiki/West_Ham_United_Football_Club).

Interpersonal background knowledge refers to shared information between people which may be opaque to 'outsiders'. The example below is taken from the final scene of the romantic comedy *Notting Hill*. The knowledge (or lack of it) of previous interpersonal communication is used for comic effect. The scene takes place at a press conference for the movie star Anna Scott (played by Julia Roberts), who is announcing her intention to stop making movies for a while. In a previous scene, the character William Thacker (played by Hugh Grant) had turned down Anna's attempt to restart their relationship. However, having realised he has made a huge mistake, he bursts into the press conference under the guise of being a journalist. Some of the phrases used in this scene (underlined) are clearly understood by these two characters, and the 'knowing' movie viewers, but not by most of the other people at the press conference. This is a comic and rather unrealistic situation but it does show how language can be used to convey 'inside interpersonal knowledge' in a way that cannot be understood by those who were not privy to the previous interaction between those people (this is sometimes referred to as dramatic irony):

Jeremy	Right . . . er . . . yes . . . the gentleman in the pink shirt.
William	Yes . . . Miss Scott . . . are there any circumstances in which the two of you might be more than just good friends?
Anna	I hoped there would be . . . but, no, I'm assured there aren't.
William	But what would you say if . . .
Jeremy	I'm sorry, just the one question please.
Anna	No, it's alright. You were saying?
William	I was just wondering if er . . . it turned out that this . . . person . . .
Journalist	Er . . . Thacker. His name was Thacker.
William	Thanks . . . thanks . . . I just wondered whether . . . if Mr Thacker realised he'd been a daft prick, got down on his knees and begged you to reconsider, whether you would in fact then . . . reconsider?
Anna	Yes, I believe I would.
William	That's very good new. The readers of 'Horse and Hound' will be absolutely delighted.

The type of context termed co-text refers to something that was expressed earlier in a text. The text below is taken from the middle of a BBC news report. In the article, the words 'the weekend' refer to 'Thanksgiving weekend' in the United States; this article is about retail sales over this specific weekend. The words in one part of the text can only be fully understood if you have read earlier sections of the text:

Retailers, which make a large portion of their annual revenue during the
November/December festive period, made special efforts to entice shoppers over
the weekend, with a number of stores opened early to make the most of the sales
rush. [emphasis added]

This brief look at co-text connects well with the next topic: cohesion. We will
look at the two main ways in which cohesion is achieved in discourse: through the
use of **grammar** and **lexis**. There are four main forms of **grammatical cohesion:
reference** (or **referring expressions**), **substitution**, **ellipsis** and **conjunction**.

Referring expressions are words or phrases which enable a person, or object, or
abstract idea, to be identified. In the *Notting Hill* dialogue above, the same person
(William) is referred to in these ways: *the gentleman in the pink shirt, you, I, this
person, Thacker, Mr Thacker, he, a daft prick.* The pronouns used to identify him
(*I, you, he*) are examples of a specific type of referring expression, termed **deixis**. It
is, of course, unusual that the same person in the same conversation is referred to by
himself as both 'I' and 'he' but this relates to the comedy of this situation. These are
examples of **person deixis**. The two other main types of **deixis** are **place deixis** and
time deixis. All three kinds, and how they function, can be seen in the following
statement and its reported version:

Mary (on the phone to John):
    I'll see you there [at a party] at six p.m. tomorrow.
John (reporting what Mary said on the next day):
    She said she would meet me here at six p.m. today.

In these sentences: *I* and *she* are used to refer to Mary (person deixis); *you* and *me*
refer to John (person deixis); *there* and *here* both refer to the location of the party
(place deixis); and *six p.m. tomorrow* and *six p.m. today* both refer to the meeting time
(time deixis).

While deixis can be used to refer to entities both inside or outside a text, the
term **endophora** is used to refer to text-internal reference. This comes in two
forms: **anaphora** and **cataphora**. Anaphora occurs when a pronoun is used to refer
to an entity previously mentioned in the text: 'Mr and Mrs Dursley, of number
four, Privet Drive, were proud to say that they were perfectly normal, thank you
very much' (Rowling 1997: 7). Anaphora is far more frequent than its opposite,
cataphora, which involves a pronoun preceding a more precise description of the
referent. This is typically used for literary effect in novels. *The Hanging Garden* by Ian
Rankin begins with the line, 'They were arguing in the living room.' It is only later that
it is clarified that *they* refers to Inspector John Rebus and his ex-wife.

A second main form of grammatical cohesion is substitution. In this case, a more
general word is used in place of a more specific term. In the example below, the
word *ones* is used to avoid repeating the word *staircases*: 'There were a hundred
and forty-two staircases at Hogwarts: wide, sweeping ones; narrow, rickety ones . . .'
(Rowling 1997: 98).

Ellipsis is a type of grammatical cohesion which is more common in spoken than written language. It also involves the avoidance of repetition but in this case words are omitted from the discourse because it is assumed that the other person can understand what is meant without them. In the following example, Harry Potter does not need to say 'I am' before 'starving' because it is obvious that he is referring to himself. He is answering Ron's question and he is the only person apart from Ron in the train compartment:

> Ron stared as Harry brought it all back into the compartment and tipped it on to an empty seat.
> 'Hungry, are you?'
> 'Starving,' said Harry. (Rowling 1997: 76)

Finally, conjunction is an extremely common form of grammatical cohesion which is used to connect clauses or sentences together. We can see the former case in the example above with the use of 'and' to connect two clauses. (Some linguists call connectives 'discourse markers'; we prefer to use the term 'discourse marker' to refer to non-grammatical items such as 'anyway', 'now then' and 'well' that indicate topic change, emphasis and attitude.) Sentence-level cohesion, while common in most registers, is particularly important in academic writing where ideas are being connected together. In the text below from Spada (2011: 233), an article on the topic of form-focused instruction in the *Language Teaching* journal, the adverb *nonetheless* is used at the beginning of the second sentence to add a modification to the argument expressed in the previous sentence:

> In response to the question 'Are particular features more affected by form-focused instruction?' the results of the Spada & Tomita (2010) meta-analysis suggest that explicit instruction is equally beneficial for different language forms. Nonetheless, it will be important to explore whether different definitions and operationalizations of 'simple' and 'complex' lead to similar findings in future research.

Moving on to **lexical cohesion**, there are various ways in which lexical items are interconnected within texts, including the use of **synonyms** and **general words**. In some languages, but not all, it is considered 'good style' to avoid repeating the same word to refer to the same thing. As a result, in academic writing authors typically introduce research findings with a range of verbs with **synonymous meanings** such as *show, indicate, suggest, demonstrate*. In *Harry Potter and the Philosopher's Stone*, Rowling uses a range of words to describe things which are 'not usual' (frequencies are given in brackets): *strange* (23), *funny* (17), *odd* (17), *mysterious* (6), *unusual* (5), *peculiar* (4), *weird* (2). The publisher would not have been impressed if she had used *strange* on all 74 occasions.

General words such as *place, stuff, thing* are used in place of specific terms. These often function in a similar way to pronouns. They are also sometimes used as a way to avoid being specific. For example, in the novel *About a Boy* by Nick Hornby

(1998), the expression 'hospital stuff' is used three times in describing the thoughts of Marcus (an 11-year-old boy) in reference to his mother's attempted suicide. Clearly, in this case, the general noun 'stuff' avoids direct reference to a very bad memory.

While cohesion is achieved by using lexical and grammatical resources to connect texts in a bottom-up manner, **coherence** is a part of 'top-down planning and organization' (Celce-Murcia and Olshtain 2000: 8), and refers to the overall unity of a text and the way in which the sentences and paragraphs 'hang together and relate to each other'. Coherence is an important aspect of effective communication, but at the same time it can be difficult to pin down precisely what contributes to coherent communication. Unlike cohesion, it cannot be located in specific words. There are broader patterns of textual organisation such as 'problems followed by solutions', 'causes followed by effects', or 'arguments followed by counter-arguments' which contribute to coherence. However, it is also the case that, 'coherence may . . . depend in part on patterns and strategies of text development that are very culture specific' (Celce-Murcia and Olshtain 2000: 8). Broadly speaking, coherence refers to the degree to which a text 'makes sense' as a whole unit of communication. Very often coherence depends on the listener or hearer knowledge. Take, for example, this excerpt from a common room conversation between applied linguistics students:

AM   I mean what what was what were they trying to find out? I mean they said in the end all they said was yes that in a in a three consonant w-word group three syllable word word group two syllable word with three consonants.

AF   Yes.

AM   They the third consonant is the least remembered or something when you when you're when you only get it orally.

AF   I think you're trying to establish a pattern of errors and what the real point is.

To AM and AF, this is coherent. An outsider to the conversation, who did know about the article that they were discussing, would possibly evaluate this exchange as incoherent.

Task 5.1 Applying the concepts to teaching

Choose a short scene (one or two minutes) from a movie that is popular with your class of learners, and prepare a transcript of this scene. After watching the movie once, give the learners the transcript and ask them to identify occasions where reference is made to something outside the immediate context. Ask them to underline the expressions which are used to refer to the outside context and then compare their answers in groups. Discuss how it went, with colleagues. If you do not have access to a class, discuss the potential implications of such a task.

Task 5.2 Trying out research

You can carry out some research on the frequency of linking adverbials in different registers by going to the Brigham Young University website to analyse the British National Corpus (see Chapter 2).

1. Go to http://corpus.byu.edu/bnc/ and click on ENTER.
2. In the DISPLAY box, click on CHART; this enables you to create a graph comparing the frequency of a word in different registers.
3. Type 'nevertheless' in the box to the right of 'WORD(S)'; this means that your search will focus on occurrences of 'nevertheless' in the British National Corpus.
4. Make sure that in the SORTING AND LIMITS option, both tabs are set to FREQUENCY.
5. Click on SEARCH.
6. Make some notes on the frequencies of 'nevertheless' in the different registers. What does this tell you? What questions does it raise?
7. Repeat the process for other linking adverbials so that you can compare their frequencies in the different registers (note that you can also search for adverbials which consist of more than one word, e.g., *on the other hand, in spite of*)
8. If you wish to carry out more qualitative analysis on the way the adverbials are used, you can click on a relevant bar chart; this will bring up the concordance lines. This may help you to answer some more of the questions raised.

Compare your findings with those of colleagues.

Task 5.3 Using the internet

Go to the *Lexical Tutor* website set up by Thomas Cobb (http://www.lextutor.ca/vp/eng/). Take an example of your own academic writing and copy and paste it into the text window, and then press on SUBMIT. You will see a list of word frequencies for your text; go through this list and identify all those words (e.g., pronouns, linking adverbials, general nouns) which are used to achieve cohesion. What do you notice about your own use of cohesive markers? Bring your findings to discuss with colleagues.

5.2 COMMUNITIES OF PRACTICE, REGISTER AND GENRE

In this section our focus moves on to the way language is used in varying ways according to the group of speakers who are communicating, the situational context and the communicative purpose. We explore the ways in which choices of vocabulary, grammar and expressions vary according to these factors. Most of the findings reported in this chapter come from the analysis of corpora of language used for a wide variety of purposes (e.g. emails, lectures), in different contexts (e.g. academic, service encounters) and among different groups of people (e.g. university students, families).

A community of practice is a concept which was introduced by Lave and Wenger (1991). Cutting (2008a: 60) explains that communities of practice are groups that are 'brought together by a common interest and mutual engagement, sharing knowledge, values and beliefs, and maintaining membership through their linguistic and behavioural social practices.' It has been noted that such groups often use words and expressions that constitute an **in-group code** which, while being clearly understandable to members of that group, may be opaque to 'outsiders'. For example, among the English-speaking expatriate population in Japan, creative expressions can be found which are presumably rare outside this group. Here are a couple of examples attested by the author:

'I'm going to <u>shink</u> it up to Tokyo.'

The verb *shink* comes from *shinkansen* which is the Japanese word for the bullet train.

'I <u>blackcatted</u> my snowboard to Sapporo airport.'

This one takes some explaining: in Japan it is quite common to have your luggage sent ahead using a delivery company when you go on a trip. One of the biggest delivery companies in Japan is called 'kuro-neko' which means 'black cat' in English. These examples show that communities of practice often develop creative ways of communicating meaning which may only be understandable to other members of that community.

We now turn to **registers** and **genres**, which reflect variation in the language used in different situational contexts. While there is some inconsistency in the way these two terms are defined in the literature, in this book we follow Biber and Conrad (2009: 6–16) by defining a register as 'a variety associated with a particular situation of use (including particular communicative purposes). The description of a register covers three major components: the situational context, the linguistic features, and the functional relationships between the first two components.' In contrast, a genre perspective is oriented towards specific linguistic features which 'are used to structure *complete* texts' (emphasis added). To take an example, while a frequent linguistic feature of the register of emails is first- and third-person pronouns, and ellipsis of pronouns and verbs, from a genre perspective we might say that an email is expected to contain an informal opening (e.g. 'Hi' + first name of receiver) and closing (e.g. 'Love and hugs' + first name of sender + xxxxx, to indicate kisses):

<u>Hi Debbie</u>
How about lunch on 5th August? <u>I</u>'ve put it in my diary but <u>. . .</u> always flexible.
What a busy time table for the summer! <u>. . .</u> Hope <u>we</u> can see John and family
while they are up here!
Keep in touch and I'll think about all <u>you've</u> said!
<u>Love and hugs</u>
<u>Pippa xxxxx</u>

The following two texts exemplify two different academic registers. The first is taken from an anthropology textbook (nouns are <u>underlined</u>, verbs are in *italics*) while the second is from 'graduate-level humanities teaching' ('oral discourse' features are <u>underlined</u>) (Biber 2006: 190):

LEARNING ABOUT THE PAST – THE MATERIAL RECORD.

This book *focuses* on the human past, but how do we *learn* about the past? How do we *collect* and *analyse* data about the ancient past of our species? In this book our approach to *understanding* the human past will *be* through the field of anthropology, *defined* properly as the study of humanity. If you *think* about it, though, nearly all the courses you *are* now *taking deal* in some fashion with people or their works. What *makes* anthropology different?

Instructor: I think some of us feel sort of really caught in a bind between agency and acculturation, sort of um, because you know I think a lot of us do want to use writing, use literacy to um, say what we want to say and to help other people say what they want to say but at the same time I think um, we're caught because we, I think we're questioning well, well you know, if, if we, if we teach X-genre are we promoting it? If we don't at the same time question it and dismantle it and kind of take it apart and look at it, and are there, are there other ways?

Both of these university registers involve knowledge transmission. However, the differences between them demonstrate what is considered to be the most fundamental register division: between the spoken and written **modes** (Biber and Conrad 2009: 260–4). The high frequency of nouns in the first text is typical of written language while frequent features in the second text, such as personal stance expressions ('I think'), hedges ('sort of', 'kind of'), first-person pronouns ('I', 'we') and lexical bundles starting with 'what' ('what we want', 'what they want') are more typical of spoken language.

As well as the spoken/written distinction, research has shown that the language used in different registers relates to a number of other characteristics of text varieties. Biber (1988) has been at the forefront of introducing a technique called multidimensional analysis in which advanced statistical techniques are used to identify the most important factors in determining register variation as well as the linguistic features which cluster on to those factors. In his original study, which looked at the frequencies of 67 different linguistic features in 23 different registers, he identified seven different dimensions of variation. In Table 5.1 the three dimensions with the strongest factor loadings are presented together with registers which typify the far ends of these dimensions and linguistic features which have statistically strong associations with these dimensions.

The findings from this kind of research can inform textbook writers (especially in areas such as English for Specific Purposes or English for Academic Purposes) who are aiming to prepare second language learners to produce language in targeted registers. The textbook writers can make sure that the materials contain an authentic coverage of language features typical of these registers. This information can also help language teachers to assist learners in establishing relevant form–function connections in the language they are learning.

We now turn our attention to genre markers. In some cases, they are quite clearly defined: for example, formal business letters typically begin with 'Dear . . .' and end with a polite sign-off such as 'Yours sincerely' or 'With best regards'. Genre markers

Table 5.1   The three strongest dimensions of variation

Dimension	Registers	Language features (examples)
Involved vs. informational	Involved: telephone conversations, face-to-face conversations, personal letters Informational: official documents, academic prose, press reportage	Involved: private verbs (e.g., *believe*, *think*); *that* deletions; contractions; present-tense verbs; second-person pronouns Informational: nouns; (long) word length; prepositions; (high) type/token ratio*
Narrative vs. non-narrative discourse	Narrative: fiction Non-narrative: broadcasts, official documents, academic prose, professional letters, telephone conversations	Narrative: past-tense verbs; third-person pronouns Non-narrative: present-tense verbs; attributive adjectives
Explicit vs. situation-dependent reference	Explicit reference: official documents, professional letters, press reviews, academic prose Situation-dependent reference: broadcasts, telephone conversations, face-to-face conversations	Explicit reference: wh- relative clauses on object positions (e.g., *people who know him*); pied piping constructions (e.g., *the way in which food is digested*) Situation-dependent reference: time adverbials; place adverbials

* The type-token ratio is a measure of the linguistic variety of a text; a high type-token ration means that the text contains a high variety of different words, i.e. that there are not many repeated instances of the same word throughout.

can also be found in spoken registers such as telephone calls: it is typical to say who you are at the beginning of the call, and it is unusual to put down the phone without having said goodbye in one way or another.

The genre markers described above are quite obvious and are typically expressed with formulaic expressions (for example, 'Hi . . .', 'talk to you soon', 'take care', 'all the best'). However, a more complex kind of genre marker is the **discourse move** (also referred to as **rhetorical move**; Swales 2004). One example of this can be found in the register of the academic abstract which is found at the beginning of a research article (see Bhatia 1993) and typically includes information about:

- the research gap
- what the researchers did
- how they did it
- what they found
- what they concluded

This is exemplified by the abstract below from Schulz (2008: 343).

While the professional literature abounds with treatises for and against the values of explicit grammar instruction and error correction in foreign or second language classrooms, few researchers have investigated student and teacher beliefs regarding the benefit of these pedagogical procedures. [research gap] This paper reports on an exploratory study, conducted at the University of Arizona, which examines and compares foreign language student and teacher beliefs regarding the benefit of a focus on form in language learning. [what we did] A total of 824 students and 92 teachers of the commonly taught as well as the less commonly taught languages were included in the study. [what we did] Results reveal that the students surveyed are relatively favorably disposed toward a focus on form, regardless of language. [what we found] However, some surprising discrepancies surfaced in teacher beliefs and in a comparison of student and teacher beliefs. [what we found] The author recommends that in order to establish pedagogical credibility and increase their students' commitment to and involvement in learning, teachers make an effort to explore students' beliefs about language learning and to establish a fit between their own and their students' expectations. [conclusions based on research]

Although the organisation of **discourse moves** is by no means always the same for a specific genre, or as tightly structured as in the case of academic abstracts, when you start analysing texts in detail you will start to find them in various registers, both spoken and written.

This section has identified patterns of similarity and difference in spoken and written text. Explicit knowledge of register features and genre markers, whether as a first or second language user of a language, can enable greater control in the production of texts and can be particularly useful in academic and business contexts.

Task 5.4 Applying the concept to teaching

The aim of this task is to focus learners' attention on the use of 'spoken genre markers'. Ask them to consider phrases (if any) which they would typically use in their L1 in these situations:

- when knocking on the door and entering a teacher's/professor's/doctor's office; and also when leaving that office
- when leaving home or arriving home, assuming that somebody is at home
- to a waiter/waitress in a restaurant when
    a. getting his/her attention
    b. complaining that a dish is not warm enough
    c. asking for the bill

If the learners have different L1s, ask them to get into groups and make comparisons. After this, introduce phrases that would be used in English in each of these contexts. If you do not have access to learners, carry out this task in your student group and compare with phrases that would be used in a variety of English that you know.

Task 5.5 Trying out research
Pick up (or find online) an English language daily newspaper and select one news article and one editorial. Underline all the expressions which express an authorial viewpoint (e.g. 'it seems that', 'it is probably true that', 'I believe', 'apparently'). Discuss with colleagues:

- the differences that you notice between these two sub-registers of newspaper writing as regards this linguistic feature
- other linguistic differences between the report and the editorial (e.g., the use of tenses, the use of adverbs)

Task 5.6 Using the internet
Look at a specialist web forum such as those for Lego enthusiasts (http://news.lugnet. com/), cyclists (http://www.cyclechat.net/), bonsai practitioners (http://ibonsaiclub. forumotion.com/) or one of your own choice. Look at some exchanges in the forums and identify words or phrases which can be considered as 'in-group' markers. Note down your most interesting findings and discuss them with a classmate.

5.3 ELECTRONIC COMMUNICATION REGISTERS

This section gives a special focus to registers which have emerged in recent years as computers, the internet, mobile phones and other technological innovations have changed the ways in which millions of people communicate. These registers include emails, texting, online chat, wikis, blogs, podcasts, Facebook, Twitter and other social media tools. In this section we will look at features of some of these registers in order to answer questions such as:

- Do these electronic registers (henceforth, 'e-registers') have more in common with written or spoken language?
- What features do e-registers have that are rarely found in more traditional registers?
- What similarities and differences are there between various e-registers?

We will begin by focusing on **emailing**, which is arguably the most dominant e-register, and which has had a particularly huge impact on the way in which communication is carried out in both formal (for example, business and universities) and informal (for example, among friends and family) contexts. Emails appear to offer a hybrid form of communication which contains elements of both conversation and letter-writing. We begin by comparing emails and conversation, which is interesting because nowadays people will often choose to send and exchange emails instead of using the telephone, or even instead of getting out of their chair to walk two doors down the corridor to talk to a person face-to-face.

As regards **situational characteristics** (cf. Biber and Conrad 2009: 178–80), emails and conversation are similar in that they are both interactive: a series of emails can be compared to a set of turns in conversation. However, the two registers differ in that

1) emails are written and conversation is spoken; 2) unlike face-to-face conversation, email communication is typically carried out by people who are separate in time and space.

Turning our attention to **linguistic features** of emails and conversation, there are again both similarities and differences between the two registers. Obviously the off-line nature of email communication, that it is non-synchronic, means that the use of backchanneling (feedback that listeners give speakers to indicate that they are listening, for example, 'uhu', 'mm', 'oh really?', 'right') is much rarer than in conversation. On the other hand, the two registers are similar in that both have a much greater frequency of pronoun use (especially the use of first- and second-person pronouns) than academic prose (Biber and Conrad 2009: 192–3); this reflects the high degree of interactivity in email communication. Biber and Conrad (2009: 187) also identified a clear continuum of variation in the use of language features with emails from friends and family towards the 'conversation' end of the continuum and emails from 'strangers' more similar to academic prose.

The main genre markers used in emails are openings and closings. Biber and Conrad (2009) found that around 70 per cent of emails to friends and family do not use the name of the receiver; they either have no salutation (30 per cent) or just 'Hi' (40 per cent). On the other hand, in professional emails to 'strangers' the name of the recipient was always used, with over three-quarters using 'Dear' + Title + last name (for example, 'Dear Professor Biber'). Similar patterns of variation can be seen for closings, with the majority of emails to friends and family ending with the first name only, while around half of the 'professional email' groupings end with 'sincerely' + name or 'thanks' + 'sincerely' + name. These findings again demonstrate that emails tend to be slightly more informal than letters, but at the same time there is a great degree of variation depending on the email recipient and the context in which it is written. It has also been observed that, as many emails are part of an ongoing communicative exchange, they typically begin with an acknowledgement of a previous email, for example 'Thanks for this', 'Sorry for the delay', 'That's great news', 'Thanks for your fast response'.

There are other elements to emails which differentiate them from letters. One example is the use of an automatically generated 'signature' placed at the end of each email. This may include the sender's full name, address, email address, website and also, in some cases, a slogan or a favourite quotation (Crystal 2006: 109). As Crystal (2006: 110) points out, such slogans can quickly lose their novelty value and appropriateness if not frequently updated: '"Cool dude" might have suited John Doe as an office junior, but he may not like to be reminded of his former e-identity now he is a company vice-president.'

While many email replies are written, as with letters, in one block of text, the technological set-up for email provides the respondent with the option of breaking up their reply and inserting comments to separate parts of the email they are replying to. Email software will often insert right-facing brackets ('>') to the left of the text of the original email so that the responses are typographically distinct (Crystal 2006: 120). In this way the medium of email allows written text to assume a dialogic form that would be extremely time-consuming in letter-writing:

>I hope to be there by six, though everything depends on the
>trains.
I know – remember last time?
> Will you be coming by train yourself, or are you driving this
> time?
Car
>I know Fred is bringing his car. (Crystal 2006: 122)

It seems clear that, while emails do indeed contain elements of both conversation and more formal written registers, they represent a distinct register which enables new ways of communicating, and a register with large variation in linguistic features depending on the communicative context.

We now turn to the register of **e-forum postings**. These are messages written on websites as part of a discussion about a specific topic. E-forums (also referred to as chatgroups; Crystal 2006) are the online equivalent of a club where people who share an interest (e.g., cycling, stamp collecting, bonsai) can 'meet' to discuss that interest and share information. In most cases, e-forums consist of a series of 'threads' which each begin with a member of the community posting a question or comment designed to begin a series of responses. Here is an example taken from a bonsai forum (retrieved from http://forums2.gardenweb.com/forums):

newby needing help
Posted by ***** on
Tue, Nov 20, 12 at 23:53

I received this tree about a week ago, and know almost nothing about bonsai. I can tell it was beautiful at some point, and would like to get it back there if that's even possible.
Can anyone tell me what kind of tree this is so i can do some research? And of course any advice here at all would be greatly appreciated.

In some cases, forum postings are also multimodal. For example, the message above was accompanied by a photo of the plant without which it would be impossible for the sender to receive any responses because s/he is asking for help with identifying the type of tree.

Empirical research on this register has identified a number of distinguishing features (Crystal 2006; Biber and Conrad 2009):

- interaction is usually 1-to-many, unlike emails which are typically 1-to-1
- the permanence of the text written in a public space is likely to lead writers to reflect on and edit their text before posting (although this is clearly not always the case)
- as a result of the above, more attention is likely to be given to writing an interesting topic title for forum postings as compared to emails
- unlike emails, a reply, although usually wished for, is not expected

- the length of contributions is usually quite short (in one analysis, Crystal (2006: 150) found an average length of 3.5 lines)
- postings are more likely to have closings than greetings
- it is important not to stray too far from the main topic being discussed; indeed a moderator may intervene to keep things focused
- capitalisation is not always used (note the use of 'i' in the bonsai example above)
- there is common ellipsis of subject pronouns (for example, 'Any suggestions?', 'Having trouble getting used to Word 2010')
- punctuation (':)'), emoticons (L) or block capitals ('SOLVED THE PROBLEM!!!') are sometimes used to convey emotions

These features demonstrate that e-forum postings can be clearly distinguished as a register from emails, and also from face-to-face conversation. Crystal (2006: 154) states that 'The language of asynchronous messaging is a curious mixture of informal letter and essay, of spoken monologue and dialogue', and he considers it to be an emerging linguistic register.

Text-messaging involves the sending of written messages by mobile phone (cellphone). These messages tend to be very short (in fact there is often a limit on their length) and are also referred to as 'SMS' ('short messaging services'). As with other e-registers, to date there has been relatively little published analysis of text-messaging corpora. Therefore, we again turn to Biber and Conrad (2009), who compiled a small corpus of 300 text messages sent by 130 different people with a variety of ages, nationalities and professions.

As regards their situational characteristics (Biber and Conrad 2009), text messages are more like emails than e-forum postings because they are usually targeted at one specific individual rather than a community. They tend to be more interactive than emails in that they often involve brief exchanges of two or three messages:

A: just arrived at café
B: great – on the way right now
A: ok – c u soon J ☺

In its interactivity, texting is closer to conversation than email. Yet, as with email, its written medium allows the sender the opportunity to plan and edit the text. As regards linguistic features, texts are notable for their use of abbreviated forms (e.g., 'r' = 'are', '4' = 'for'), non-standard punctuation (commas and full stops are sometimes omitted), lack of capitalisation (see example above) and the use of emoticons (e.g, L, ☺). These features may well change, once the use of predictive text becomes more commonplace. Biber and Conrad's (2009) corpus suggested that emoticons may not be as common as they are generally thought to be; only 3 per cent of the texts included them. Genre markers were also rare in this corpus: 90 per cent of the texts did not begin with a greeting, and those that did usually started with 'hey', 'heya', or 'hi'; closings were even rarer – only 5 out of 300 texts had one.

Emails, forum postings and texts can all clearly be considered as separate registers. It is also apparent that other e-registers exist or are coming into existence. For example, Twitter, a microblogging service launched in 2006, has a limit of 140 characters for any one 'tweet'. This communicative restriction is likely to cause users to use language in new and different ways. At the time of writing, empirical research on the linguistic features of tweeting has only just begun. Another social networking service, Facebook (launched in 2004), has also had a huge global impact on communication. Unlike Twitter, which involves one main form of communication, Facebook contains a range of ways of communicating, many of which involve multi-modality. Again, research on the language of Facebook posts is in its infancy.

The hybrid nature of e-registers leads Crystal (2006) to use 'Netspeak' as an overarching term. He also highlights the emergent nature of many e-registers and that their precise features are still evolving: 'As a new linguistic medium, Netspeak will doubtless grow in its sociolinguistic and stylistic complexity to be comparable to that already known in traditional speech and writing. But it is too soon to be certain about the form these new varieties will take' (Crystal 2006: 272).

Task 5.7 Applying the concept to teaching
Get into groups with colleagues and brainstorm ways in which their language use in their L1 in emails and text messages is different from more traditional forms of written communication. Move the discussion to English and discuss the use of abbreviations, punctuation variation and emoticons in emails and texts. Finally, discuss what sort of guidance you would give your learners on the use of these features.

Task 5.8 Trying out research
Look at the most recent 20–30 tweets on the Twitter account of 1) a famous pop or movie star; 2) a politician. Do a comparative analysis of the language used in these tweets. For example, what do you notice about:

- the use of abbreviated forms (e.g., 'cuz' instead of 'because')
- the (non-)use of capitalisation
- the use of formal or informal vocabulary
- any other features of note

Compare findings with colleagues.

Task 5.9 Using the internet
Identify one online forum which seems to cover a more formal subject (for example, saving for retirement) and one which has a more informal subject (for example, Japanese manga comics). Look at the list of e-forum features described above and analyse the degree to which these features occur in the two online forums. Discuss the similarities and differences that you notice between them.

5.4 FURTHER READING ONE

Liu, D. (2008), 'Linking adverbials: an across-register corpus study and its implications', *International Journal of Corpus Linguistics*, 13(4): 491–518.
This study compares the use of linking adverbials (henceforth, 'LAs') in five different registers: spoken English, academic writing, fiction, news writing and 'other writings'. The aim of the research was to find out more in-depth information about these adverbials which enable writers and speakers 'to make semantic connections between spans of discourse of varying length' (Biber et al. 1999: 558). Liu argues for the importance of understanding how to use linking adverbials with special reference to the case of second language learning. He emphasises the difficulties LAs can present for ESL learners, including the issue of 'register-inappropriate use, e.g. using informal colloquial LAs in academic writing' (2008: 494). As a result, his study sets out to identify more precise information on the use of LAs in different registers including both formal and informal registers. In his study, he adopts Celce-Murcia and Larsen-Freeman's (1999: 530) four-category classification of LAs (itself based on Halliday and Hasan 1976): 1) additive ('in addition', 'similarly'); 2) adversative ('however', 'instead'); 3) causal ('therefore', 'in that case'); and 4) sequential ('first', 'finally').

In order to carry out his analysis, Liu searched for the frequency of linking adverbials in sub-corpora from the BNC (British National Corpus) for each of the five registers outlined above. Some of the most relevant findings from his overall analysis were as follows:

- the highest frequency for LAs was found in academic writing; this included a particularly high proportion of additive LAs;
- some LAs had noticeably high frequencies in academic writing (for example, 'however' and 'moreover') while others were very frequent in the speaking sub-corpus (for example, 'so' and 'then');
- overall LAs were less frequent in the fiction corpus than the speaking and academic writing corpora; in spite of this, fiction had the highest frequency of sequential LAs;
- although speaking and academic writing have the two highest frequency counts for LAs, there is considerable difference in the forms used in each register.

The article goes on to report on findings related to specific LAs. Some differences in the use of LAs in speaking and academic writing are reported:

One more interesting finding is related to the use of the concessive adversative *yet*. The BNC data shows that although the frequency of *yet* is about the same in both speaking and academic writing (307.21 versus 307.46 tokens per million), the positions in which it appears differ significantly between the two registers. While in speaking, it is seldom used sentence-initially (only 8.42 times per million words), in academic writing, the frequency of its appearance in the sentence initial position is very high (116.40 per million words). Conversely, in speaking, the use of yet in other positions is much higher than in academic writing with a ratio of 278.90: 190.06.

Another noticeable finding deals with a group of LAs that often co-appear with a conjunction (usually right after it), e.g. *and finally, and/but of course, and then, and yet, but . . . all the same.* The BNC data suggest that the use of this type is mostly found in speaking and seldom in writing, especially academic writing. There is, however, one interesting exception. In the use of *and also* and *but also* (either as part of the *not only . . . but also* structure or as the independent conjunction *but* plus LA *also* structure), the former (*and also*) is used far more frequently in academic writing than in speaking (130.13 vs. 22.42 in the case of *not only . . . but also* and 19.26 vs. 6.99 in the case of the independent conjunction *but* plus LA *also* structure). (2008: 504)

The article also looks at some LAs which can be used for more than one function, and therefore the authors go beyond frequency counts to look at how these LAs ('of course', 'at the same time', and 'as a matter of fact') are used in different contexts for different communicative purposes.

The findings from this study provide insights into how linking adverbials are used and also into their relative frequencies in different registers. In the conclusion, the author discusses the relevance of the findings to language teaching:

For example, the finding that news makes an extensive use of some sequential and summative LAs indicates that, in teaching journalism, it will be advisable to focus on sequential and summative LAs, especially those used most frequently in news such as *in the mean time, meanwhile,* and *in short.* As another example, the finding that fiction sometimes overuses colloquial LAs may be an issue worth a close look by fiction writers and those in the business of learning and teaching fiction.

Furthermore, the finding of a general low use frequency of summative adverbials might make us wonder whether it is advisable to give them so much prominence both in the teaching material and in the classroom. I am not suggesting that we do not teach them, though. I am just wondering about the wisdom of having them occupy such a prominence in our teaching of LAs when there are many other far more useful ones that have been neglected. In order to avoid the problem of focusing on seldom used LAs and to make sounder decisions regarding which idioms to include for instruction, language educators and materials writers may want to look at LAs' frequency and usage patterns. The information in Appendix 2[2] should be especially helpful for deciding the sequence in which LAs need to be taught. It is paramount to note, however, that I am not suggesting that the selection of LAs for instruction should be based exclusively on the frequency order. Yet it should be one criterion to consider along with others such as students' learning needs and a curriculum's objectives. (2008: 509)

---

[2] Appendix 2 (Liu 2008: 517–18) provides a list of individual LAs by frequency levels.

As with many corpus-based studies, the findings reported here question the *intuitive* presentation of language in textbooks and grammars for second language instruction. The author acknowledges that frequency should not be the only criterion in determining what is taught and the order in which it is taught. However, the results from empirical studies on form–function use in different registers can provide valuable information for the development of pedagogical materials.

Task 5.10 Applying the concept to teaching
What are the advantages and disadvantages of using 1) intuition and 2) corpus-based findings, when making decisions about what linking adverbials to use in textbooks? Discuss in groups.

   When developing their skills at writing compositions, many second language learners are taught to begin paragraphs with a series of phrases such as: 'Firstly', 'Secondly', 'Thirdly', 'In conclusion'. Discuss how learners can be helped to move on from this stage to producing writing which aligns itself more closely with the way linking adverbials are typically used in authentic texts. Discuss what kinds of materials you could bring to class to help learners with developing these skills.

Task 5.11 Trying out research
Find out why your learners (or your colleagues, if you do not have access to learners) make their lexical choices as regards cohesion in their writing. This can be done by carrying out what is called a 'retrospective verbal protocol': getting learners to talk through the reasons why they made certain choices. This research will work best with learners at an intermediate level or higher who are able to write longer compositions. After learners have completed a piece of written work, arrange to meet some of them individually for around 30–45 minutes each (if you are working with colleagues on this, you could each bring a page of an assignment that you have written). Go through the composition/assignment and ask the learner to explain their use of these markers by asking questions such as:

- Why did you choose this cohesion marker?
- What other words could you have used instead of this one?
- Do you find yourself translating forms from your first language when you write?
- Have you been taught these forms or have you picked them up by yourself from reading?
- Are you aware of differences in the level of formality of different cohesion markers?

After you have analysed your findings from several learners/colleagues, summarise the main issues, and discuss possible implications for the teaching of cohesion in second language writing.

5.5 FURTHER READING TWO

Waldvogel, J. (2007), 'Greetings and closings in workplace e-mail', *Journal of Computer-Mediated Communication*, 12: 456–77.

As discussed above, one of the interesting features of emails is their hybrid status between conversation and letter-writing. They are often written and answered at much greater speed, and with greater frequency, than letters; at the same time, unlike conversation, they are written, they can be edited by the author and interpersonal elements cannot be communicated through non-verbal communication (smiles, body language, etc.). As a result of these factors, there can be great variation in the degree to which writers of emails attend to interpersonal communication (e.g., through writing greetings such as 'Dear . . .', 'Hi!', or closings such as, 'Best Regards', 'Cheers'). In her comparison of the use of greetings and closings in corpora of emails produced in two different workplace settings in New Zealand, Waldvogel investigates the relationship between the (non-)use of greetings and closings and broader issues in the organisations, such as staff morale and the degree of trust in the management. She argues that:

> A study of greetings and closings can . . . provide valuable insights into people's relational practices at work, and, on an organizational level, into the organizational culture of the workplace, since the aggregate tone of individual e-mails plays a constitutive role in constructing the organizational culture. (2007: 457)

There is a tension between the transactional and interactional elements in email communication. They provide a fast and efficient method of communicating, but the heavy traffic of email can lead to them becoming like memos with interpersonal elements disregarded for the sake of efficiency:

> In as much as greetings and closings pay attention to the recipient and are oriented to the addressee's face needs (see Goffman, 1967), they are politeness markers. Like other politeness markers, they serve an important function in constructing and maintaining workplace relationships. Greetings and closings enable the writer to express warmth or distance, expressions that are otherwise difficult to do in e-mail, and they are a strategy for personalizing messages as well as a means of reinforcing status relationships and underlining positional expectations. (2007: 458)

Waldvogel also mentions previous research which suggests that workplaces 'tend to develop their own unique email style, reflecting organizational differences' (2007: 459). This reflects the idea of a community of practice with its own in-group code which is discussed above. The two workplaces investigated in this study were an educational organisation (SCT) and a manufacturing plant (Revelinu). The following data was collected:

> Each organization provided two e-mail samples: One was a week's inward and outward messages from a senior manager (SM); the other was a set of e-mails related to a particular issue. Because of the greater use made of e-mail in the educational organization (Waldvogel, 2005), the SCT corpus (394 e-mails) was

over three times as large as that from Revelinu, the manufacturing plant (121 e-mails). (2007: 460)

Their results showed that greetings and closings were used to a much greater degree in the manufacturing plant than the educational organisation. Some of the main findings for greetings are described:

At SCT, 59% of the greetings started without any form of greeting, and an additional 21% started simply with the person's name. Only 20% of the greetings contained any general greeting. *Hi* was the most popular general greeting (10% of messages), followed by *Dear* and *Hello* (about 3% each) and *Good morning* (2%). Two messages used the Maori greeting *Kia ora*.

At Revelinu, in contrast, the figures were almost reversed. Most messages (58%) began with a greeting word, usually accompanied by the addressee's name (53%). Another one-quarter began with a name only, and in sharp contrast to SCT, only 17% began baldly. Here, too, *Hi*, found in half of the messages, was the most popular greeting word. The second most favoured greeting word – starting 7% of the messages – was *Dear*. However, with only one exception, *Dear* was used to start messages to a group. Eighteen per cent of the messages addressed to a group began in this way. *Good morning* was used twice, including once to a group, and *Hey*, once. (2007: 462–3)

The results for closings mirrored those for greetings. While at SCT, nearly three-quarters of the emails ended with no closing or just the writer's first name, at Revelinu, 'three-quarters of the e-mails signed off with a closing word such as *Cheers* or *Regards*, a phatic comment such as *Have a nice day* or *Thanks*, and the person's name' (2007: 465). In her discussion of these results, Waldvogel offers possible explanations for the low frequency of greetings and closings at the educational organisation:

There are several possible reasons for the low use of greetings and closings at SCT. One is that less friendly and more impersonal e-mails are part of its culture and may reflect the social distancing strategies people use when they feel alienated from what is going on. Another is that because of the greater volume of messages they receive relative to their Revelinu counterparts, managers in particular respond to them under pressure. The key person, from whom the bulk of the e-mails came, averaged over sixty e-mails per day. In these conditions, niceties such as greetings and closings may be the first to be sacrificed. E-mail may thus assist in constructing a less personalized culture. A third possibility is that greetings and closings are omitted because there is an assumption that they are unnecessary in exchanges among professionals engaged in a common purpose. However, this runs counter to what most of those surveyed felt. (2007: 472)

The findings are also connected to a related study (Waldvogel 2005) which found that there was a much more supportive and harmonious environment between the staff and management at Revelinu, and the author suggests that the findings regarding greetings and closings in emails represent a culture in which more effort is put into the maintenance of friendly interpersonal relationships. In her conclusion, Waldvogel offers this observation:

> The importance of greetings and closings as a linguistic resource lies in the affective role they play. The choice of greeting or closing and its presence or absence in an e-mail message conveys not only an interpersonal message enabling the writer to negotiate his or her workplace relationships but also contributes to the creation of a friendly or less friendly workplace culture and, in turn, reflects this culture. (2007: 474)

Task 5.12 Applying the concept to teaching

Plan a 50-minute class in which your aim is to teach your learners to email and text effectively in English. Think about (and then discuss with colleagues):

- what linguistic features of emails and texts you will introduce
- how you will introduce them
- how you will get your learners to practise their new knowledge
- what advice you will give to them as regards the use of abbreviated forms, emoticons and punctuation

Task 5.13 Trying out research

Carry out an analysis of the last 50 emails you have sent and the last 50 emails you have received which relate to the context of your work or study. Focus on (non-)use of greetings and closings in these emails. What conclusions can you draw from your analysis as regards the level of attention given to interpersonal relations in these emails? Bring your findings to class and compare findings.

5.6 SUMMARY

This chapter has helped you to:

- recognise the variety of ways in which texts are connected to their contexts, and also internally connected through the use of various cohesion markers
- develop your awareness of how registers vary both in terms of their situational contexts and linguistic features
- learn about registers which have developed and are continuing to develop as technological developments change the ways in which people communicate

As regards teaching English in the classroom, your greater understanding of context and register variation will help you to:

- critically evaluate textbooks and language tests as regards the authenticity of language used in the various registers that are represented
- raise learners' awareness of cohesion, register variation and genre markers

- provide learners with tools which enable them to adapt their language between different registers
- prepare teaching materials which introduce learners to various registers and the linguistic features which are typical of those registers
- inform learners about the latest developments in the use of language in e-registers, and to advise them on how to communicate in those registers.

Chapter 3 looked at the variety of Englishes in existence around the planet, and this chapter focused on the variety that exists in the linguistic make-up of texts used for various purposes and in various contexts. Both chapters share the key point that understanding language in TESOL involves continually developing your awareness and knowledge of linguistic variety.

5.7 ADDITIONAL READINGS

Biber, D. (1988), *Variation across Speech and Writing*, Cambridge: Cambridge University Press. (This book reports on Biber's powerful contribution to our understanding of the linguistic features of spoken and written registers.)

Biber, D., and S. Conrad (2009), *Register, Genre, and Style*, Cambridge: Cambridge University Press.
(This brings Biber's research up-to-date through his longstanding collaboration with Susan Conrad. In particular, it demonstrates the variety of ways in which corpus analysis can be utilised in researching how language is used in different contexts.)

Celce-Murcia, M., and E. Olshtain (2000), *Discourse and Context in Language Teaching: A Guide for Language Teachers*, Cambridge: Cambridge University Press.
(This is an excellent guide for teachers in helping them give pragmatics and discourse a central role in language teaching.)

Crystal, D. (2006), *Language and the Internet*, 2nd edn, Cambridge: Cambridge University Press.
(Crystal leads the way in presenting features of the new e-registers. He describes and celebrates the new ways in which language is used in internet communication.)

6

EXCHANGE THEORY AND CONVERSATION ANALYSIS

INTRODUCTION

In spoken language, utterances tend not to occur in isolation. With the possible exception of 'Help!' shouted by someone leaning out of a building or 'Sorry' muttered by someone pushing through a crowded street, most utterances are a response to what has been said before and a trigger to what is said after. This chapter explores ways of analysing the structure of discourse in everyday interactions, including those in the classroom, looking at the units within those structures and the way that that they follow on from each other in predictable patterns.

Exchange Theory (ET) and Conversation Analysis (CA) differ in two ways. First, whereas ET starts with a model and sees how real data fits it, CA starts by observing the data and then describes the patterns that emerge. Secondly, whereas ET focuses principally on classroom interaction, and the theory has been applied to other domains in a limited fashion, CA has focused on a wide range of interaction genres and has more recently also been applied to classroom interaction.

The relevance of these systems of analysis to EFL teachers is self-evident. Walsh (2011: 1) contends that 'language teachers can improve their professional practice by developing a closer understanding of classroom discourse and, in particular, by focusing on the complex relationship between language, interaction and learning'. An English teacher who knows how teacher-centred classroom interactions tend to be structured will be more self-aware and able to give learners enough space to talk fluently and creatively. A teacher who understands about typical patterns of turn-taking, pauses and overlaps in English conversations will be in a position to explain to their learners about how they differ from those in their own culture, and thus prepare them for social and professional interactions.

6.1 EXCHANGE THEORY

ET was first proposed by Sinclair and Coulthard (1975), who analysed primary classroom interaction and devised a hierarchical framework of analysis. At the top of the hierarchy is the lesson, which consists of a series of 'transactions', each of which consists of a string of 'exchanges'. The exchanges break down into three 'moves': Initiation (I), Response (R) and Follow-up or Feedback (F), sometimes

Table 6.1   Exchange Theory acts and their functions

Move	Act	Function	Form
Initiation	Inform	gives information	'To change to past, add "ed"'
	Direct	gives orders	'Get into groups of four'
	Elicit	requests response	'What does that mean?'
	Cue	encourages	'You'll easily solve this problem'
	Nominate	names responder	'Li-fen?'
	Check	checks progress	'Have you nearly finished?'
	Prompt	reinforces directives	'Go on, say it!'
Response	React	non-linguistic reply	[nod], [raise hand]
	Reply	to an elicitation	'France'
Feedback	Accept	heard correct info	'Yes, exactly, good!', 'That's right'
	Evaluate	evaluates answer	'Not quite, Rafaella!'

known as Evaluation (E). Each of the moves is carried out by 'acts', which are somewhat similar to speech acts (see Chapter 7), in that they 'inform', 'react', 'accept' and so on. The pattern that Sinclair and Coulthard predicted was that the teacher initiates with a statement or question, the learners respond verbally or non-verbally, and the teacher gives feedback on the response. This, as Walsh (2011: 76) points out, is 'even today, regarded as the very fabric of classroom interaction by most practitioners'. Table 6.1 gives examples of the acts and explains their functions with illustrations.

The Feedback move is usually verbalised and explicit, although it can be an implicit evaluation, as in a repetition, an error correction or repair, or simply the absence of a repair. However, it is often non-verbal, taking the form of nods, head-shakes and smiles. Johnson (1995: 23) gives an example of Feedback that corrects without stalling the interactional flow because it sounds like an Initiation:

1 T: Vin, have you ever been to the movies? What's your favourite movie?
2 L: Big.
3 T: Big, OK that's a good movie, that was about a little boy inside a big man, wasn't it?
4 L: Yeah, boy get surprise all the time.
5 T: Yes, he was surprised, wasn't he? Usually little boys don't do the things that men do, do they?
6 L: No, little boy no drink.
7 T: That's right, little boys don't drink.

Here, 'Yes, he was surprised, wasn't he?' and 'That's right, little boys don't drink' are cleverly phrased to sound more like an 'accept' or 'inform' than a negative evaluation or correction.

The transaction:

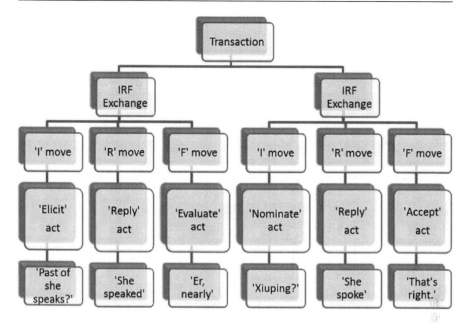

Fig. 6.1   Tree illustrating transaction, exchange, move and act

Teacher:	Past of she speaks?
Learner 1:	She speaked
Teacher:	Er, nearly. Xiuping?
Learner 2:	She spoke.
Teacher:	That's right.

can be analysed using ET as in Figure 6.1.

Note that 'act' in ET means something quite different from 'speech act' in Speech Act Theory (see Chapter 7). The former refers to sub-units of 'I', 'R' and 'F' move, principally in classroom exchanges. The latter refers to all social functions of language is everyday use, such as 'predicting', 'threatening', 'requesting' and 'apologising'.

ET has several limitations. One is related to the coding of data using the hierarchy. Some say that ET wrongly suggests a one-to-one function–form relation, stating that one utterance performs one speech act. However, one utterance can perform several speech acts. Others declare that it is difficult to determine where one exchange ends and another begins. McCarthy (2003: 33–63) points out that small response tokens such as 'Yes', 'Really', 'Right', 'Good' and 'I see' can be both Response and Initiation, and sometimes they have discourse functions such as marking transactional or topical boundaries, and signalling 'affective and social well-being between interlocutors'. In the following excerpt from CANCODE (the Cambridge and Nottingham Corpus of Discourse in English), 'lovely' is both Feedback and discourse marker:

B: What time do you want us then?
A: When were you planning?
B: Well you said about fiveish didn't you?
A: Yeah.
B: Yeah.
A: Lovely.

Another limitation is that ET reflects the teacher-centred classrooms prevalent until the 1970s with their question-and-answer routines, and it does not cater for learner-centred classrooms of the twenty-first century, in which the teacher encourages maximum learner involvement in communicative interaction and interactive decision-making. In learner-centred classrooms, learners work in pairs and groups, Initiate and Respond to each other, solve problems, discuss issues and so on, while the teacher monitors without impinging on the learners' interactional space.

Another drawback is that ET does not easily accommodate the unpredictable nature of the classroom. Sometimes learners do not respond when asked but answer with another question or ask a peer to respond. In addition, 'overlaps, interruptions, back-channels, false starts, repetitions, hesitations are as common in language class-rooms as they are in naturally occurring conversations' (Walsh 2011: 77–8). In the following example, taken from Hunt's 2010 corpus of primary school reading-hour interactions in Scotland, the children's responses are more than the teacher asked for. The class had just read the lines 'Sam put the lid on the jam. He put the jam in the sack.'

Teacher	All I can say is I'm glad he put the lid on first, or there'd be an awful mess in the sack. I wonder what kind of jam it was.
Children	{mingled responses} . . . raspberry . . . strawberry . . . apricot
Teacher	That's my favourite. Any others? You can make jam out of anything – any kind of fruit that is.
Children	{mingled responses} . . . peach . . . plum
Teacher	Lovely.
Child 1	Carrot jam!
Teacher	That would be interesting . . .
Children	{mingled responses} cabbage jam, lettuce jam, pea jam, q jam
Child 2	Mrs Lawson – you know my favourite is letter jam!
Children	{laughter}
Teacher	Oh dear – let us get on with our reading.
Children	{louder laughter}

Child 2's input constitutes an Initiation; the teacher does not respond, but dis-misses it rather with a non-related Initiation of her own, in an effort to regain control. Hunt makes the point that this is an example of the teacher constraining the children's language play and the children struggling with the asymmetry of participation rights.

One of ET's main limitations is that, in general, it cannot be used to describe interactions outside the classroom. However, it has been suggested that ET *can* be used to describe interaction in doctor–patient interviews and TV or radio quizmaster–contestant exchanges, because they are ritualistic and there is a high power differential. The quiz does tend to have Feedback, as this excerpt from BBC TV's *Mastermind* demonstrates, with its quick 'Yes' 'accept' acts:

Quizmaster	The *Titanic*, the largest moving man-made object in the world at the time, was launched on 31st May 1911 from the Harland and Wolff shipyard, in which city?
Contender	Belfast.
Quizmaster	Yes. What was the name of the look-out in the crow's nest who spotted the iceberg that led to the sinking of the *Titanic* in April 1912?
Contender	Frederick Fleet.
Quizmaster	Yes. Which –

(http://www.bbc.co.uk/iplayer/episode/b01nwndk/Mastermind_2012 _2013_Episode_13/)

The following excerpt from a doctor–patient communication illustrates that although the Initiation–Response routine is prevalent, there is little Feedback in the sense of 'accept' or 'evaluate', although the reformulation to check comprehension, 'So a little heat from the coffee cup is helpful', can be seen as a form of Feedback:

Doctor	How – how does it influence your life – your daily life and your sleep?
Patient	I'm always conscious of it. I'm always kind of favouring that side. I put my hand there, cos my hand is warm. I'll put my warm coffee cup there. And just constantly my eye sometimes waters on that side.
Doctor	So a little heat from the coffee cup is helpful.
Patient	Well whether it's a placebo or not, I do it anyway, yeah.

(http://www.youtube.com/watch?v=kFGGFyP-l_c&feature=related)

Interviewer–interviewee exchanges and judge–defendant examinations have an I–R–F structure. However, as the next courtroom example from Cotterill (2007: 100) illustrates, the Feedback again tends to be missing, unless the repetition comprehension check 'In 1996?' can be understood as Feedback:

Judge	Mr S, can you help us at all as to which year this was?
Defendant	1996.
Judge	In 1996?
Defendant	Yes.
Judge	Can you tell us, please, as to what month it might have been?

Defendant   Roughly, to be honest, I can't know. At the time I was receiving treatment for depression.

Indeed, Tsui (1994) maintains that, outside the classroom, Feedback moves are not evaluative. They acknowledge the outcome of the interaction, confirming and re-confirming the understanding of one another's actions.

Another criticism of ET is that it does not take into account the cultural context (the pragmatic, sociolinguistic, social world and the identity of participants), the interpersonal context (why and how people say what they say) and the context of the situation (the physical situation around the speakers).

Task 6.1 Trying out research
Try coding the turns in the following excerpt from a primary reading hour class (Hunt 2010) in terms of I, R and F moves. Discuss any difficulties that occurred as you tried to use this system of analysis, and say whether you think the I–R–F framework could be adapted to learner-centred classrooms.

Child 2   I know why Wilf is good at that game. Cause it's his game and he plays it

Teacher   Nadim you mean. Aha yes – it's just what exactly you were saying a wee minute ago. That Nadim, because it's his game, he's played it a lot, he's becoming quite an – What do you call it when you're good at something, you become an e-

Child 2   Expert

Child 1   An expert

Teacher   That's it.

Child 2   That that – once I was playing with my friend's Gameboy and I can't really work Gameboys and he's better.

Teacher   I would need somebody to show me how to do it anyway.

Child 1   I'm good at it.

Teacher   Yes – guess what's going to happen now?

Task 6.2 Using the internet
Type 'EFL classroom interaction structure' into an internet search engine and make a survey of the material that appears, taking into account whether they are journals, EFL teacher education websites, blogs or Masters dissertations, and noting the country of origin. Decide whether the majority are in favour of teacher-centred class-rooms or learner-centred, and what the main arguments are in each case. Discuss why you think the balance is as it is.

6.2 CONVERSATION ANALYSIS
Conversation Analysis began with Schegloff and Garfinkel in the 1960s, continued with Goffman (1981) and Sacks (1992), and is still being used. CA deals with surface

features, studying how linguistic forms are structured into interactive sequences and how they operate as mechanisms of social behaviour (Chapman 2011). It examines interactions as linear ongoing processes, unfolding little by little, based on the understanding that 'social contexts are not static but are constantly being formed by the participants through their use of language and the ways in which turn-taking, openings and closures, sequencing of acts, and so on are locally managed' (Walsh 2011: 84).

One aspect of interaction structure that CA studies is **turn-taking**, or the way that one person finishes what they are saying and cedes the floor to the next person, with normally only one person speaking at a time. The point where a change of turn occurs is called a **Transition Relevance Place** (TRP) and it is generally marked by intonation (usually falling), semantic completeness, lengthening of syllables, pausing (generally 0.5 second or less), signals such as 'mm', 'anyway', eye contact and body position.

When hearers take the floor before the TRP, there is an **overlap** or an **interruption**. Overlaps occur if the new speaker's words run simultaneously with the preceding speaker's. It can be an expression of solidarity. An interruption, on the other hand, causes the preceding speaker to stop speaking before they have finished their utterance or train of thought. It can be, but does not necessarily have to be, competitive. Stubbs (1983: 184–6) found that interruptions are often prefaced by a term of address, by 'Could I' and 'Let me', as in 'Can I add to that er'; by self-referential meta-statements (language about what language is doing) such as 'If I can just come in here'; and repeated syllables, for example 'Look – look – let me – let me – make it patently clear.'

Speakers often stop hearers interrupting them by using **floor-holding devices**, such as 'um' or by indicating that there is more to come, as in 'There are three points I'd like to make. First . . .' (Yule 1996: 75) and 'Hang on – let me just finish what I'm trying to say.' They can try to stop the hearer taking over the discourse by not pausing at the end of the utterance, by pausing within an utterance, by increasing volume, or by speaking over someone's attempt to interrupt (Paltridge 2012: 96). Take, for example, this excerpt from the Obama–Romney pre-election televised debate on 3 October 2012, chaired by Jim Lehrer:

President Obama	And one of the things I suspect Governor Romney and I probably agree on is getting businesses to work with community colleges so that they're setting up their training programs –
Mr Lehrer	Do you agree, Governor?
President Obama	Let – let – let me just finish the point.

In political interviews in the media, some news presenters are so skilled at interrupting that the interviewee does not have time to use floor-holding devices. Witness this BBC1 interview (1 July 2012), in which Jeremy Paxman, a famous British interviewer, cross-examines Chloe Smith, the then British Treasury Minister. Note that // indicates interruption (see Transcription Symbols, p. 00):

Chloe Smith	That figure will er progress, if you like //
Jeremy Paxman	// Well just name me a few departments
Chloe Smith	No I won't do that because //
Jeremy Paxman	// You don't know?
Chloe Smith	we'll be giving you the full details // in er
Jeremy Paxman	// Are you waiting to be told that as well?
Chloe Smith	No because //
Jeremy Paxman	// You know do you?
Chloe Smith	Those //
Jeremy Paxman	// You know which departments have underspent?
Chloe Smith	It is not possible to give you a full breakdown at this point because the figure is evolving somewhat.

Pauses are also of interest to CA researchers. They can be of any length, from 0.5 seconds to 13 seconds (this, at least, is the longest pause that I have witnessed in a group of speakers). When a pause is intended to communicate meaning, analysts call it an **attributable silence**.

CA theorists believe that interaction tends to occur in **adjacency pairs**. These are pairs of acts, such as when the speaker makes 'an invitation' and the interlocutor's words constitute 'an acceptance'. In this example, the 'acceptance' is expected; it is the **preferred response**. The corollary is that 'a refusal' is more unusual and is a **dispreferred response**. Here are some more examples of adjacency pairs:

an assessment prefers	an agreement
a blame	a denial
a complaint	an apology
a greeting	a greeting
an offer	an acceptance
a proposal	an agreement
a question	an answer
a request	an acceptance

If the hearer gives no response, the speaker may assume that they are taking some time to think about it, that they have not heard, that they are not paying attention or that they are, in fact, being un-cooperative. Hearers who, for whatever reason, cannot provide the preferred response tend to use politeness forms (see Chapter 8, Politeness Theories) such as prefaces ('well', 'oh'), expressions of doubt ('I'm not sure'), token 'yes' ('I'd love to but'), apologies ('I'm sorry'), alternative obligations ('I must do X', 'I'm expected to do Y'), non-personal statements ('everybody else is doing Z'), excuses ('I've got no time') and mitigators ('I guess not') (Yule 1996: 81).

CA also considers **sequences** of interaction. These are like exchanges in ET, except that they not hierarchical and they are not seen as predictable. The literature mainly addresses four types: **pre**-sequences, **insertion** sequences, **opening** sequences and **closing** sequences. Pre-sequences indicate or announce that a particular act is about the follow. If a speaker says 'Are you doing anything tonight', they are about to invite the hearer to do something; if they say 'Do you have a minute?', that is a pre-request; and if they say 'Wait till you hear this!', that is a pre-announcement asking for the go-ahead to say something particularly interesting. Insertion sequences are exchanges of utterances that occur within another series of turns and differ in topic or focus.

Clive	You – you don't have the processor to do it.
Mike	But – but why don't I?
Clive	Cos (0.5) in technical terms you own an // eighty-eight.
Mike	// Say. You shouldn't be here.
Rowan	I got the job.
Mike	How come she got back so early. (0.5) That was yesterday.
Clive	In technical (1) terms you own a what's called an eighty-eight six processor.

'Say. You shouldn't be here' and 'I got the job' constitute an insertion sequence. Sometimes the insertion sequence is necessary so that a speaker can interact efficiently, as in:

Sue	You coming tonight?
Liz	Where?
Sue	We're all going to that Italian place on Cockburn Street eight o'clock.
Liz	Yes OK! I'd love to. See you there.

Here the last line is a response to the first, and all the interaction in between is an insertion sequence.

Opening and closing sequences are more ritualised in that the words for opening or closing an interaction are limited. Openings tend to contain a greeting, an enquiry after health and a past reference ('Hi. How are you doing? Did you have a nice weekend?'). As Paltridge (2012) explains, Schegloff found that telephone openings contain summons (the phone rings), answer, identification, recognition, greeting, 'how are you' and the reason for the call. An example of a less ritualistic opening is:

Penny	Hello! (0.5) Long time no see.
Aoife	Mm. It seems ages doesn't it?

Closing sequences generally contain a farewell, an evaluation of the encounter that is ending and a future reference ('Bye. Nice seeing you. I hope you get your assignment done tonight'). Button (1987) asserts that the archetype closing is 'pre-closing' ('OK', 'all right'), then 'closing' ('bye bye', 'goodbye'), although pre-closings on the telephone can also include the making of an arrangement, referring back to something said in the conversation, the initiation of new topics, good wishes, restatement of reason for calling or thanks for calling. Some closings can be quite brief:

| Kim | See you then. |
| Ibtihal | Yeah see you Kim. |

Some telephone closings can be extended. You may recognise this sort of routine:

Roger	Bye.
Nicola	Bye – love you.
Roger	I love you so much.
Nicola	Sleep well.
Roger	You too. Night!
Nicola	Night night my darling.

As with all approaches to language analysis, CA has **limitations**. One is that it lacks systematicity. It does not give a clear account of how adjacency pairs or TRPs might be recognised (Eggins and Slade 1997). It tends to suggest that forms have fixed functions. Paltridge (2012) reminds us that 'hello' is not always a greeting and 'thank you' is not always an expression of thanks. 'Like – hello?' can mean rejection of a suggestion and 'Well, thank you!' can mean anger at an intrusion. By focusing on the minutiae of language in a rigid way, it misses out the complexity of language and it fails to allow for a quantitative and generalisable study. Walsh (2011: 88–9) finds CA over-selective, dealing with snatches of discourse rather than exploring how it relates to discourse as a whole.

A criticism frequently levelled at CA is that it is unable to describe the bigger picture because it fails to take into account the situational and background context. CA theorists consider talk as something that creates context, rather than seeing it as something created by context. It thus places little emphasis on the pragmatic and sociolinguistic aspects of interaction. CA ignores the dimensions of power and the effects of inequality and social disadvantage, stance and social and cultural values.

Recently, solutions have been put forward to compensate for these limitations by combining CA methodology with CL (see Chapter 2) and relating it to a wider view of context; these solutions, in turn, have had implications for language teaching. CL combines well with CA because it examines lexis and word patterns in empirical data. It improves on CA in that it enables a description of language that is not dependent on an a priori model.

As suggested earlier, a knowledge of CA can make an EFL teacher aware of their own classroom interaction. Walsh's SETT framework (Self Evaluation of Teacher Talk) aims to 'get teachers to think about classroom interaction as a means of improving both teaching and learning' (2011: 110). This is discussed further in *Developing Practice in TESOL* by Fiona Farr in this series.

Task 6.3 Applying the concept to teaching

Here is a simple task that you could try out in class, aimed at making intermediate learners aware of the implications of pre-sequences. Get learners (or colleagues if you do not currently have access to learners) into pairs and give them a piece of paper with the following utterances:

- 'You'll never guess who I bumped into yesterday!'
- 'Do you know the one about the panda in the bar?'
- 'You doing anything this afternoon?'
- 'You know that book she gave you last week?'
- 'Do you see those muddy boots on the carpet?'

Ask them to predict what the next words might be. For example, if a speaker says, 'You know the man I was talking to last night?', they are most likely wanting to relate an incident. They might follow it with 'It turns out that he is the uncle of a very good friend of mine!' or such like.

Finally, ask them to consider, in their own language if necessary, whether they use pre-sequences in another culture and language or a variety of English that they know well. If pre-sequences are not used so frequently, you could ask them to consider if there are language forms that serve the same function. If the function does not exist, they could discuss why this is so.

Task 6.4 Trying out research

Analyse with colleagues the following excerpt from Cutting's (2000) Applied Linguistics common room conversations. The title is 'New Year's Eve Celebrations in Edinburgh':

1	Jon	Did you go to Manchester over Christmas?
2	Lyn	I did yeah. Just for a week. (0.5) A short visit.
3	Jon	Came back here for Hogmanay?[3]
4	Lyn	Yeah.
5	Jon	Was it good?
6	Lyn	It was good yeah. It was a bit crowded though. Cos we all met
7		up er in the town centre at ten o'clock. (0.5) And when we
8		got there (0.5) they'd stopped serving. (1)
9	Jon	Ten o'clock?
10	Lyn	About ten o'clock. All – all pubs had stopped serving. We-//
11		we really!
12	Jon	//(heh heh)
13	Lyn	We hadn't had anything to drink and sort of and we couldn't
14		believe it. What this is Scottish New Year you know? (0.5)
15		Anyway eventually after walking round the pubs for about an
16		hour (0.5) we got to one that Dave and I usually go to. (0.5) It
17		can be a bit rough but it // it has
18	Jon	//Which one is it?
19	Lyn	It's the Royal Oak. Right and they have live music. (0.5) We got
20		there and they were serving so everybody desperately ran to
21		the bar and got a drink.

---

[3] A Scottish word for New Year's Eve

Look at the pauses (with the number of seconds indicated in brackets) and interruptions (indicated with a //), and decide what their function is, what they show and what they imply. For example, the half-second pause in 'Just for a week. (0.5) A short visit.' might serve the function of giving Lyn time to think of how she might rephrase her 'Just for a week.' On the other hand, she may have a pause and a rephrasing simply because she can think of nothing else to say.

Task 6.5 Using the internet

Find a short dialogue on the internet that has been specially written for an English-language learning book. Print it out and discuss with colleagues whether:

- You would tell your learners about adjacency pairs, preferred responses, and opening and closing sequences, and ask them if they can see what is going on in this regard in the dialogue
- You would ask them to spontaneously perform dialogues with opening and closing sequences, and adjacency pairs with preferred responses.

6.3 STRUCTURE AND SOCIAL VARIABLES

Interactions vary according to the cultural context, the interpersonal context and the context of situations. These contextual dimensions can be taken into account when using ET and CA to analyse data.

One year, I asked my TESOL students to write cultural journals after each class of our 'Text, Discourse and Language Teaching' course. They wrote about the relevance of approaches to language analysis that they were meeting in class to their own cultural context. I shall be referring to their journal entries throughout the rest of this volume.

Interestingly, after the class on ET, some students from the same culture contradicted each other. One Chinese student said:

> It has been a tradition that students should listen to what the teachers say without any interruption in the whole class. Students are used to keeping silence without revealing their response. Thus the structure is only 'I' or 'I, F', there is no 'R'.

Another protested:

> The exchange structure can't apply to all real-life classroom discourses. Sometimes, in a lower power position, students still can play the role of initiation by eliciting a question and the teacher replies. For example, if the teacher asks if there is any question, and one of the students raises another question about the part he doesn't know very well, the teacher then has to reply to the student's initiation (I), perhaps followed by the student's reaction (F)

Students indicated that the language of the Feedback move in language classrooms varies across cultures. Two of the Chinese students wrote:

If the student's answer is wrong (middle school) the response from teacher may be like this, 'No it's wrong. Have you listened to me seriously?' However in UK, the response from teacher is like 'well, maybe but there is one thing you should notice that . . .'

The words Chinese teachers use are quite strict and criticisms of language are always to be heard in Chinese class. However, things are different in UK. Assertive teachers always use indirect language to show the respect to learner's presentation and using suggestive tone.

As far as CA is concerned, the conventions about whether overlaps and inter-ruptions are acceptable, and how long inter-turn and intra-turn pauses can and should be, vary from culture to culture. This goes some way to explain why in intercultural communication, people from one culture might feel that people from another are rude because they interrupt, or that they are frustratingly slow to speak to because they want a pause before speaking. Günthner (2000: 218) examined interactions between Spanish people and Chinese people speaking Spanish, and quoted the following example of a breakdown in communication (I have changed the names):

Pedro   What do you want to do?
Xiang   (2)
Pedro   What shall we do now?

The '(2)' indicates a two-second pause. Pedro the Spaniard concluded from Xiang's pause that he had not understood the question and so rephrased it. Xiang, on the other hand, explained later that he had in fact understood; he was just giving some thought as to what he was going to say.

A study that I carried out on a mini-corpus of multicultural interactions in TESOL workshops (Cutting 2009) showed that interruptions and overlaps functioned differ-ently according to the culture of the students and the power relation between partici-pants. Lecturers interrupted the students in a way that fulfilled their role as a teacher; they did it to scaffold, rephrase, encourage, echo and sympathise, and sometimes to disagree and correct, as in:

Jiali   Then that can happen, that can be happening in the same class at the same time.
Lecturer   Could be, you could differentiate questions. =
Jiali   = So, actually speaking is very difficult to be done in //
Lecturer   // Ehm, no because you can still put them in groups and they can all do a speaking activity based on what you give them. =
Jiali   = Ah, I see.

The Egyptian students seemed to interrupt the lecturer in order to disagree, clarify and change topic. Here is an example:

Lecturer	So, but the point is that they are learning that kind of structure, they are learning how to put it together, and they are learning how to //
Ayman	// Can we role play after that? It's easy to role play =
Lecturer	= Yeah, it could be. Yeah. There is a whole (0.5) other ehm aspect to this way of introducing stories

The East Asian students rarely interrupted the lecturer, and when they did, it was only to clarify and request clarification, an example being:

Lecturer	That's open to debate. But what I think you could put // if it's a project
Yukako	// So just like this?
Lecturer	Eh, no.

Furthermore, while the Egyptian students were quite comfortable with interrupting the lecturer in plenary sessions, the East Asian students preferred to reserve that behaviour for one-to-one exchanges during poster sessions.

The literature on adjacency pairs also shows cross-cultural differences. An example is the preferred response to an offer. Japanese people tend to refuse the first and second time, and only accept when the offer is made a third time, whereas many English people will not offer a second time if the first offer is refused. The response to the phone ringing also varies from culture to culture. American and British speakers tend to answer the phone with 'hello' whereas Swedish (Lindström 1994) and Dutch speakers (Houtkoop-Steenstra 1991) identify themselves by their name in the first turn.

My TESOL students on the 'Text, Discourse and Language Teaching' course commented on opening sequences. One explained them in terms of cultural and social differences:

'Where are you going?', 'going to work?', 'what are you doing?', 'are you busy?', 'have you eaten?' – these polite Chinese greetings may be viewed by westerners as an invasion of privacy. The natural reaction of westerners to these greetings would most likely be 'it's none of your business!', since in western culture such questions are private questions and asking them could be interpreted as an invasion of privacy, to which westerners are very sensitive. These phrases are very normal and common to the Chinese because Chinese culture emphasise concern for others. They show manners and politeness.

The Saudi Arabian students also made the point that conversation openings have important social dimensions: 'In some regions of Saudi Arabia where people are farmers, they greet each other by using "How's the milk?" because if their sheep have milk that means everything is OK.'

As for conversational closings, my Chinese TESOL students mentioned the different conventions for closings after an evening at a friend's house:

One interesting thing I find is that the host seldom initiates farewell language. The guests are always saying, 'I must leave now, it's too late' at first. Although the host is already feeling sleepy or tired, he or she may still keep on saying 'not late at all, don't hurry to leave, stay here longer'. Such issues always happen in my family – I just complain silently, but I still wait for the guest to say farewell at first.

I remember one translation class when the teacher told us not to translate directly 'end of the party' (in Chinese) into 'end of the party' (in English). He said it would be more natural to say like 'We've had a good time. We all enjoyed ourselves' etc. in the English speaking context.

Task 6.6 Applying the concept to teaching
One student made the observation that cross-cultural differences as regards interruption conventions can lead to misunderstandings and negative impressions:

In Chinese–western encounters, Chinese appear to interrupt more and in a more marked way. In these contexts, westerners would inaccurately conclude that Chinese are rude since many western people regard interruptions impolite. Rather than associate rudeness with Chinese linguistic behaviour, however, westerners associate rudeness with Chinese themselves. Their reasoning may be as follows: Chinese interrupt, interruptions are rude, therefore Chinese are rude. Such reasoning is unfortunate for Chinese, who come from a culture where interruptions may be associated with friendliness, indicating the conversationalists' active involvement in the interaction.

Discuss whether you agree at all with this student's analysis. Design a simple class-room task for advanced-level Chinese learners that would make them aware that people of other cultures might misunderstand their interruption conventions, and that would encourage them to explore ways of explaining their behaviour to non-Chinese people. Discuss to what extent you agree with the adage 'When in Rome, do as the Romans do' or whether you think that it is more a case of 'Romans need to be aware that non-Romans come with different social conventions which are polite in their own context'.

Task 6.7 Trying out research
Write, as a whole class if you can, a ten-item questionnaire to be circulated either among staff within your school or university or among people outside the institution. Design the questions so that participants have to describe their own preferences about opening and closing routines, and so that they offer descriptions of what they understand people from other countries to say and how they say it. Aim to get five completed questionnaires back for each member of the class. Collate your findings as a class and try to draw conclusions about cross-cultural differences and stereotypical impressions.

Task 6.8 Using the internet
Find a recording (in English) of an interview (for example, a news interview or a pop star interview) on the internet. Make sure that it involves two people of different cultural backgrounds, one of whom considers English to be their L1. Transcribe about five minutes of it and analyse it in terms of adjacency pairs. Prepare an intermediate EFL class task that asks them to notice cultural differences between the preferred responses that the speakers recorded seem to favour and the preferred responses in the learners' own language. Warn your learners (or your colleagues if you are simply presenting your findings to them) that there may not be many differences.

6.4 FURTHER READING ONE

Barraja-Rohan, A.-M. (2011), 'Using conversation analysis in the second language classroom to teach interactional competence', *Language Teaching Research*, 15(4): 479–507.
Barraja-Rohan's article focuses on the use of CA in teaching interactional competence in English to adult second language learners, demonstrating its effectiveness 'initially in raising students' awareness of both the mechanisms and norms of spoken interaction, and also eventually in helping them to become analysts of conversation and more effective conversationalists' (2011: 479). She points out that 'CA offers teachers insights into this interactional machinery, and they can then transfer this knowledge to L2 students by making it explicit' (2011: 481).

Barraja-Rohan feels that 'many of her ESL students lived rather isolated from the L2 community, and this impacted negatively upon their welfare and/or livelihood; language seemed to be a contributing factor to this isolation' (2011: 486) and so she designed a 12-week course for twenty adult migrants aged 20–60, training them in Intercultural Competence (Group 1), and for a class of students from their late teens to early twenties from China, Hong Kong, Japan, Korea, Thailand and Vietnam (Group 2). The course aimed to train students to be conversation analysts, and to interact better with NESs and NNESs of English. It covered:

> social action, affiliation, adjacency pairs, polarity, repair mechanism, turn-taking system, topic management and sequential organization (opening, centring, pre-closing, closing), sociocultural norms such as greetings (in openings), invitation, apology, and leave-taking (in closing), as well as the role of paralinguistic features, prosody, and response tokens (not necessarily in that order). (2011: 488)

Here are her results:

> Judging from students' responses to tasks, the results were very encouraging. There was a high level of participation and interest, they made very positive comments in both groups, and positive discussions took place between the teacher-researcher and students. Students' performance improved throughout

the course, which was particularly noticeable in the post-instruction conversations. Positive changes occurred in many areas, as illustrated by the two post-instruction conversations analysed below and their responses to the questionnaire.

/. . ./

b Post-instruction conversations: The next conversation, which focuses on Truc, is taken from Group 1, and it took place at the end of the course, i.e. post-instruction. Note that Truc is interacting with another student from his group. Students were free to choose their own topic but were reminded of the structure of conversation. This conversation illustrates the concepts taught in the conversation course: greeting with appropriate sociocultural norms, adjacency pairs, topic management, affiliation, use of assessment, pre-closing sequence, and leave-taking.

> Conversation 3 (Group 1: Truc and Hung, both Vietnamese males):
> 1. Truc: hello Hung. how are you today.=
> 2. Hung: =good thanks.
> 3. Truc: are you are er you going back er the next course?
> 4. Hung: yes of course.
> 5. Truc: what did you plan to do on the holiday.
> 6. Hung: o::h, my holiday? em I–I will looking er for a job_ if I
> 7. Hung: don't get a job I come back this school;
> 8. Truc: oh yes that good.
> 9. Hung: how about you?
> 10. Truc: mm I:: stay home, listen the music an I review my lesson.
> 11. Hung: oh:: I'm sorry, I–I'm busy I must go now.
> 12. Truc: okay.
> 13. Hung: s[ee you], bye bye.
> 14. Truc: [see you.]

As a reminder, Truc had not given any feedback in conversation 1, which took place early in the conversation course. In this conversation he starts with an opening by using a greeting, which incidentally is not reciprocated in line 2. However, the second part of the greeting, the pseudo health inquiry 'How are you?' receives a second pair part with 'Good thanks'. Then, once the greeting is over, in the next turn at line 3 Truc introduces a topic, which was relevant as it was the end of the year and the course. Note that he introduces the topic by using a question, and then the topic moves on to the holidays at line 5, which turns out not to be so for Hung who in the event of not getting a job will attend more English classes (line 7). It is interesting to note that at line 8 Truc is able to produce an assessment ('Oh yes that good'), which is appropriate because going back to learning more English is deemed a positive outcome. This is indeed a vast improvement from not using response tokens at all, as mentioned before, since assessments are more complex to produce than continuers or other types of response tokens (see Ohta, 2001). At line 9, Hung keeps the conversation going by asking Truc about his plans. Then at line 11, Hung starts to move into closing by launching into a pre-closing sequence 'Oh I'm sorry, I–I'm busy I must go now'; then, in the following turn (line 12), Truc responds appropriately by using 'Okay' with a falling intonation and moving into closing. Again this is a response token that Truc did not use at the start of the conversation course, nor did Group 2 students in their pre-instruction conversations. Then, at line 13, Hung initiates leave-taking, which is reciprocated by Truc in the next turn at line 14 and which ends the conversation. Given what the students accomplished in the conversation, this conversation certainly shows a reasonable level of interactional sophistication, particularly for lower intermediate students. (2011: 493–5)

Barraja-Rohan then goes on to analyse a long conversation that Group 2 had engaged in and invited the students to analyse what was going on in it: 'openings to greetings, topic management (introducing topic, topic shift and ending topic), invitation with a pre-sequence, preference organisation, display of affiliation, use of assessments, co-construction, turn-taking strategies by using overlaps, repair to clear any misunderstanding or mishearing, moving into pre-closing and leave-taking' (2011: 496). Here is the conclusion to the article:

The comparison of the two students, Truc and Kim, first interacting in conversations 1 and 2 and then at the end of the course in conversations 3 and 4 illustrates the interactional accomplishments achieved by them over the period of 12 weeks of a CA-informed pedagogical approach. When including the responses given at the end of the course evaluation questionnaire it is apparent that the L2 students who participated in the two groups gained much knowledge about interaction, language and intercultural communication as well as confidence in speaking English, judging from their comments.

Not all aspects of IC were discussed in the particular cases shown above due to lack of space; however, they were nonetheless part of the conversation course as discussed previously. The focus of the course was clearly on communication and not accuracy, an approach advocated by Kramsch (1986), which reflects what the interactants orient to in naturally occurring conversations. We know from fine-grained conversation analyses of native speaker interactions that the interactants orient to the communicative aspect of the interaction and are found to commit syntactic errors on occasions. Only when intersubjectivity is threatened do the interactants resort to the repair mechanism to restore it. Hence it is imperative that the L2 learners are shown how to orient to the communicative aspect of the interaction and not only to grammatical accuracy. (2011: 498–9)

Task 6.9 Applying the concept to teaching
Look at a dialogue in an EFL textbook that you have used, or that you might use:

- Check to see if there is an I–R–F structure, and see how much there is in terms of CA categories.
- If any of these are missing, add them into the dialogue to make it sound more authentic.
- Discuss with your classmates whether you think this is an improvement and whether your learners would benefit from meeting a dialogue like this.
- Discuss whether the dialogue now looks as if it belongs to one variety of Inner Circle English more than another, and whether it could be said to look like Outer Circle English.

Task 6.10 Trying out research
Do a survey of each member of your class, or each member of your department if you are at work, to see which of the features listed in the first task here 1) should be taught, and 2) could be taught. Draw a graph of each feature and the number of staff that agreed they should be taught. Draw another for the features that they agreed could be taught. Discuss possible causes of differences between the graphs.

6.5 FURTHER READING TWO

Bowles, H. (2006), 'Bridging the gap between conversation analysis and ESP – an applied study of the opening sequences of NS and NNS service telephone calls', *English for Specific Purposes*, 25: 332–57.
Bowles examines 'the way in which participants in service telephone calls to book-shops negotiate their requests' in native-speaker (NS) and non-native-speaker (NNS) corpora, concentrating on the part of the call opening in which the business of the phone call begins to be addressed by callers and receivers. He analyses and compares 'the pre-sequences which introduce reason-for-call and the strategies deployed by NS and NSS in formulating their pre-sequences'. The research questions were:

- What are the differences, if any, between the NS–NS and NNS–NS patterning of pre-sequence types?
- Are NNS–NS differences attributable to the influence of the L1 (Italian) or to more general pragmatic considerations regarding the interaction as a whole? (2006: 337)

Bowles classified the data according to whether or not pre-sequences formed a turn constructional unit (TCU), a semantically and syntactically complete unit of talk. This was of interest because a pre-sequence which is a TCU ('*I would like some information please. Have you got the story of Pinocchio?*') can be interrupted, whereas a pre-sequence which is not a TCU ('*I was wondering if* you have got the story of Pinocchio') cannot be interrupted. Some pre-sequences could not be classi-fied as TCU or non-TCU; direct questions without a pre-sequence ('Do you happen to have the story of Pinocchio?') were classified as 'direction question', and straight-forward descriptions ('I'm looking for the story of Pinocchio') were classified as 'story'. The four pre-sequence types for NNS–NS and NS–NS were also classified in terms of whether they occurred on their own (single) or in combination with other pre-sequence types (combined), and whether they took place over one or more turns.

He starts by making some general observations:

> Firstly, NNS use more combined pre-sequences than NS (54% NNS vs. 30% NS) whereas NS prefer individual pre-sequences (70% NS vs. 46% NNS). Secondly the non-TCU pre- is the preferred single pre-sequence type for NS (67.5%), and NNS (50%), though NNS also show a strong preference for non-TCU pre, TCU pre and story (occurring in 42%, 46% and 46% of the calls respectively). Thirdly, the frequency of use of the TCU pre, which is only used in combination with other pre-sequences, is greater for NS (46%) than for NNS (20%). (Bowles 2006: 339)

He finds that 'reason-for-call is a particularly difficult area for NNS and that the correct management of pre-sequences is crucial for successful negotiation of a request'. As regards the direct question pre-sequence, 'NS use the direct question format exclusively in combination with other pre-sequence types whereas NNS sometimes use it on its own'. As for non-TCU pre-sequences, NS are almost twice as likely as NNS to use it (57.5 per cent vs. 30 per cent) on its own in one turn, which suggests that it is an effective pre-sequence for NS. NNS tend to use the non-TCU pre-sequence with greater hesitation phenomena, as in:

> Call 7 (NNS corpus)
> ((ring))
>
> 1. R: paul main the xxxxxx bookshop?
> 2. C: .hh eh:good morning.hh ehm:: i was
> 3.   wondering if you have compu- eh:: books on computer
>   <science>.hhh
> 4. R: ehm::[()
> 5. C: [on the:::hm::.hh ecdl particularly xxxxxxx
> 6. R: which one? (2006: 344)

TCU-pre-sequence is always used in combination with other pre-sequence types, and NS use the TCU-pre-sequences much less frequently than NSS. The following is therefore typical of NNS:

> Call 11 (NNS corpus)
> (ring)
>
> 1. R   () bookshop
> 2. C: h yes hello is this xxxxxxx bookshop
> 3. R: yes [it is]

4.   C: [.h a] i was wondering if you could give me some information
          please
          .h do you happen to have any books for teaching english to italian
          students? .h I've heard of one that's called on stage. h an i think the
          editor is petrini
          (1.2)
5.   R: it's called on stage (2006: 348)

Storytelling is different because it requires suspension of the turn-taking system of ordinary conversation. The caller has to extend the turn until the story has been satisfactorily completed, and the receiver can negotiate 'a way between cutting a story off short if sufficient information has been obtained and encouraging a story if he/she agrees that it needs telling' (2006: 345). NS use the story as a last resort and feel that they should not let the story 'drag on' and compromise the economy of the call; NNS do not appear to use the story as a last resort and seem to feel less pressure to conclude in the first turn (2006: 47)

Bowles then describes the language of TCU and non-TCU pre-sequences. NNS speakers had a wide variety of expressions, and they were mostly in TCU-pre:

I wonder if you can help me
I need some information
I'm looking for a book
I need an information
I need a bit of information (2006: 350)

Non-TCU are more frequent in NS talk, frequent expressions being:

I was wondering
Can you tell me if
Could you tell me
I'm wondering if
I'm just wondering

In the last part of his article, Bowles moves on to a discussion of the applications of findings to EFL. He suggests that producers of Language for Specific Purposes (LSP) materials include his findings and that other areas of institutional talk could be examined in this way:

9.1. Collecting and analysing data from different languages
LSP materials writers need a description of the conventions of English service telephone calls. This involves distilling the Schegloff-style NS–NS data on English sequencing into usable format and providing authentic transcripts as illustrative material. This process will produce basic sequencing information for English. Materials writers also need a similar description for languages other than English.

/. . ./

In order to combat the problem of specific L1 interference, the basic sequencing information then needs to be subjected to an analytical process such as the following: (a) compare the telephone conventions of English with the telephone conventions in the L1 of the NNS (b) establish points of possible difficulty where the respective conventions of English and the L1 of the NNS do not coincide; check NS–NNS studies for particular languages (if available) to see whether these difficulties for the NNS do in fact arise. This kind of analysis will produce sequencing information modified for speakers of particular languages.

9.2. Writing the materials

The materials writer will now have enough information with which to produce accurate materials for practising service telephone call openings with ESP students of different native languages. However, writers are still faced with the problem of organising the language input and producing appropriate tasks which will make the most of the description.

9.2.1. Grading the language

As mentioned in 8.5, lists of pre-sequence types and tokens in both NS and NNS are useful data for ESP material. However, the sheer variety of linguistics forms used in pre-sequences needs careful presentation and handling. Four areas in which applied work on language input needs to concentrate are suggested:

- This study has shown that a variety of pre-sequencing strategies are possible but that the default pre-sequence expected by NS receivers is the non-TCU pre to be completed in one turn; since this is the pre-sequence which appears to be most expected by English receivers, students should be given specific practice in using it.
- There is some evidence (see discussion in 8.2) to support a hypothesis that presequences may be learned by NNS in pre-learned chunks; an awareness of the more typical TCU and non-TCU pre-sequence forms such as I was wondering if . . . is therefore important for economical formulation of pre-sequences.
- Tables 6–8 also highlight interesting and authentic NS alternatives to the more typical forms, which show the subtleties of variations on the prototype (e.g. 'I was wondering if' vs. 'I'd like to know if', 'I was wondering' vs. 'I was just wondering'; 'wondering if' vs. wondering whether and so on). This kind of language also needs to be carefully analysed, graded and presented.
- Since acceptability (justifying the request) plays an important part in successful request negotiation, students' attention needs to be focused on this area. In order to justify a request, NNS need to have a variety of possible forms to use with which to modify the degree of politeness which they wish to inject into the request; for example, this study has shown that a

pre-sequence such as 'I was just wondering whether' is a more frequent, and therefore more acceptable, NS token than a standard textbook introduction such as could you tell me please... This in turn would imply that the production of indirect forms after wonder should be given greater focus.

9.2.2. Producing appropriate tasks
The present study also suggests a number of specific task types that could helpfully be included in materials:

(a) Role-based tasks. CA studies have consistently shown that successful negotiation skills involve the correct management of turn taking; in order to heighten students' awareness of turn taking management, they should carry out practice in the role of both caller and receiver in order to experience call management from both points of view.

(b) Pre-sequence strategy tasks. The study has also shown that pre-sequences other than the non-TCU pre are possible and preferred in certain circumstances; practice exercises should therefore involve the use of different pre-sequencing strategies. For example, students might be given a particular problem (e.g. 'you want to buy a book for your mother') and asked to practice using different pre-sequence strategies (e.g. story or TCU pre-sequence) before making the call to the bookshop.

(c) Storytelling tasks. This study also suggests that production practice needs to develop students' micro-skills in the area of storytelling. Though not the most frequently used pre-sequence, storytelling has been shown to be a flexible and important pre-sequence for dealing with requests, particularly the less precise ones. Students need practice in using the storytelling pre-sequence in both short and extended first turns and over two or more turns. This is important because although the present research has dealt with bookshops, where extended stories and longer turns may be more acceptable, receivers in other types of institution, such as call centres, may be unwilling to allow callers to extend the reason-for-call sequence into more than one or two turns. Students therefore need two kinds of practice: the first is in keeping a story economical but appropriate – a 'storytelling summary' skill – and the second is in strategies for coping with being cut short by receivers. Both these skills are highly complex and require considerable preparation and analysis by both teacher and student. (2006: 353–4)

Task 6.11 Applying the concept to teaching
Discuss the issues that arise in this article and decide to what extent you agree with them. Discuss what aspects could be applied to the language classroom and why. Think of tasks that you could design that would take these aspects into account.

Task 6.13 Trying out research
Discuss to what extent this project would be replicable in a similar interactional genre. What genre would be of interest to you and why? What aspect of CA would you investigate and why? Discuss with colleagues how you would design such a project.

6.6 SUMMARY

Exchange Theory:

- is a language analysis system that sees the lesson as a hierarchy of categories, with series of 'transactions', which consist of 'exchanges', which break down into Initiation (I), Response (R) and Feedback (F), carried out by 'acts' such as 'inform', 'react', 'accept';
- has limitations: there is no one-to-one function–form relation, it reflects the teacher-centred classrooms, it does not accommodate easily to the unpredictable nature of the classroom, it cannot generally be used to describe interactions outside the classroom, and it does not easily take into account the cultural context (the pragmatic, sociolinguistic, social world and the identity of participants), the interpersonal context (why and how people say what they say) and the context of the situation.

Conversation Analysis:

- is a system that deals with surface features, studying the structure of interactive sequences, examining turn-taking, overlaps, interruptions, floor-holding devices, pauses, repairs, adjacency pairs, preferred and dispreferred responses, as well as sequences (pre-sequences, insertion sequences, opening sequences and closing sequences);
- has limitations: it lacks systematicity, it is unable to take into account the bigger social picture, it examines language from the outsider's point of view. As we saw in the section on ET, interactions vary according to the cultural context, the interpersonal context and the context of the situation. These contextual dimensions can be added to ET and CA when data is being analysed.

As far as social variables are concerned, studies have shown that each culture has its characteristics as regards the structure of language, and the generally accepted rules vis-à-vis pauses, interruptions etc. These cultural differences need to be handled sensitively in teaching English as a Foreign Language.

6.7 ADDITIONAL READINGS

The following three texts provide general introduction to ET and CA in a clearly accessible way, well illustrated with authentic data:

Chapman, S. (2011), *Pragmatics*, Basingstoke: Palgrave Macmillan.
Paltridge, B. (2012), *Discourse Analysis*, London: Bloomsbury Academic.
Yule, G. (1996), *Pragmatics*, Oxford: Oxford University Press.

7

SPEECH ACT THEORY AND
THE COOPERATIVE PRINCIPLE

INTRODUCTION

Why, as an EFL teacher, would you want to know about Speech Act Theory (SAT) and the Cooperative Principle (CP)? The reason is that it is not enough to be able to use grammar and vocabulary accurately and fluently, and to pronounce intelligibly. In order to communicate successfully, you need to know about the meaning under the surface features, because sometimes what the words say and what they imply are different. And what is more, it is essential that you pass on to your learners something of the social rules of linguistic interaction so that they can understand the full meaning that speakers intend to communicate. In addition, your knowing how to analyse language from the point of view of SAT and CP also enables you to investigate how communication works.

SAT and CP are described together in this chapter because they are both about underlying meanings of language. The chapter explains the linguistic features that each of these approaches to data analysis relate to the underlying meaning. These linguistic features are seen in conjunction with their sociocultural variables in a way that explains cross-cultural communication and enables teachers of English to evaluate their ELT methodology, syllabus, course and materials.

7.1 DIRECT AND INDIRECT SPEECH ACTS

SAT is the product of two thinkers, Austin (1962) and Searle (1969). Austin defined speech acts as doing things with words. Communication works on three levels:

- The **locutionary act**, or the act of saying something, for example saying 'I'm sorry', 'Can I help?' and 'Come here.'
- The **illocutionary force**, or 'what is done in uttering the words', that is the function of the words, for example apologising, offering and giving orders. These are generally known as the speech acts.
- The **perlocutionary effect**, or 'what is done by uttering the words', that is the effect on the hearer; for example, the hearer feels less annoyed, the hearer gets help, the hearer walks towards the speaker.

In an early version of SAT, Austin saw utterances as **performatives**. He proposed that there are two types, the first being explicit performatives which contain performative verbs, such as 'to apologise', 'to offer', 'to order' and 'to promise', as in 'I promise I'll support you' and 'I order you to come here'. The second are implicit performatives, with no performative verb, as in 'I'll support you' and 'Come here'.

Searle (1976) proposed macro-categories of speech act:

- **Declarations**, or acts that change the world by their very utterance, such as 'I declare this museum open' and 'I hereby pronounce you husband and wife'.
- **Representatives**, in which the words state what the speaker believes to be the case. Examples of speech acts here are 'describing', 'claiming', 'hypothesising', 'insisting' and 'predicting', as in 'She got 7 in IELTS' and 'He teaches in a small rural primary school.'
- **Commissives**, which commit the speaker to future action. Here the speech acts are 'promising', 'offering', 'threatening', 'refusing', 'vowing' and 'volunteering', for example 'I'll lend you my laptop' and 'I'll be back!'
- **Directives**, with which the speaker attempts to influence the hearer's action: 'inviting', 'suggesting', 'ordering', 'requesting' or 'forbidding' the hearer to do something, as in 'Come round to my place about eight tonight' and 'Please don't eat in here.'
- **Expressives**, which contain an overt evaluation or reflect an emotion, as in 'apologising', 'praising', 'regretting', 'congratulating' and 'deploring'. Examples are 'That tweet of yours was really, really nice' and 'I wish it hadn't come to an end.'

Classifying naturally occurring utterances into SAT macro-categories and speech acts is not straightforward because they can be categorised in various ways. For example, 'You look wonderful tonight' for one analyst might be a representative, but for another it might be an expressive, and for yet another it could be both.

Central to SAT is the difference between direct and indirect speech acts (remember that 'speech acts' in SAT are not exactly the same as 'acts' in ET: check out Chapter 6). In the case of **direct speech acts**, speakers want to communicate the literal meaning of the words, and so the form relates directly to the function. Thus:

- declarative forms which have the function of a statement, as in 'I'm experimenting with task-based learning' and 'My learners don't speak much in class'
- interrogative forms with the function of a question, such as 'Have you tried it before?' and 'What are your learners like?'
- imperative forms that have the function of a command, for example 'Give it a go' and 'Don't force them to speak in plenary'

In the case of the **indirect speech act**, speakers want to communicate a different meaning from the apparent surface meaning, and the form does not relate directly to the function. Here are some examples:

- Declarative forms such as 'I'd like to borrow your book' do not usually have the function of a statement (no hearer would reply 'Oh really? That's interesting'); they have the function of a command, meaning 'Lend me your book.' (Hearers tend to respond along the lines of 'Yeah no problem. Take it.')

- Interrogative forms such as 'Can you lend me your book?' do not have the function of a question (hearers are unlikely to respond 'Yes I have that ability. It's not difficult for me to lend people books'); they have the function of a request or command, meaning 'Lend me your book.' (Again, hearers might respond 'Yeah no problem. Take it.')
- Imperative forms such as 'Enjoy your class' should not make hearers feel that they are being given a command (they are unlikely to respond 'OK, I'll do as you say!'); they function as a statement, meaning 'I hope you enjoy your class.' (Hearers tend to say something like 'Thanks!')

Indirectness is used as a politeness strategy, as we will see in Chapter 8. It usually aims at enabling smoother social interaction.

Both Austin and Searle believed that for speech acts to be carried out successfully, certain **felicity conditions** had to be met. For Austin, these conditions were that the context and roles of participants must be recognised by all parties, the action must be carried out completely and the persons must have the right intentions. Searle added that the hearer must understand the language, and the speaker must believe that it is possible to carry out the action, that they are performing the act in the hearer's best interests, and that they are sincere about wanting them to do it. Thus if you say to your learners 'Learn your irregular verbs', they will respond appropriately because they recognise you as qualified to demand that and they know why you are saying it. A friend who says to them 'Learn your irregular verbs' might not be taken so seriously. They might think 'She's got no right to tell us what to do – what does she care?'

Since the 1990s, linguists have noted that some indirect speech acts contain forms that are so routinised that they function like direct speech acts, because hearers do not have to rely on inference alone to understand the meaning. For example, requesting in English is rarely performed by means of an imperative; 'can you' and 'could you' as in 'Can you pass the salt?' and 'Could you answer the phone?' are so often used in requests that they function like conventionalised direct requests (Aijmer 2009; O'Keeffe et al. 2011).

SAT has been accused of focusing on single utterances in isolation rather than taking into account the co-text (the preceding and following utterances) and the context (the immediate surrounding situation and the background knowledge). CL has made it possible to examine the most frequent co-text and context of speech acts, as explained in Chapter 2. SAT has also been accused of attempting to describe universal norms when in fact the model does not apply worldwide, being based on Anglocentric viewpoints. See Section 7.3 for speech acts and their realisations in other cultures.

Another problem with SAT is that it can be difficult for an analyst to categorise the 'messiness' of everyday spoken language. Utterances such as 'Do you know what I mean?' and 'Here we all are then' are fillers with little semantic content. They cannot be said to be representative, expressive or otherwise; they have an interactional function of keeping the conversation going or showing social cohesion. Similarly, utterances such as 'Cool!' and 'Oh really?' are backchannels, which do not have an obvious SAT category but simply indicate that the hearer is listening. Incomplete sentences such as 'Where did you put the er' and 'I was wondering – oh no never mind' are almost impossible to categorise, and yet they are a natural part of spontaneous talk.

Task 7.1 Applying the concept to teaching

It is straightforward to incorporate an awareness of indirect speech acts into your teaching. Try this junior school role-play task called 'Asking for things politely in your friend's grandparent's house', either with your learners or with your colleagues. The objective is to develop the learners' ability to produce indirect speech acts. Decide which of the chapters of the coursebook that you use could be related to this task.

Three learners read aloud the dialogue to the class as a demonstration:

Visitor	<u>I'd like to</u> have a look at your atlas.
Grandparent	Would you dear? You must be a very clever girl.
Visitor	<u>Can I</u> look at it then?
Grandparent	I'm sure you can. You've got good eyes, unlike me.
Grandson/daughter	Grandma, <u>give</u> Emma your atlas!
Grandparent	Oh sorry! Here you are.

In a group, analyse what happened in terms of direct and indirect language, and note the forms used (the ones underlined). Then divide learners into groups of three and assign roles – grandparent, grandson/daughter and visitor. Give the visitor a prompt card. Here are prompts to go on the cards:

- You want to wash your hands
- You want to check the football results on television
- You want a drink of water

Ask your learners to discuss, in their L1 if necessary, whether this indirectness exists in other varieties of Inner Circle or Outer Circle English that they know, and whether it exists in another language that they are familiar with. Ask them to think about how indirectness relates to the culture (the values and norms) of the speakers. If this discussion is too difficult for your learners, you could make mention of any cross-cultural differences that come to your mind.

Task 7.2 Trying out research

A technique frequently used with speech act research is Discourse Completion Tests (DCTs). These ask the subjects to read a small scenario and fill in the words that they would use in the situation described, in order to carry out a linguistic analysis of their choices. Here are two examples:

1. You are at a friend's house having coffee and you spill some on her cream-coloured carpet. There's now a brown mark the size of a finger. Your friend is very fussy about her clean carpets. You say

---

2. Your friend proudly shows you a painting that she did herself. You feel that the colours are too loud and the topic somewhat boring. You say

---

The first scenario might elicit an apology such as 'I'm terribly sorry about your carpet. Can I clean it for you?' with an indirect offer. The second will most likely elicit an expressive of complimenting, such as 'That is lovely! Well done.'

Choose one speech act and justify why you chose that particular one. For example, you might say 'I've noticed that when peers from my country apologise to Australian learners, the Australian people do not look satisfied. I need to raise their awareness of cross-cultural differences.' Write three DCT scenario questions with the speech act in mind. Ask each of your learners or your peers what they would say in each situation. Find out what proportion of answers are indirect. Then think what your results might show. You might say, for example, 'The content of the apology reflects more the learners' home culture than British cultural norms.'

Task 7.3 Using the internet

Go to the COCA corpus (http://corpus.byu.edu/coca/) and run a search for 'I 'm sorry' (remember that the corpus demands that you put a space between 'I' and ''m'). Examine the concordance lines (see Chapter 2) to find the main speech act that 'I'm sorry' fulfils, and see whether it is always expressive of apologising. Choose ten lines that represent the most frequent speech acts involved and bring them to class. Discuss what classroom task you would design for 15–16 year olds, and what part of their current syllabus and coursebook would accommodate this task.

7.2 OBSERVING AND FLOUTING THE COOPERATIVE MAXIMS

The Cooperative Principle (CP) stems from the work of Grice (1975). He understood that, in successful communication, interlocutors assume that they are obeying four maxims. These maxims are illustrated here with data from the COCA corpus:

- The maxim of **Quantity**, which says that speakers should be as informative as is required, and give neither too little nor too much information. When speakers point to the fact that they are adhering to this maxim, they use expressions like 'in brief' or 'Anyway, <u>to cut a long story short</u>, th – they deported me, they put me on a plane back home.'
- The maxim of **Quality**, which says that speakers are presumed to be sincere, to be saying something that they believe is true. Some speakers emphasise the truth value of their words, as in 'he didn't return after that, <u>as far as I know</u>' and '<u>To be honest with you</u>, we have a lot left to do.'
- The maxim of **Relation**, which says that speakers are expected to be saying something that is relevant to what has been said before. Some point to the relevance: 'Oh you know what, that reminds me of something.'

- The maxim of **Manner**, which says that we should avoid ambiguity. Speakers emphasising this use expressions such as 'When I say couple of times, I mean, like ten or twenty.'

Classical Gricean theory claims that, much of the time, speakers appear not to obey these maxims. When hearers are expected to infer a meaning other than the one in the words themselves, we say that the maxim is **flouted**, and this is known as **conversational implicature**. Flouting CP maxims is similar to indirect speech acts, in that the speaker assumes that the hearer understands the underlying meaning. The difference is that whereas indirect speech acts can be explained by the grammatical choice of declarative, interrogative and imperative, CP maxim flouting implies a whole different meaning that is not necessarily predictable linguistically. Let us take each maxim in turn:

- A speaker who flouts the maxim of Quantity seems to give too much or too little information, knowing that the hearer can guess the rest. For example, if a friend responds to your invitation out with 'I haven't finished my assignment yet', you can understand the rest of the meaning: 'so I can't come'.
- A speaker flouting Quality may appear to say things that cannot be true. Exaggeration, or **hyperbole**, is a case in point: if a parent playing with a child says 'Get off – you're going to squash me flat!', the child knows that the adult just means that the child is heavy. **Metaphors** are another instance: a hearer knows that if someone is described as a 'live wire', it does not mean they are electrical but, rather, enthusiastic. **Irony** and **banter** are other examples. 'While irony is an apparently friendly way of being offensive (mock-politeness), the type of verbal behaviour known as "banter" is an offensive way of being friendly (mock impoliteness)' (Leech 1983: 144). Witness the irony in 'I really love the way you whistle when I'm trying to study' and the **banter** in 'You must bore your learners so much when you talk like that!'
- When the maxim of Relation is flouted, speakers know that hearers can do the work to make one utterance relevant to another. When a friend of mine came to stay, I asked her one evening 'Is it warm enough in here for you?" and she replied 'Um, I brought slippers.' I took that to mean 'no'.
- When flouting Manner, speakers' meaning appears obscure, and they are often trying to exclude someone who does not have enough information to see through the ambiguity. An example is 'Did you bring the "you know what"?'

Sometimes a speaker does not observe the maxims, but they know that the hearer thinks that they *are* observing them; this is known as **violating** the maxims. Generally in these cases, the speaker is lying:

- Violating the maxim of Quantity means giving the hearer less information than they need, while the hearer thinks that they have the full picture. If, in a court of law, the accused person answers the question 'Where were you on the night of the murder?' with 'In my apartment', knowing that the lawyer does not know that he has two apartments, one that the lawyer knows about, ten kilometres from the scene of the murder and another on the site of the murder, he is being economical with the truth.

- The same accused could have answered by violating the maxim of Quality, saying 'I was visiting a friend in hospital' when in fact he was at the murder scene. Some violations of the maxim of Quality amount to white lies; these are untruths used in order to not hurt the hearer, as when someone asks 'Do you like my painting?' and the speaker replies 'Yeah, it's great!' when in fact they do not like it.
- When the maxim of Relation is violated, the speaker believes that the hearer will think that their response is relevant, when in fact it is not. This is often the case in political interviews in which the interviewee avoids answering the question by saying something unrelated, as in this excerpt from a 2002 BBC *Newsnight* programme when Tony Blair was British prime minister:

Jeremy Paxman   But where is the justice in taxing someone who earns £34,000 a year, which is about enough to cover a mortgage on a one-bedroom flat in outer London, at the same rate as someone who earns £34 million. Where is the justice?

Tony Blair   The person who earns £34 million, if they're paying the top rate of tax, will pay far more tax on the £34 million than the person on £34,000.

Jeremy Paxman   I am asking you about the rate of tax.

- The maxim of Manner is violated when the speaker uses ambiguity to cover the truth. An example would be if Hamish asks 'When're you coming?' and Callum answers vaguely 'Later', meaning 'not for at least a month' and knowing that Hamish will think he means 'some time today'.

There are two other forms of non-observance of maxims, which are not related to implications of further meaning or avoidance of the truth. The first is **infringing** a maxim, which happens when the speaker cannot speak informatively, truthfully, relevantly or clearly because they are not speaking their first language; because they are tired, excited, nervous, drunk or cognitively challenged; or because they wrongly assume the amount of information that the hearer needs. Take the following example from a MICASE tutorial interaction:

S4   we, we have also get this probability so, my question is this (query) used is correct or no?
S2   is that s- [S4: i mean] what correct? is that
S4   yeah i mean, is this is correct or not i mean here it's, equal to <PAUSE:04> um (that) (xx) (times) (xx)
S2   yeah plus the other three? [S4: yeah] yeah that's that's right.
S4   that's right? [S2: mhm] oh okay, yeah.

The second form of non-observance is **opting out**. This is when a speaker cannot speak informatively, truthfully, relevantly or clearly because they are unable to cooperate, for political, legal or ethical reasons, as in 'I'm unable to say for certain whether he will survive' (COCA).

Gricean theory has its limitations. When analysing naturally occurring data, researchers can find it difficult to determine which maxim is operating and may decide that two or more are operating at once. I had an unemployed friend who used to try to give the impression that he was busy. When asked 'What did you do this afternoon?', he would invariably reply 'I was just organising bits and pieces.' He could be said to be violating the maxims of Quantity or Manner or both.

Grice was accused of suggesting that his maxims are universal. He denied this, yet his examples are all Anglo-American, so one might suspect that he understood the maxims used in the UK and the US to apply worldwide. See Section 7.3 for an exploration of how far the model can be applied to other cultures.

Neo-Gricean pragmatics theorists have suggested adaptations of the CP model. Some have recommended that there should be more maxims, some prefer the maxims to be collapsed into two or three maxims, and others suggest that there are two types of conversational implicature. One is **generalised**, when no special knowledge of the context is required in order to infer the meaning, as in:

Mary   Did you invite Pete and Ken?
Sue   I invited Pete.

which implies that Sue did not invite Ken. The other is **particularised**, when the hearer has to draw on specific shared knowledge for the meaning, an example being:

Mary   Did you invite Pete and Ken?
Sue   Ken's parents are here.

where Mary knows that when Ken's parents visit, he stays at home and so it is pointless to invite him.

A major challenge to Grice's theory came from Sperber and Wilson (1986), who developed **Relevance Theory**, which suggested that interaction works because hearers assume that speakers are trying to be as relevant as possible, and because when maxims are flouted, speakers know that hearers know that speakers are being cooperative at a deeper level. They proposed:

- the **Cognitive principle**, which says that relevance is a function of two factors:
  - contextual effects: the more communication adds new information, strengthens or contradicts an existing assumption, the more relevant it is
  - processing effort: the less effort the hearer has to make to access the new information context, the more relevant the communication is
- the **Communicative principle**, which claims that the context stops utterances being ambiguous, helping the hearer understand the connection between utterances.

Relevance Theory also has several limitations. Because it is all-encompassing, referring to everything that is said and written, it loses its explanatory force as a theory (Mey 1994: 81). It is another universal theory, which assumes that non-Anglo-American cultures give the same importance to relevance and disregards dimensions of social variation, such as age, gender and status.

Task 7.4 Applying the concept to teaching

Here is a task that you could use with first-year English students at university (or some of your peers if you do not have access to a class), based on the film *Bend it like Beckham*. The objective of the class is to make learners aware of the maxims of Quantity and Quality and the importance of access to context. As you go through the task, consider how it would fit into the curriculum.

Tell the learners the background before they read the excerpt: Jess likes playing football. The first time that Jules saw her, Jess was playing football in the park. Jules asked Jess if she would like to join her football team, and Jess said 'yes'. Jess did not ask her parents for permission. In this scene, Jules has brought Jess to meet Joe, the trainer of the girls' football team. Jules has played in Joe's team for a long time. Before you show them the excerpt, ask them to read the transcription individually, and write notes about why:

- Joe says 'Jesus!' in line 8
- Joe and Jules have a disagreement in lines 13–20
- Jess answers 'Yeah, they're cool' in line 24

The transcription that you give to the learners will not have the underlinings: these are here to help you, the teacher, with the answers. You could provide your learners with a glossary of the new vocabulary. You will probably find that they have difficulty understanding the excerpt and think that there has been an argument.

1	Jess	Hi
2	Joe	<u>Where do you normally play?</u>
3	Jess	<u>In the park.</u>
4	Joe	<u>I mean what position.</u>
5	Jess	<u>Oh sorry. I usually play all over but up front on the right is best.</u>
6	Joe	Get your boots on.
7	Jess	I haven't got any
8	Joe	Right join in. Start warming up. Jesus!

(Jess plays football with the team)

9	Joe	How did you feel out there?
10	Jess	Brilliant. Really, really great!
11	Joe	I've never seen an Indian girl into football
12	Jess	I didn't even know they had a girls' team here.
13	Joe	*(Looking at Jules)* <u>It's all her fault. I used to play for the men's club</u>
14		<u>and she used to hang around here whining that there was no team</u>
15		<u>for her to play on.</u>

16	Jules	Oh! I wasn't whining! <u>No, there was nothing here for us girls. I mean</u>
17		<u>there was Junior Boys stuff. But when he busted his knee, he set up</u>
18		<u>a girls' side. And he's been on my case ever since.</u>
19	Joe	<u>See they made me start at the bottom. You can't get much lower</u>
20		<u>than her.</u>
21	Jules	Oh! You're so full of it! No, we get just as many trophies as the
22		men's side do. So does she pass?
23	Joe	*(Looking at Jess)* Are your folks up for it?
24	Jess	Yeah they're cool.
25	Joe	Suppose you'd better come back then. I got to go and open the bar.
26		Some real work.

Play the film excerpt to your learners and ask them to check whether they were right. In the second group discussion they will probably show that they realise that there was a certain amount of playing and joking going on. Tell them that the dialogue is all about who knows what. It is about what information is shared by whom. Then tell them to work in pairs and:

- Underline once the lines which show that <u>Jess lacks information</u> and that a) Joe does not know this, or b) Jules has to fill in the information for her.
- Underline twice the lines which show that <u>Joe and Jules are playing with the information</u> that they share, in order to joke with each other.
- Underline with a dotted line the lines in which <u>Jess is lying</u>.

You can ask them to do this simply with the transcript or at the same time as you play the film clip for a second time.

A follow-up task would be to facilitate a discussion of whether the dialogue suggests that the rules in Britain are:

- Give the right amount of information so that people understand.
- You can say something that is not true, if people know what the truth is, if you want to play and joke.
- You can say something that is not true, even if people do not know what the truth is, if you want to do something.

Remind them that one has to be careful when generalising about 'rules in Britain', with its many social and regional varieties, and its wide range of ethnicities (Jess is Indian, and the other two are white English).

Then move on to these cross-cultural questions:

- Are the social rules in your country the same or different?
- It what situations might it be important to know the differences between Britain (noting the caution mentioned above) and your country?

Task 7.5 Trying out research

Record some family members, friends or colleagues talking in their L1, informally and as spontaneously as possible, for about ten minutes. Before you analyse the talk, predict what you think you might find in terms of flouting and violating maxims, for example, 'Half of the lines contain maxim flouting' or 'Most lines are to do with the maxim of Quantity', and discuss why you think that this will be the case. Analyse utterance by utterance what maxims are being observed, flouted and violated. As you analyse, consider whether there are maxims that they are observing that are not in the CP model. Discuss your findings with colleagues.

Task 7.6 Using the internet

Go online to YouTube and search for 'Sitcoms Full Episodes'. Find one that you think would be suitable for your learners. If the sitcoms are not suitable for your learners, find one on an Outer Circle site on the internet. Think about it from the point of view of CP maxims, flouting, violating and Relevance Theory. Formulate a rationale for giving your learners the following task; justify it, in terms of usefulness. Decide how exactly it would fit in with the syllabus and textbook that they tend to use.

Write a list of ten very simple questions that you could put to your learners, so that they would have to look for implied or underlying meaning and/or lies. Then ask them to compare their way of interacting with how people interact in their own culture.

7.3 FUNCTIONS, MAXIMS AND SOCIAL VARIABLES

Throughout this chapter, it has been suggested that SAT and CP depend on social variables and that they are not universally applicable to all cultures. Although greetings, apologies, suggestions, requests and thanks exist in most cultures, as do flouting and conversational implicature, the linguistic realisations and the elements involved, and the contexts in which they are used, vary. In the following brief survey of some of the literature and anecdotal illustrations on this topic, note that each observation is based on a relatively small study or on personal experience (either mine or those described in TESOL students' journals from a 'Text, Discourse and Language Teaching' course). These observations cannot be generalised to any great degree, and no observation is intended to cover all the people of that culture. Researchers and observers are very careful not to fall into the trap of stereotyping. Likewise, you are invited to consider the observations critically.

Social variables have an important influence on Anglo-American indirect directives (see Chapter 8, for the relationship between indirectness and politeness), for example:

- A **lack of familiarity** with an interlocutor can make someone say 'Could you pass me the water?' rather than 'Pass me the water.' I was once on a train and a passenger wanted to sit on the seat next to me; instead of saying 'Move your bag', she said 'Is this bag yours?'
- The **reasonableness of the task** is a factor: the bigger the request, the more likely the directive will be indirect: compare 'Lend me £10!' and 'I'm in desperate need

of £1,000 – my daughter needs a deposit on her flat. You don't have that amount spare, do you?'

- The **formality of the domain** influences whether an indirect speech act is used or not. In a meeting, a speaker might say to someone who is trying to interrupt 'I wonder if you could wait until I finish making this point?' whereas in the cafeteria, they might simply say 'Hang on – I haven't finished.'
- **Social distance** has an impact too. Differences of status, role, age, education and class can require indirectness. Social distance can give speakers power and authority, and it is generally those in the less dominant role who use indirectness.

Let us turn now to a discussion of speech acts and cultural differences. We start with differences as regards directness and indirectness. In intercultural exchanges, pragmatic failure can occur when hearers infer the wrong indirect speech act. To take an example, I was once showing some Chinese visitors the sights of Edinburgh. After an hour of walking, one said 'You're tired.' I said I was not, but soon learned that this was not an indirect question about me so much as an indirect request for the tour to stop. Breakdowns in communication can also occur when the direct speech act is the same but the realisation is different. For example, a student wrote in her journal about a command used to console:

> Sometimes when the Taiwanese say 'Ni xiang tai duo le' they try to tell you not to worry too much. But if you translate the expression word by word, it says 'you are thinking too much' in English and it has a negative implication. I once translated it word by word and offended my friend.

Some cultures embed directives in politeness expressions more than others. Spencer-Oatey (2008) carried out an experiment with Japanese students which required them to write a letter asking a professor to read a thesis chapter. In English they simply asked if the professor could do it. In Japanese, they prefaced their directive with a reference to the weather, so as not to be too blunt, and then used several hedges and apologies, because of the greater social distance.

Expressive speech acts are particularly well investigated from a non-Anglo-American point of view. Let us begin with 'thanking'. Huang (2007) notes that, on leaving a dinner party, English-speaking guests tend to say 'thank you' and offer compliments, whereas Japanese guests apologise for intruding with 'itashimshita'. Wierzbicka (2003) points out that 'thanking' in English means the speaker feels good and wants the other person to feel good too, whereas Japanese speakers' 'thanks' are often expressed as a kind of 'sorry' because they feel indebted and must then repay it. Kim (2008) explains that in Korean, there are two types of 'thank you': 'mainhada' which indicates that returning the debt will be difficult, and 'gamsahada', which indicates that the speaker can return the benefit.

'Complimenting' and 'responding to compliments' have also been researched. Huang (2007) has found that a compliment generates acceptance and thanking in English, but self-denigration in Chinese and Japanese. When I first arrived in Cuba,

I went to a party where I complimented another guest on her necklace. Her response was 'It's yours.' I protested that I could not possibly take it off her and then realised that this was not an offer but simply a 'responding to compliments' formula.

'Apologising' has also been widely discussed and investigated. To take an example, Paltridge (2012: 47–8) tells an anecdote of a Japanese student in the UK who was upset because a builder had done a bad job and would not apologise. The student then learned that a British apology implied 'both taking responsibility for the faulty work and agreeing to do something about it', and explained that this is not implied in Japanese, but that a simple apology is always expected.

Differing conversational implicature can cause pragmatic failure across cultures. Interestingly, the following illustrative anecdotes centre mainly on the flouting of the maxim of Quality. Again in Cuba, this time during the campaign to control the *Aedes aegypti* mosquito that was spreading dengue fever, I joked in a deadpan voice when the fumigation plane was going back and forth across the sky, 'I think that plane is just fumigating our house.' 'No-no' came the answer, 'It's doing the whole of Havana.' This way of flouting the maxim was apparently not Cuban. Metaphors and hyperbole seem culture-specific, as these two TESOL student comments suggest:

> There are also many 4-word phrases in Chinese used to express one's opinions but they're just metaphors, not really mean what they mean on the surface. For example, 'women's heart is a needle in the sea' which means women are unpredictable and changeable, cannot be explored thoroughly.

> The use of hyperbole or exaggerated expression in spoken language is quite common, in the talk between couples in particular. Males are often asked to prove to their lovers how deep their love is. Lots of four-word-idioms in Chinese are also invented to show the concept of true love. For example 'hai ku shi lan' means that even if the seas run dry and the rocks crumble, they still love each other.

Task 7.7 Applying the concept to teaching

Take a moment to think of any stereotypical preconceptions about social norms with relation to SAT and CP that your learners may have about an Inner Circle country (see Chapter 3) where English is spoken as a first language (Australia, anglophone Canada, Ireland, New Zealand, South Africa, UK, USA). Describe them to your peers, and suggest which you think are right and which are in fact just stereotypes.

Design a task for your learners that requires them to do a group project to find out more about these IC social norms. Evaluate how practical this task would be, taking into account:

- the age and language proficiency of the learners
- the syllabus, coursebook and assessment in your teaching context

Task 7.8 Trying out research

The six comments below were made by a UK TESOL student about his understanding of social norms in Japan, where he had lived and worked for a number of years. Read them with the following issues in mind and then discuss:

- Do they refer mostly to SAT or CP? Are they mostly concerned with directness and maxim observation, or indirectness and maxim flouting? Which speech acts and cooperative maxims are involved?
- If you are Japanese or have lived in Japan, do you concur with his observations? Do you find any of the generalisations offensive? Are they typical of how non-Japanese people perceive Japanese people? Whether or not you are Japanese or have lived in Japan, how would you evaluate his comments, in terms of cross-cultural understanding? What might have made him have these opinions, do you think?
- Would you say there are any limitations to this case study, in terms of research design? Do you have any suggestions for further research?
- What applications can you think of, in terms of a short course to prepare EFL teachers going to Japan?

UK: polite for person making request to assume effort. Japan: polite/respectful to recognise addressee's effort, time and ability. Means that requests can seem very direct and almost like commands when translated into English. Japanese English: 'Please read my essay.' British English: 'Could you read my essay?'

Japanese indirectness – not imposing your opinion on someone else makes evaluating explaining something much more subtle process than in English – ie speaker presents facts, descriptions, gives lots of examples and leaves listener to draw own conclusions, pick up inferences. Rude to tell listener what he should think/get out of something. Can make Japanese sound vague and non-committal when speaking English.

Putting forth your opinions very assertively is frowned upon in Japan. The key is to appear to agree with everyone – this is very important to keep harmony within a group. In order to avoid disrupting the harmony it is essential to be vague so as to feel your way around a conversation. Once you sense the opinions of the group you can be more clear in what you're saying. This is why Japanese do not like to use the words 'yes' and 'no' so much – they're too direct.

Apologies – making excuses doesn't seem to go down very well in Japan. An explanation of why you were late for example, no matter what it is, traffic jam, etc. doesn't seem to be heard. The key seems to be to apologise and say if such and such happens again, things will be done differently, i.e. it will not happen again.

Unfinished sentences – when I first arrived in Japan I would ask for a product in a store, I would sometimes be told 'ima chatto . . .' meaning literally 'now it's a little . . .' I would stand and wait for the person to finish the sentence with a quizzical look. This would cause the person some anguish, especially if they were a shop assistant and have to be very polite to me. I would literally force them to say 'no we don't have any' or 'you can't have that service' in the politest way they could. I soon came to realise that the vague unfinished sentence was in fact a complete sentence and could even be said with some finality. This is a common set phrase in Japan.

Japanese generally do not place a lot of importance on the spoken word; they try to work out what's really going on, how the person really feels. It's called interacting through your stomach – maybe like your gut feeling. This is related to the focus on the listener when communicating. It seems to be the listener's responsibility to understand what someone is saying. The speaker is not really asked to clarify or repeat or paraphrase. Being puzzled at what someone is saying is rude and you wouldn't normally ask someone to repeat what they have said.

Task 7.9 Using the internet
Find an EFL task on the internet from an IC or OC country that illustrates a point about cross-cultural differences in terms of SAT and CP. Think how you might adapt it for your learners, again taking into account:

- the age and language proficiency of the learners
- the syllabus, coursebook and assessment in your teaching context

Here is an example of the sort of thing you might do. This task is taken from www.wilderdom.com/jamesneill.

Hello in Different Languages

- The goal of this activity is to heighten cross-cultural awareness, celebrate cross-cultural knowledge, and to say 'hello' in many different languages.
- This can be used a fun, warm-up, get-to-know-you activity with a cross-cultural theme.
- Within a group, you may be surprised how much knowledge there is of different languages for basic phrases.
- Optional: Ask participants to see if they can guess how many people there are in the world and how many different languages are spoken. (There are ~2800 languages and ~6 billion people. If an equal number of people spoke each language, that would be ~2 million people per language. You might relate this to local city/town size.)
- Challenge the group to come up with as many different languages for 'hello' as possible. When somebody volunteers (e.g., Bonjour!), make sure they say it or repeat it clearly for the rest of the group who then repeat.
- Optional: Before people start making suggestions, ask the group to have a guess how many collective languages the group will be able to come up with. Don't allow discussion – just do a quick whip around each person's guess and take a rough average – that's the group's estimate.

- The group leader keeps count on his/her fingers.
- Was the final number of 'hellos in different languages' close to the group's guess? If the group underestimated, they may not realize the knowledge within the group that might be used to their advantage. If the group's guess was an overestimate, why did they overestimate their knowledge resources? Discuss.
- Optional – to make more difficult or to add variation, try asking for these basic phrases:

  - Hello . . . Goodbye
  - Hello, my name is . . .?
  - Hello, how are you?
  - Yes . . . No
  - Please . . . Thank you
  - Do you speak English?
  - Numbers 1–5 or 1–10

- Optional, but recommended – have a list of hello in lots of different languages from which you can read out (see Jennifer's Language Page). This is especially useful for groups who don't know many different languages, as well as to learn, have fun, and illustrate the range of different languages.
- Variation: Can be run as a competition between groups.

Ways of adapting this would be to substitute the 'Hello' phrases and greetings with any one of the following, according to the characteristics of the learners and your teaching context:

- 'Thank you'
- 'I'm sorry'
- 'You look good'

7.4 FURTHER READING ONE

O'Keeffe, A., B. Clancy and S. Advolphs (2011), *Introducing Pragmatics in Use,* **London: Routledge, Chapter 8, 'Pragmatics and Language Teaching', pp. 137–43**

This reading explores the uses of pragmatics in language teaching. It begins by emphasising that pragmatics is related to 'a set of internalized rules of how to use language in socially cultural appropriate ways, taking into account the participants in a communicative interaction and features of the context within which the interaction takes place' (Celce-Murcia and Olshtain 2000: 19). It adds that pragmatic competence involves pragmalinguistic competences (knowledge of the range of forms available for performing pragmatic actions) and sociopragmatic competences (knowledge of the right forms for a particular goal and setting).

O'Keeffe et al. say that it is important to teach pragmatics in the language classroom because there is a need and it has proved to be effective. They highlight that pragmatic transfer from the L1 can make a learner appear insincere. Without knowledge about pragmatics, learners can appear rude; pragmatics errors can be seen by native speakers as social or personal blunders. Pragmatic competence development needs input but it does not happen on its own by exposure only; it needs explicit teaching to draw pragmatic considerations to the learners' attention. In the short term we can raise awareness, while in the long term we can help learners to perform by using explicit instruction.

EFL methodology in the classroom tends to focus on micro-level grammatical accuracy rather than macro-level grammatical appropriateness. Learners and teachers tend to rank grammatical errors more seriously than pragmatic errors partly 'due to the prevalence of examinations as indicators of success' (O'Keeffe et al. 2011: 139). Textbooks are generally not a reliable source of pragmatic input, because they have based any pragmatic advice on intuition rather than analysis of corpora of naturally occurring language.

The first excerpt claims that textbooks give little information on speech acts:

Vellenga (2004) maintains that despite a decade of complaint regarding the authenticity of the language contained in textbooks, little seems to have changed. Vellenga examined eight ELT textbooks in order to determine the amount and quality of pragmatic information included. She found a dearth of information for students in the areas of politeness, appropriacy, register, cultural information and speech act information, and maintains that 'in some cases, the focus on speech acts in textbooks may actually be pragmatically inappropriate for students' (Vellenga, 2004: 10). Crandall and Basturkmen (2004) also underline the inadequate approach for the teaching of speech acts taken by most English for Academic Purposes (EAP) textbooks. They claim that EAP textbooks appear to assume that learners know when it is appropriate to employ a particular speech act. Instead of being shown when and for what purposes to use a speech act, learners are instead provided with a list of 'useful expressions'. As discussed elsewhere in the book (Chapters 5 and 6, in particular), so much research into speech acts shows that non-native speakers find it very challenging to navigate the nuances of enacting a speech act in a foreign language (see for example, Boxer, 1993; Bardovi-Harlig, 2001; Félix-Brasdefer, 2003). While NNSs might easily know when an apology, invitation, or expression of gratitude is required, they may inadvertently end up over-apologising, being too forceful in an invitation, not expressing the right amount of gratitude, and so on, based on their L1 pragmatic norms. Vallenga (2004) concludes that a 'pragmatically friendly' textbook should include pragmatic awareness-raising activities that equip learners with the contextual information, variety of form and in-depth cultural information necessary to make the correct pragmalinguistic (the range of forms available) and sociopragmatic (the right form for the right situation) choices.

The second excerpt describes websites for teaching speech acts:

The language teacher also needs to consider the context of the classroom itself when designing pragmatic awareness exercises. The teacher–learner relationship is both an institutional and hierarchical one, in which the teacher is the power-role holder and this context normally produces a limited range of discourse patterns (see Lörscher, 1986; Ellis, 1990). Indeed, Cohen (2008) recommends that the teacher give the learner initial guidance in the form of direction to, for example, specific websites where learners can interact with different speech acts enacted in different situations and leave the actual meaning of pragmatics to the learner according to their own interests. Cohen and his associates have built an excellent online resource for teaching Spanish pragmatics which is well worth exploring for ideas on how to approach teaching areas of pragmatics in a learned centred way (see website for the Centre for Advanced Research on Language Acquisition, CARLA). For example, students can explore speech acts such as expressing gratitude, leave-taking, apologising, requesting, inviting, advising, suggesting, disagreeing, complimenting, complaining and reprimanding, as well as the social context of service encounters. For example, in the case of expressing gratitude, students are asked to assess when an expression of gratitude is needed in Spanish. Tick box options include borrowing an item, having someone else buy your lunch, getting a tour of the city, receiving a gift, the use of someone's time, borrowing money, receiving a favour, having someone serve you dinner. Students can then check their answers for feedback.

Task 7.10 Applying the concept to teaching

Analyse an EFL textbook that you know well, or one that you can easily get your hands on, to determine the amount and quality of pragmatic information included about speech acts:

- Are the learners 'shown when and for what purposes to use a speech act'?
- To what extent does the book 'include pragmatic awareness-raising activities that equip learners with the contextual information, variety of form and in-depth cultural information necessary to make the correct pragmalinguistic ... and sociopragmatic ... choices'?
- Is the picture presented to learners one related to a specific Inner Circle English or is it related to the country of the learners?

Task 7.11 Trying out research

Explore the CARLA website (www.carla.unn.edu/speechacts/definition/html). Choose one of the speech acts there (leave-taking, apologising, requesting, inviting, advising, suggesting, disagreeing, complimenting, complaining or reprimanding) and design a 50-minute lesson around it.

7.5 FURTHER READING TWO

Nunn, R. (2003), 'Intercultural communication and Grice's Principle', *Asian EFL Journal*, 5/1 (unpaginated)

The abstract summarises this article:

Grice's theory of implicature has been considered ethnocentric, but this paper will argue that it is highly relevant to intercultural analysis. The Principle of Cooperation, and its subordinate maxims, focus on the rationality of discourse, but Grice also includes linguistic and nonlinguistic context, conventional meaning and 'other items of background knowledge' in the inferential process. This notion of background knowledge is radically refined by Sperber and Wilson. Within a theory of relevance, interlocutors share only some contextual clues in a 'mutual cognitive environment'. In intercultural negotiation a high level of awareness of assumptions about what is 'mutually manifest' is of central importance to performance.

Teachers of intercultural communication skills attempt to establish a balance between providing meaningful practice and a useful rationale for improving theoretical awareness of the inferential process. This paper uses recordings of a classroom simulation involving foreign and Japanese students of intercultural communication taking part in a traffic accident insurance negotiation. Two data extracts are examined in detail, in which the failure by a foreign student to recognize radically different background assumptions had a decisive negative impact on his ability to negotiate, but a positive impact on his ability to analyse his own intercultural performance.

The first excerpt presents 'extracts from recordings of simulations involving foreign and Japanese students of intercultural communication in a Japanese University. One American student (AM) and three Japanese students (JP1, JP2 and JP3) played the role of insurance agents, each representing a driver in a traffic accident. Their aim was to negotiate the lowest possible percentage of blame for the driver they represented. (Numbers in the transcript represent percentages proposed by negotiators.)'

Transcript Part 1

JP1: |Why | |Ah . . . I think . . . {.er . . . Escort..} . . . {you . . . Escort

AM: Yes.}

JP1: ::Escort is forty to fifty|

AM: |Tell me why |

JP1: |Tell me why |

AM: |Tell me what laws I broke first |

JP1: |I don't know {I don't know that, I don't know} about er the situation in other country :: but er in Japan ::especially in Japan :: er . . . er You were drunk, {drunk.}|What is drunk is . . . er . . . driving

AM: Ah

JP1: . . . is most severe situation|

AM: |Okay| Where does it say ::I was drunk then |It doesn't say {er my er client does not say} :: he was drunk|

JP1: |Ah . . . even a little bit {er couldn't er }you couldn't admit That in Japanese law ::I think|

Transcript Part 2 (6 minutes later in the same conversation)

> AM |You should be more cautious:: when you're {when you're} coming into this lane :: because I'm driving . . . |In Japan these lines here . . . :: well according to what {the VW} the representative for the VW was . . .|
> JP1 (Interrupting) |::Even if you are driving main road you are drunk . . . | you are drunk . . . | Okay | Er {you have} you did have a drink :: even a little bit :: so I think er your responsibility is er 40 to 50, {er 40 to 50 and er} . . . |
> AM |{How do you} how do you know :: I was drunk though :: or my client was drunk | I mean :: how do you know |
> JP1 |You said . . . before|
> AM |I didn't say :: he was drunk| I said :: he had a drink|
> JP1 | In Japan a little bit drink means drunk:: |Okay| {. . . in Japanese law}|
> (laughter from other JP students)

The second excerpt suggests that the notion of common knowledge is untenable.

> Sperber and Wilson point out that even members of the same linguistic communities using the same language do not share the same assumptions as no two people share identical 'life histories'. They conclude that the notion of common knowledge is untenable and the idea of shared knowledge too vague. In our extract, the Japanese student's contributions indicate an assumption that drinking is incompatible with driving, however little has been drunk, based on his knowledge that it is illegal in Japan to have consumed any alcohol when driving. The American student brings the assumption that 'having a drink' or a 'couple of drinks' before driving is not a serious issue in this negotiation based on his assumption that a driver is allowed to have a few drinks up to a legal limit.

The third excerpt argues that for communication to succeed there have to be mutually manifest assumptions.

> A mutual cognitive environment (41) (i.e. what actually intersects in the cognitive environments of two people) does not mean that two people make the same assumptions, but 'merely that they are capable of doing so'. Hence a 'mutually manifest assumption' is not a 'mutual assumption'. One desired result of intercultural communication, if not of all communication, is to modify and to expand mutual knowledge of each other's assumptions. What is actually required, activated and made mutual in a particular conversation is subject to the appreciation and skill of participants and is also subject to constant negotiation. In this sense the negotiation in the first data extract fails. The challenge by the American student (Where does it say I was drunk then?) indicates that he has missed the relevance of the Japanese student's assumption. JP1, however, immediately confirms its relevance in relation to 'Japanese Law', but does not convince the American student, as some six minutes later in the second extract a similar exchange is initiated with unchanged assumptions. However, the Japanese

student's insistence on 'in Japan' allows us to conclude that he has an inferential advantage in that he is aware of an assumption that the American student does not share.

The last excerpt aims to show that 'skilled intercultural negotiation involves bringing out into the open, ostensibly making manifest or available for inference what is not shared'.

We have already noted that the American student did not consider the Japanese student's assumption of the 'drunkenness' of the Escort driver as true or possibly true in any relevant sense. (I didn't say he was drunk, I said he had a drink.) The repeated act of ostension by the Japanese student in the second extract obliges the American student to re-consider his assumption. The strong ostensive behaviour of the Japanese student has successfully made the American student recognize the relevance of the contribution 'you were drunk' in spite of the fact that this contradicts the background assumption his own argument was grounded in and his assumption that language was the major problem of understanding. Skilled intercultural negotiation involves bringing out into the open, ostensibly making manifest or available for inference what is not shared. The discovery of radically opposing assumptions may represent the cultural equivalent of an electric shock. In this context, the American student, a hitherto able and articulate negotiator with considerable intercultural experience, admitted (in later analysis) that he was 'paralysed', leading him to accept a very high percentage of blame for his driver with little further negotiation.

Task 7.12 Applying the concept to teaching

If you are in a class with people from a variety of cultures, ask one to give a short presentation about an event that is very culture specific to where they come from. Instruct the other learners to ask questions about that culture-specific event, not in order to find out more, but to check that they have fully understood what the presenter was saying. Keep in mind that 'skilled intercultural negotiation involves bringing out into the open, ostensibly making manifest or available for inference what is not shared'.

Task 7.13 Trying out research

If you have access to a class of English language learners, describe something about an English-speaking country that you know they might have difficulty understanding. Leave a few aspects unclear and ask the learners to draw a picture of what you have just talked about and check that they have fully understood what you have described. Find a way of telling your learners in simple language that 'skilled intercultural negotiation involves bringing out into the open, ostensibly making manifest or available for inference what is not shared'.

7.6 SUMMARY

This chapter has helped you to:

- recognise the speech acts that utterances are enacting, and the cooperative maxims that interlocutors appear to abide by
- think about the underlying meaning implied, whether in indirectness or in conversational implicature
- consider how the social norms of interaction vary from culture to culture

As regards using SAT and CP to improve your EFL teaching, you have considered how to:

- evaluate syllabuses and coursebooks along the lines of these theories, so as to build an understanding of language in context into them
- design tasks based on an aspect of the theories to enable learners to understand underlying meaning, for example tasks based on a film in order to raise learners' awareness of conversational implicature
- analyse films and sitcoms using these theories of data analysis
- carry out research on learners' ability to express underlying meaning using DCTs, study naturally occurring data using Excel spreadsheets, and carry out a qualitative analysis of learner journals describing cross-cultural experiences
- run a concordance on a corpus to discover the illocutionary force of everyday expressions and design a task for learners, and adapt an online task on everyday expressions across cultures.

It should be remembered that SAT dates from the 1960s and CP was developed in the 1970s. Research on the social norms of interaction have taken theories forward in the last fifty years, partly inspired by Corpus Linguistics, which has highlighted the need to analyse naturally occurring data. However, the classic theories still live on, as you will find as you read current linguistics and language-teaching journals in your quest for ways to improve your understanding of language and teaching methodology.

7.7 ADDITIONAL READINGS

The following texts have chapters that are pertinent to SAT and CP. They provide excellent introductions and present the various debates involved in a highly comprehensible way:

Chapman, S. (2011), *Pragmatics*, Basingstoke: Palgrave Macmillan.
O'Keeffe, A., B. Clancy and S. Adolphs (2011), *Introducing Pragmatics in Use*, London: Routledge.
Paltridge, B. (2012), *Discourse Analysis*, London: Bloomsbury Academic.

8

POLITENESS THEORIES

INTRODUCTION

Most adults have an understanding of how politeness functions in their society. They teach it to their children as part of their social upbringing ('Say thanks to Auntie Lil for your nice present') and they know when someone breaks the rules ('He just barged through the door in front of me!'). This everyday understanding of polite formulae ('Please', 'Thank you') and behaviour is not generally the focus of politeness studies. Politeness in linguistics is concerned with theories about linguistic expressions of closeness, solidarity, respect and consideration, used to save face and maintain relational rapport. Impoliteness theories, an emergent field, are concerned with verbal aggression and other threats to face.

Politeness has been a theme running throughout this volume. In Chapter 4, we noted that 'In some cultures it is considered more polite to decline a compliment ("Oh, don't be so silly!") whereas in others compliments are typically accepted ("Thank you very much!")'. In Chapter 5, we read that 'In as much as greetings and closings pay attention to the recipient and are oriented to the addressee's face needs (see Goffman 1967), they are politeness markers'. In Chapter 7, we pointed out that 'Flouting CP maxims is similar to indirect speech acts, in that the speaker assumes that the hearer understands the implied underlying meaning, and it tends to be associated with politeness.' Some linguists suggest that the social rules of politeness underlie the majority of approaches to language analysis, pointing out that the conventions of conversation structure are about politeness, that the maxims of cooperation are in fact politeness maxims, and so on.

As an EFL teacher, you will find it helpful to know about politeness in order to:

- make your learners aware that the politeness principles of other cultures may be different from their own, so that they can interact sensitively with English speakers;
- enable your learners to use English expressions of solidarity and respect, and to recognise linguistic manifestations of rudeness and verbal aggression;
- evaluate your current EFL syllabus, materials, tasks and assessment from the point of view of politeness, and build an understanding of politeness into the curriculum.

This chapter introduces you to politeness and impoliteness theories, and explores the influence of contextual variables and cultural variation on the concepts and linguistic expressions of (im)politeness. It ends with a focus on EFL teaching applications.

8.1 POLITENESS THEORIES

The study of politeness began in the 1970s, inspired by Goffman (1972: 5), who defined face as 'the positive social value a person effectively claims for himself' and proposed a **'social norm' model** comprised of two rules: 'show self-respect' (maintain own face) and **'show considerateness'** (maintain face of interlocutors). Lakoff (1972) expanded this model by proposing one of **'conversational maxims'** with rules of pragmatic competence: 'be clear' (obey Grice's four cooperative maxims) and 'be polite' ('don't impose', 'give options' and 'make the hearer feel good – be friendly').

Brown and Levinson's 1987 **'face-saving' model** has been the most influential to date. Brown and Levinson saw face as the public self-image that an individual projects and that is attributed by others. They introduced the notions of **'positive face'** (the desire to be liked or appreciated) and 'negative face' (the desire not to be imposed upon or impeded), and postulated that if a speaker needs to carry out a **face-threatening act (FTA)** such as an order, request, offer, promise, disagreement or complaint, they tend to soften it with indirectness and hedges. Brown and Levinson believed that if the weight of the threat is estimated to be minimal, speakers can use a strategy that is bald-on-record, whereas if it is great, they can avoid the FTA altogether. The range of strategies in between these two extremes is illustrated below with examples from the following scenario: a man is standing at a bus stop, and a bus is approaching but he cannot read the number in time to know whether to stop it or not. He has the option of asking another person for help.

The strategy **do not perform the FTA** means avoiding it altogether by saying nothing. The problem can be indicated non-verbally: the man at the bus stop can screw up his eyes and crane his head, or he can 'tut' and sigh, in the hope that the other people around him will realise his plight and offer to help. If the others at the bus stop do not respond, he has not threatened their face by asking for a favour or threatened his own by risking lack of cooperation.

Strategies	Examples
Do not perform the FTA	[screw up eyes, crane head at bus]
Perform the FTA	
• Off record	'I've left my glasses at home'
• On record	
• With politeness strategies	
• positive	'Aren't bus numbers small? Can *you* see what that says?'
• negative	'Would you mind telling me that bus number?'
• Bald	'Tell me the number of that bus.'

The strategy **perform the FTA off record** implies using indirectness or conversational implicature (see Chapter 7). The man at the bus stop can, if he feels that asking for help is not a major imposition, say in a loud voice, 'Oh dear, I've left my glasses at home!' or 'I can't see what that says.' These declaratives have the function of a command, indirectly telling people to tell him the bus number. He is flouting the cooperative maxims of Quantity and Manner by hinting. If the people at the bus stop desire not to be imposed upon, they can ignore the hint, and nobody's face has been threatened.

A frequently used strategy is **perform the FTA on record with positive politeness**. This is an involvement strategy showing solidarity and closeness that attends to positive face, the need to be accepted and liked by others, treated as a member of the group, and to know that one's wants are shared by others. Sub-strategies within this category include claiming common ground, seeking agreement, avoiding disagreement, exaggerating approval, assuming reciprocity, offering or promising action, being optimistic, intensifying interest, joking, using in-group identity markers (for example, in-group terms and abbreviations) and using inclusive 'we' and 'let's' forms. Thus if the visually challenged man says 'Aren't bus numbers small! Can *you* see what that says?', he is claiming common ground and seeking agreement.

Another frequently used strategy is **perform the FTA on record with negative politeness**. This does not mean being impolite. It is an independence strategy showing distance and respect for the hearer's negative face, their need to have freedom of action and not be imposed on by others. Here, sub-strategies are minimising the imposition, not interfering, being pessimistic, giving options, giving a chance to say 'no', showing deference, apologising, impersonalising, stating the imposition as a general rule, going on record as incurring a debt, and using mitigation and hedges ('I mean', 'you know', 'actually') to downtone and soften. Thus the bus stop request would be 'Would you mind telling me that bus number?' or 'Sorry to bother you – you couldn't possibly tell me the number of that bus, could you?'

The last strategy that Brown and Levinson mention is **perform the FTA bald on record**, without redress or mitigation. This means using imperatives, as in 'Tell me the number of that bus', direct questions, as in 'What's that number?', and verbless questions/commands such as 'Number of that bus?' Here, the speaker does not disguise what he is doing or to take any steps to avoid the face threat. However, not all bald-on-record language is face-threatening. It can be the norm for speakers who consider themselves equals ('Show me the spreadsheet') and friends ('You gotta be kidding me!'). Imperatives can be used when the positive consequences of carrying out the action outweigh the face threat, because the speech act is an indirect offer ('Have some more rice'), a passionate plea ('Give me a kiss') or a potentially life-saving warning ('Fire – get out!').

Any authentic interaction, spoken or written, can be analysed using this model. I illustrate it here with a Facebook interaction to show how the very public nature of virtual social interaction demands careful FTAs. In mid-February 2013, a university accompanied a poster advertising a panel discussion on women's equality with a message beginning '5th March is International Women's Day'. An alumnus posted a comment:

Alumnus	Sorry but 5th March is not International Women's Day
Editor	They didn't want to clash with the big lecture on the 8th. Details of that here: [web link]
Alumnus	I imagined there were very good reasons for the event being on 5th. My comment was about the accompanying text to this lovely poster, which reads '5th March is International Women's Day'
Editor	I see what you mean. Good spot. The poster people will be informed of their error.

Correcting an internationally accessible institutional public posting is potentially a major face threat, as is defending the institution without appearing defensive. The alumnus performed the FTA on record with negative politeness: the 'Sorry but 5th March is not International Women's Day' mitigated with threat with an apology, impersonalised the correction and stated the imposition as a general rule. Both the alumnus and the editor performed the FTA on record with positive politeness: they claimed common ground and sought agreement ('I imagined there were very good reasons', 'I see what you mean') and exaggerated approval ('this lovely poster', 'Good spot').

It is often not possible to obey both the politeness principle and the cooperative principle. Take the example of a self-conscious man, dressed up to go out, who asks his partner 'How do I look?' If she feels that he looks awful, she can still protect his positive face by saying 'You look great', thus violating the maxim of Quality. Alternatively, she can obey the maxim of Quality and answer bald on record ('You look awful') or with politeness strategies ('Well, I'm afraid you don't look all that cool, my love'), either of which risks offence. The strategy that allows for both minimal face threat as well as CP observance is 'perform the FTA off record'. Here the response might be 'You looked awesome in that black linen shirt you wore to Hank's party'.

Brown and Levinson's 'face-saving' model has several limitations. One is their assumption of the universality of the model: although they insisted that it was based on studies of more than one culture (Tamil, Tzeltal, US and UK English), their model implies that there are comparable linguistic strategies in each language. It assumes that all societies are individualist like Western ones, with a focus on the need of the individual to be free and autonomous. See Section 8.3 for a discussion of politeness rules in other cultures.

Another criticism of Brown and Levinson's model is that it focuses on the speaker at the expense of the hearer. Critics point to the fact that speakers are constrained by politeness conventions encoded in turn-taking patterns and the expectation that they will respond to the interlocutors' initiations. They hold that it is often the hearer who decides whether the speaker's words contain acceptable politeness, and that the audience factor is important.

Leech (1983) proposed an alternative model of politeness, based on six **polite conversational maxims**, which can also be expressed in Brown and Levinson's terms:

- **Tact** ('minimise cost to other' and 'maximise benefit to other') amounts to Brown and Levinson's strategies of minimising the imposition and attending to the hearer's wants. The man at that bus stop could have asked 'Would you be kind enough to tell me that bus number?'
- **Generosity** ('minimise benefit to self' and 'maximise cost to self'). Here the man at the bus stop could indicate the cost to his own face of making the request thus: 'I hate having to do this but I just need you to tell me the bus number.'
- **Approbation** ('minimise dispraise of other' and 'maximise praise of other') echoes Brown and Levinson's politeness strategies of avoiding disagreement and making others feel good by showing solidarity. The bus-stop request could have been 'You look like you've got good eyes – what's that number?'
- **Modesty** ('minimise praise of self' and 'maximise dispraise of self'): 'I very stupidly left my glasses at home – could you tell me the bus number?'
- **Agreement** ('minimise disagreement between self and other' and 'maximise agreement between self and other') again echoes Brown and Levinson's politeness strategies of seeking agreement: 'Aren't bus numbers small! Can *you* see what that says?'
- **Sympathy** ('minimise antipathy between self and other' and 'maximise sympathy between self and other') requires a request such as 'Sorry to be a pain, but you couldn't possibly tell me the number of that bus, could you?', sympathising with the effects of the imposition.

Leech's model also has its limitations. It has been suggested that the list of maxims is not exhaustive. Cruse (2000: 366) adds a maxim of 'consideration', expressed as 'minimise discomfort/displeasure of other' and 'maximise comfort/pleasure of other', which is related to the positive politeness strategy of making other people feel good. Since devising his model, Leech (2005: 12–13) has clarified his position: 'these are not a set of distinct constraints or maxims, but rather variant manifestations of the same super-constraint, the GSP [Grand Strategy of Politeness]', explaining that 'In order to be polite, S [self] expresses or implies meanings which place a high value on what pertains to O [other] or place a low value on what pertains to S.'

Spencer-Oatey (2000: 11–44) has devised an interactional model of politeness that is not solely concerned with the face of the individual. Her **rapport management model** is about politeness in a community; it entails management of:

- **Face**, the positive social value that people claim for themselves, such as worth, dignity and individual, collective and relational identity
- **Sociality rights and obligations**, the social entitlements that people claim for themselves, and the expected normative behaviour prescribed by a particular context

- **Interactional goals**, specific tasks and relational goals within the community

There are four types of rapport orientation in Spencer-Oatey's model. The first two relate to politeness:

- **Enhancement**, a desire to strengthen or enhance harmonious relations, as in the case of starting a romantic relationship or winning a business contract
- **Maintenance**, a desire to maintain or protect harmonious relations, as in preserving a current relationship

The third and fourth types of rapport orientation are related to impoliteness (see Section 8.2).

Watts (2003, 2005) has propounded a **model of 'appropriateness'**. He introduces the notion of 'politic' behaviour, which is behaviour that is appropriate to the ongoing social interaction and aimed at establishing and maintaining relationships between individuals of a social group. He understands 'polite' behaviour as a marked form of 'politic' behaviour, which exceeds the participants' expectations of what is appropriate in the context for the social group.

Task 8.1 Applying the concept to teaching

Here is a junior/senior school writing task that you could try with your colleagues or your learners. Imagine that in the previous class, you had told them very simply about the Anglo-American principles of positive and negative politeness, as envisaged by Levinson. Draw two columns on the blackboard, one headed 'showing closeness and sharing experience and feeling' and the other 'establishing distance and not imposing'. Write in the columns a few linguistic expressions that can be used for these purposes.

Read out to the class the following Letters A and B, and ask them which is 'showing closeness and sharing experience and feeling', and which 'establishing distance and not imposing'. Ask them which linguistic expressions gave them the clue. Ask them to think about why a speaker would choose one of these strategies over the other.

LETTER A
Hi Sara
Lend me your book for tomorrow's class – I've got to give a presentation and you know what she's like if you haven't got your book. I'll give you my notes after!
Love Lynda

LETTER B
Dear Sara
You couldn't possibly lend me your book for tomorrow's class, could you? I've got to give a presentation. If you need it yourself, it doesn't matter.
Regards Lynda

Ask the learners to get into pairs, and decide on something that someone needs to ask someone to do. Ask them to write a letter either 'showing closeness and sharing experience and feeling' or 'establishing distance and not imposing', and to indicate which it is. Take in all the letters and read them out. The first pair of learners that suggest correctly which strategy is used wins a point.

Ask them to consider whether these letters sound very British and to think how politeness is expressed in their language. This discussion could be in their own language if their English level is not high enough.

Task 8.2 Trying out research
Record your family or close friends talking at dinner and choose randomly a five-minute section for analysis. Categorise each utterance according to which of Leech's six maxims are obeyed. Decide which maxim is most in evidence. Discuss with colleagues how easy Leech's model was to work with and whether you were inclined to create a new maxim to fit part of your data.

Task 8.3 Using the internet
The following text is an authentic chat exchange from an online ticket-booking site for a train service. The name of the support team member in India and the customer and cities in the UK have been removed to preserve anonymity. Analyse it using one of the politeness theories. Discuss the issues involved in communicating effectively, solving problems and maintaining politeness in official online chat:

Support	Hi, my name is *[Support]*. How may I help you?
Customer	Hi I booked a ticket today 16.52 *[City 1]* to *[City 2]*. I'm feeling a bit ill and am thinking of cancelling. When I click on refund online, it just offers me a fresh booking. Does that mean I can't actually have a refund but that I have to make a new booking with the refund money?
Support	I will check this information.
Support	Are you the card holder for this booking?
Customer	Thanks
Customer	Yes I am
Support	May I take your name please?
Customer	*[Customer]*
Support	Thank you.
Support	You have booked an Off-Peak Return ticket to travel from *[City 1]* to *[City 2]* today and return.
Customer	Yes
Support	This ticket is refundable less £10 admin charge.
Customer	OK can you answer my first question now?
Support	This is a refundable ticket, you should get the option to cancel this ticket online.
Support	The amount refunded would be credited to the same payment card within 5 working days.

Customer	Unfortunately I don't – it just offers me the chance of a fresh booking
Support	I will check this information, please give me some time.
Customer	Thank you very much
Support	You will need to login to your account then go to 'My Account'.
Support	Then you will need to click on 'My Bookings'.
Support	Then click on the journey that you wish to cancel and you should get the option to cancel.
Customer	OK thanks. I'll give that a try.
Support	You are welcome.
Support	Is there anything else I may assist you with?
Customer	No that's all – thank you for your help
Support	Thank you for contacting us. Have a nice day.
Support	Please click on the 'Disconnect' button to end the chat session.

8.2 IMPOLITENESS THEORIES

In the twenty-first century, the study of politeness has broadened out to include impoliteness. Theorists tend to describe impoliteness in the same terms that they use to describe politeness. Leech (2008) incorporates impoliteness into his polite conversational maxims model, seeing it as either **non-observance** or **violation** of maxims. Spencer-Oatey (2000: 32) outlines two types of impoliteness in her rapport-orientation model:

- **Neglect** – a lack of concern or interest in the quality of relations, possibly because of focusing on the job at hand, caring more about self
- **Challenge** – a desire to challenge or impair harmonious relations, to assert personal independence or repay previous offence

The neglect orientation amounts to 'not being polite' and is similar to Leech's non-observance. The challenge orientation means 'being impolite' and reflects Leech's violation of maxims.

Others perceive impoliteness in terms of **face**. Culpeper (2008) sees it as linguistic behaviour either intended to cause 'face loss' of a target or perceived as such. A speaker causing face loss aims to devalue the positive social value that the target claims for themselves or to deny them some of their freedom. Culpeper (2005) proposes an '**Anatomy of Impoliteness**' model based on Brown and Levinson's (1987) 'face-saving' model (the examples are my own):

- **Bald-on-record impoliteness**, used when the face threat is great and there is an intention to attack it, creating maximum possible face damage, clearly, directly and unambiguously. This includes abusive, insulting, aggressive language, as in 'You've obviously got no idea what you're talking about, you total idiot' and 'Are you blind, you waste of space?'

- **Positive impoliteness**, which threatens positive face by ignoring or excluding the target, denying common ground, seeking disagreement, being uninterested, unconcerned, unsympathetic, not joking, using inappropriate identity markers, using obscure and secretive language, or using taboo words. An example would be 'I don't care what you say – I'm going out and don't know when I'll be back.'
- **Negative impoliteness**, which threatens negative face by frightening, condescending, scorning or ridiculing, being contemptuous, not treating the other seriously, belittling the other, invading the other's space, explicitly associating the other with a negative aspect or putting the target's indebtedness on record. 'You make me laugh! What do *you* know about it? You're just a woman.'
- **Off-record impoliteness**, which is sarcasm or mock-politeness ('an apparently friendly way of being offensive', Leech 1983: 144). The man at the bus stop could have said 'It's really, really nice the way you see me screwing up my eyes at the bus and don't think of telling me the number.'
- **Withhold politeness** where it is expected. An example would be intentionally not following the first part of an adjacency pair with the preferred second part, as in responding to the man at the bus stop's indirect request 'I've left my glasses at home' with not the number of the bus, but a pseudo-sympathetic 'So it goes.'

Culpeper (1996) makes a distinction between genuine impoliteness (see the aforementioned categories) and **mock-impoliteness**, which is banter and teasing ('an offensive way of being friendly', Leech 1983: 144). An example is 'You've obviously got no idea what you're talking about, you total idiot' and 'Are you blind, you waste of space?', when spoken jokingly to a friend who is expected to know that the impoliteness is not intended. Banter tends to have a rapport-maintenance orientation (see Section 8.1).

Impoliteness has also been described in terms of **appropriateness**. Mills (2003) claims that impoliteness is linguistic behaviour felt as intending to threaten the hearer's face or social identity, or going against the norms of the community of practice. Watts's 2005 model of 'appropriateness' accommodates both politeness and impoliteness:

- **'Politic'/appropriate** behaviour, which includes 'polite' (positively marked behaviour) and 'non-polite' (unmarked behaviour)
- **'Non-politic'/inappropriate** behaviour, which includes negatively marked behaviour that can be **'impolite'**, **'rude'** or **'over-polite'**.

The 'non-polite' behaviour is appropriate behaviour that is not felt as unusually polite or exceeding the norms of politeness, whereas 'non-politic' is inappropriate behaviour. In the literature, some see 'impolite' as unintentionally face-damaging and 'rude' as intentionally face-attacking (Terkourafi 2008) whereas some argue the opposite (Culpeper 2008). 'Over-polite' language is akin to sarcasm, and it can be particularly acerbic if it implies criticism, as in 'I wonder if you could possibly do me the favour of turning off the light – you may have noticed I'm trying to sleep?'

Many theorists agree that speech acts and linguistic expressions are **not intrinsically impolite**, understanding that the context (the situation and participants) determine whether the expressions are impolite or not. Even speech acts such as disagreeing, criticising, insulting and threatening cannot be said to be inherently face-threatening. Disagreeing with a compliment ('What this old thing? I bought it ages ago!') obeys the cooperative maxim of Modesty; criticising a loved one ('You drink too much coffee') can be intended to maximise the benefit to the hearer; insulting a friend ('Are you blind, you waste of space?') can be aimed at showing closeness; threatening a loved one ('Ask me if I'm cold again and I'll hit you') can be intended to reassure in a playful way. Watts (2003) holds that if a group of people negotiate and construct an unmitigated FTA as acceptable, it is not felt as impoliteness.

Some theorists maintain that if impoliteness has become **routinised**, it is no longer felt as impoliteness. Mills (2003) gives US army sergeants' **systematic impoliteness** as an example. Locher and Watts (2008) make the point that British TV political programmes contain a high level of aggressiveness and lack of respect on the part of the interviewer towards political interviewees. The excerpt from the Jeremy Paxman interview with Chloe Smith quoted in Chapter 6 demonstrates this. Viewers are so accustomed to Paxman's techniques that they have come to expect the barrage of interruptions and attacking questions, and are almost immune to his negative impoliteness. Another example of systematic impoliteness occurs in parliamentary debate in the United Kingdom. Insults are part of the discourse expectations of a good debater and are sanctioned at Prime Minister's Question Time (Harris 2001; Christie 2002).

Culpeper (2005) notes that habitual impoliteness is only neutralised if the targets of impoliteness feel it as such. We could cite the example of prisoner Wild Bill in *The Green Mile*, a film about death row in a US jail. Bald-on-record impoliteness is central to Wild Bill's idiolect. Just before the scene below, another prisoner hands round some cornbread, but does not give any to him because he has been so offensive:

Wild Bill   Hey! What about me? I'm going to get some too, ain't I? Hey! What about me? Don't you hold that on me, you big dummy nigger! Ha ha ha ha! Oooh, here come the boss man.
Warder   [Looks him in the eye] (1) You'll keep a civil tongue on my block.
Wild Bill   [Spits in his face]
Warder   [Wipes face] (1) You get that one for free. (1) But that's the last one.
Wild Bill   Ha ha! That's it? Just that little bittie one?

Here, the targets of Wild Bill's impoliteness do not appear to feel that his impoliteness has been neutralised; they engage in positive impoliteness themselves, ignoring him and being unsympathetic, in the hopes of imposing a minimal politeness rule on him. Bullying is an example of systematic impoliteness whose force does not diminish. Each aggression can augment the offence felt.

Culpeper (2011: 113) warns that to emphasise the context rather than linguistic form 'risks throwing the baby out with the bath water'. He argues that the negative effect of **conventionalised impoliteness formulae** (2011: 129–52) is not easy to eliminate by means of the context. He identified in the Oxford English Corpus insults such as 'you little dickhead', pointed criticisms such as 'that was unspeakably crap', unpalatable questions such as 'why do you make my life impossible?', condescensions as in 'that's being childish', message enforcers as in 'listen here', dismissals such as 'piss off', silencers such as 'shut the fuck up', threats as in 'I'm gonna smash your face in', and ill-wishes as in 'go hang yourself'. He notes that the offensiveness can be exacerbated by tone and manner of speaking (for example, shouting or spitting the words) and body language (for example, rolling the eyes or an 'ill-wishing' hand gesture). Culpeper also identified what he calls 'implicational impoliteness', examples being insinuations and snide remarks which flout the maxim of Manner ('We all know why *you* want to go out for a drink with the boss . . .'), and sarcasm and verbal formula mismatches which flout the maxim of Quality ('I hate to be rude but you're really pissing me off').

A central issue in the literature is the extent to which impoliteness depends on **speaker intention**. Bousfield (2008) believes that impoliteness can only be intentional, whereas Culpeper holds that impoliteness can also depend on the target's perceptions of the speaker's intentions; it comes about when the speaker communicates face-attack intentionally, or the hearer perceives and/or constructs behaviour as intentionally face-attacking, or a combination of both (2005: 38). Archer (2008) proposes two levels of face-threat:

- The prototypical one is the spitefully undertaken '**intentional**' face-threat
- The other two involve **unintentional** face-damage levels:
    - the '**accidental**' one, such as gaffes and faux pas, which the hearer perceives as face-damaging even though the speaker did not intend to offend, and which the speaker would have avoided if they had known it might have offensive consequences
    - the '**incidental**' one, in which the speaker knows that their words might have offensive consequences, but they say them anyway. This covers scenarios where there is verbal aggression, such as a cross-examination in court, in which the lawyer does not intend to offend the witness but knows that the witness might take offence.

Task 8.4 Applying the concept to teaching

Choose an aspect of impoliteness as described in the Anglo-American literature that you could tell the learners about in a class that you have taught. Design a short task that would raise their awareness of it on a receptive level. Consider whether you would also want your learners to be able to produce this type of language, taking into consideration the importance of context, and whether you would want them to make cross-cultural comparisons with linguistic impoliteness in their own culture.

Task 8.5 Trying out research

In the British House of Commons, at Prime Minister's Question Time, the prime minister can be directly challenged by any Member of Parliament, and the disagreement is managed by talking through the Speaker, who chairs the debate. Analyse the following excerpt of a debate between Conservative prime minister David Cameron and Labour leader Ed Miliband (5 December 2012), using all the models of analysis for impoliteness mentioned in this chapter, and decide which suits it best.

Miliband	Mr Speaker, the Conservative Party Manifesto published in April 2010 said, and I quote, 'We will increase health spending in real terms every year'. But the Head of the Statistics Authority says clearly and unequivocally that hasn't happened. What's today's excuse, Mr Speaker?
Cameron	[amidst cheering and jeering from members] This – this government is putting 12.6 billion pounds extra into the NHS. But let me – let me quote him the figures – let me quote him the figures directly from the Head of the Office of National Statistics, which is that in real terms spending in 2010 was 104.2 billion in real terms and in 2011 it was 104.3 billion in real terms. That is a real-terms increase and I can tell him, there will be further real-terms increases in 2012, in 2013, in 2014, whereas there'll be cuts under Labour.
Miliband	[amidst cheering and jeering from members] Mr Speaker, let me just say to the Prime Minister that, even by his standards, that was the most slippery answer you could possibly imagine. He has – that is unbelievable – he has – he's unbelievable – he has come to this House 26 times since he became Prime Minister and boasted about how he is increasing health spending every year of this Parliament. Well, well-well-well they're cheering, but he failed to keep the promise, Mr Speaker, and it's not an argument between me and him. We have a ruling from the Chair of the independent UK Statistics Authority who says it hasn't happened and I should be grateful if the Department of Health could clarify the statements made. Look, instead of his usual bluster, why doesn't he just correct the record?

Task 8.6 Using the internet

Electronic communication lends itself to miscommunication, especially when prosody and body language are not replaced by attitudinal punctuation such as '!!?' or smileys ☺ (see Chapter 3). Find examples of texts or emails that you have experienced (either in English or another language) in which the recipient was offended, even though the sender did not intend to offend. Analyse them from the point of view of impoliteness.

8.3 POLITENESS, IMPOLITENESS AND SOCIAL VARIABLES

This section deals with the contextual variables that influence (im)politeness strategy use and determine the linguistic choices that speakers make to express (im)politeness. It also deals with cultural variation in (im)politeness, examining how speakers' backgrounds affect the way that politeness is conceived and expressed.

The **contextual variables** can be grouped under two main headings, the situational context and the interpersonal context, although in reality the two are closely inter-woven. The variables in the **situational context** are the activity type, the formality and the size of the imposition. The **activity type**, be it a lecture, a job interview, a court trial, a service encounter or a casual conversation in a coffee bar, constrains the (im)politeness strategies which are available. Let us take the case of a lecturer who wishes to stop others talking while she is delivering her lecture. She might say 'If you can hold your questions for a minute, I'll just finish this point', performing negative politeness to minimise the imposition, but she would be unlikely to say, 'Be quiet – I'm talking!', as such directness and informality would be interpreted as negative impoliteness in this activity type. A judge in a trial has the power to say 'Silence in court!' without sounding offensive; the hedged 'If you can hold your questions for a minute, I'll just finish this point' is not part of the judge's script.

The variable of **formality** is usually a component of the activity type, and the rule tends to be 'the greater the formality, the more indirect the language is'. Thus, if the lecturer's request was a sarcastic 'Feel free to talk all the way through my lecture: it's not as if I ever say anything of worth', the off-record impoliteness could be quite offensive, unless the lecturer was known for using a routinised informal humorous tone. In an informal activity type, such as a casual conversation with family in a coffee bar, the lecturer or the judge might turn to the children with a direct 'Be quiet – I'm talking.'

The **size of imposition** depends on the reasonableness of the task, and the ten-dency is 'the greater the imposition, the more indirect the language is'. Thus, the lecturer who intends to discuss the issues raised in her lecture with her students can content herself with a simple 'If you can hold your questions for a minute, I'll just finish this point.' If she has no time for questions and seriously regrets restricting their freedom, her request might contain the full gamut of politeness strategies: 'I'm terribly sorry but we have a lot to get through this morning, so I'm going to have to ask you to be silent for the whole hour. If you do have any questions, you could maybe post them on the online discussion board, and I'll attend to them as soon as I can.'

The variables in the **interpersonal context** are the social identity features of the participants and the degree of familiarity. **Social identity features** include roles/status, gender, age, class and education. The choice of politeness strategy, accord-ing to Brown and Levinson (1987), is determined by the speaker's assessment of the social and interpersonal distance between them and the hearer, and of their relative power. They state that where there is social distance and/or power difference there is more indirectness. Power is usually in the hands of the person with more **status** and **authority**. Thus, one could say, simplistically, that the lecturer who asserts her authority over the students, and the employer who takes a dominant stance vis-à-vis their employees, are more likely to use bald-on-record politeness expressions when addressing them, and those in the less dominant role are liable to use more indirectness, hedges and mitigation.

Whether **gender** affects the way that politeness is expressed has been hotly debated. Holmes (1995) argues that women use more interactional solidarity language than men, finding that they use more compliments and give/receive more apologies than men. Murphy (2009) and Mullany (2011) have examined swearing and banter used by young men to express solidarity. However, Mills (2003) makes the important point that it is stereotyping to say that females use less directness and swearing than males.

Other social identity features have been less researched. **Age** difference can affect how politeness is expressed. Thus a child might say to a friend 'Give us a sweet' but to a grandmother 'Gran, could I have a sweet please?' Differences in class and education may result in the dominant class or the person who considers themselves more educated using more directness. However, Mills (2003) once again warns against stereotyping, questioning whether the social classes are fundamentally different in terms of linguistic politeness. Eelen (2001), on the other hand, suggests that politeness norms reflect dominant class views and make sure that those in power remain in power.

The degree of **familiarity** is another interpersonal variable. Generally speaking, the greater the distance between people in terms of relational intimacy, the lower the level of politeness strategies used. Thus a woman, if her husband leaves the door open, may mumble 'Door', whereas in a restaurant, she might ask the waiter, 'Excuse me, would you mind trying to keep that door shut? It's a little bit cold tonight, isn't it?' Mills (2003) notes that some women may find it appropriate for a close male friend to say 'Hello gorgeous', but offensive for a workman on a building site to shout 'Hello gorgeous!'

Moving on to **cultural variation**, studies have shown that, while there may be some universal social principles, the difference between cultures is immense. The dimensions include the concept of face, the enactment of politeness maxims and the degree of indirectness and deference built into the language. Before exploring these dimensions, it should be noted that 'the undoubted existence of culture-specific norms cannot reliably predict how a person will behave on an occasion of [interaction across cultures]' (O'Driscoll 2007: 467). There will always be individual differences.

The concept of face varies from culture to culture. To take a couple of examples, in Thailand it means dignity, self-esteem, prestige, reputation and pride (Ukosakul 2005: 119), and in China it has two sides: 'mianzi' (striving for own reputation/prestige) and 'lian' (respect of group for a person with a good reputation/prestige, ascribed face) (Mills 2003). Sifianou (2011: 43) notes that in non-Western societies, face is 'far broader than mere self-image with a positive and a negative aspect to it, since it involves social, moral and, in particular, group aspects', citing studies of face in East Asian, Nigerian, Turkish, Persian and Zulu cultures.

The enactment of politeness maxims varies across cultures. Günthner (2000: 218) found that different adherence to the maxim of Agreement could cause misunderstandings in intercultural settings. Her analysis of dissent in Chinese and German student conversations at a German university showed that the Germans contradicted and corrected the interlocutor, and that the Chinese students signalled consent and then indicated a discordant position, thus:

German   [well] do you believe there is a natural limitation?
Chinese   I belie:ve (-) not, but I (hi) I must say, there is (1.0) a bit

Interviews revealed that the German students valued overt expressions of opinions and found conversations with the Chinese students uninteresting and awkward, and that the Chinese students felt that the Germans were too willing to argue.

The importance of **indirectness** as a politeness strategy varies from culture to culture. In Japanese, for example, indirectness is a sign of mutual understanding and friendship. Directness can be felt as rude to those whose culture expects more indirectness. One Chinese TESOL student of mine recorded this story about another Chinese student living in the USA:

> One day when he entered the office which he was sharing with his professor, the professor was on the phone. The Chinese student still walked into the office and got ready to work. The professor turned to him and said, 'I'm having a private phone call, would you please walk outside for a few minutes.' This conversation shocked the Chinese student, to whom the professor was rude by directly requesting him to leave. He thought he had 'lost face'.

Indirectness can cause breakdowns in communication if the hearer's culture demands directness. To take an example, Grainger (2011: 171–93) reports on a study of English-speaking Zimbabweans interacting with British English speakers: the Zimbabweans' off-record politeness and non-conventional implied meaning was often misunderstood.

Some languages have an inventory of rapport-management strategies. English does not have conventionalised **deference and honorifics**, apart from the address forms 'Sir' and 'Madam', but many European languages do (Welsh 'ti'/'chi', French 'tu'/'vous', Spanish 'tu'/'usted' and German 'du'/'sie'). Japanese honorifics are not a politeness strategy but a part of social register, socially obligatory linguistic choices, regardless of face threats. Deference is also part of Korean politeness, honorifics establishing face through recognition of a person's ability, refinement, good character, adequate maturity and proper conduct (Brown 2011); and address forms are central to Chinese politeness (Gu 2011).

When it comes to the question of whether to **teach politeness** in EFL classes, there are three main points of view in the literature. Some say that there is no need to teach it, some claim that it is immoral to do so, and others believe that it is essential. Those who say that there is no need believe that the only way to achieve pragmatic fluency is to go to the country where the language is spoken and acquire it in action. Writers of communicative language-teaching coursebooks include texts with cultural content but use them to teach skills rather than to raise awareness of the target language culture and enable comparisons with the learners' own culture.

Those who claim that it is immoral to teach it see English as owned by BANA (Britain, Australia and North America), a global hegemonic power promoting the values of their own culture over those of other countries (Phillipson 1992; Hall and Eggington 2000; Pennycook 2001). These theorists see the teaching of politeness as part of linguistic imperialism.

Those who believe that it is essential to teach it base their position on studies that have shown that those who consider themselves to be native speakers of a language are likely to be less tolerant of a learner's politeness error than of a grammatical, lexical or phonetic one. Cross-cultural pragmatic failure can occur in interactions between speakers of different languages because of differing views of appropriateness. Learners need to understand the politeness values and conventions of the target language and to be made aware how their own language functions, so as to gain access to academic or professional opportunities (Tanaka 1997; Corbett 2003).

However, those who believe in teaching about politeness do state that teachers should keep in mind learners' attitudes and beliefs as regards the target language and their need to preserve their own identity. Learners may not want to align themselves with the target culture, and may be quite 'sensitive about having their social (or even political, religious, or moral) judgment called into question' (Thomas 1983: 104).

Task 8.7 Applying the concept to teaching

Discuss in groups what the main ethos seems to be vis-à-vis teaching about Anglo-American politeness strategies, maxims and norms, in an EFL context that you know:

- No need to teach it
- Immoral to teach it
- Essential to teach it

Discuss why the country and/or institution has this attitude, and say whether you share that general feeling.

Task 8.8 Trying out research

Design an interview or a questionnaire to use with people from different cultures to compare how norms of appropriate linguistic behaviour vary according to the situational and interpersonal context features.

Task 8.9 Using the internet

Go to the internet search engine of your choice (but not an academic one such as Google Scholar) and type in 'impolite rude language' and a non-IC-English-speaking country or nationality of interest to you, for example 'German' or 'Chinese'. Check:

- What most websites are – blogs, Wikipedia, advice sites, reports and articles.
- Who most are targeting – language learners, business people, researchers.
- What they describe – how impoliteness is expressed in that country/culture, how impolite people there can seem to people from other cultures.
- How 'right' are they – are they reinforcing stereotypes, imposing norms from another culture?
- What their purpose is – to inform people so they can do business successfully, to improve international harmony, to stir up prejudice and hatred.

Put together a short Powerpoint presentation for an imaginary group of advanced level learners of the language of that culture to counteract misinformation and/or present what you see as the correct picture of that culture.

8.4 FURTHER READING ONE

Haugh, M. (2007), 'Emic conceptualisations of (im)politeness and face in Japanese: implications for the discursive negotiation of second language learner identities', *Journal of Pragmatics*, 39: 657–80.

Haugh suggests that learners of Japanese need to understand the Japanese notion of 'place' ('basho') in '(im)politeness' and 'face'. He explains that 'place' has two dimensions: the 'place one belongs' ('uchi' or connectedness) and the 'place one stands' ('tachiba' or separateness). He adds that these two dimensions work together in interaction and that 'one's place in Japanese does not exist prior to or independently of interaction, but rather is established, maintained or challenged discursively through interaction'.

Japanese politeness traditionally includes 'teinei' (being warm-hearted and attentive) and 'reigi' (protecting the order of social life, especially manners/etiquette which express upward respect towards others ('kei'i')). Recent changes have meant that there is less emphasis on the expression of 'upward' respect, social position and relative status, and an increase in the expression of 'mutual' respect, awareness of the dignity/character of others and the place one stands ('tachiba').

Japanese impoliteness involves 'shitsurei' (lacking 'reigi', not having manners, making an inquiry, taking one's leave) and 'burei' (not correctly discerning according to 'reigi'). Impoliteness is not showing respect or consideration to the dignity/character and place of others, or not showing modesty about one's own place.

Haugh then presents an analysis of naturally occurring interactions that shows how '(im)politeness' and 'face' are indicated through 'place' in the negotiation of identities by speakers. Here are two of the analyses:

An understanding of how 'impoliteness' may arise in interaction is also important so that learners can make more informed choices about their identities. In the next example, the manner in which 'impoliteness' can arise from what one shows one thinks of others is illustrated when Kobo-chan's father indirectly criticises his mother's cooking.

(2) (Kobo-chan's father, mother and grandmother are eating dinner together)

1 Father:	Gochisō-sama. [*]
2	feast-Hon
3	(Thanks for dinner)
4 Grandmother:	Ara, mō tabe-nai no? [0]
5	oh longer eat-Neg M
6	(Oh, you're not eating any more?)
7 F:	Ko-iu abura-kkoi ryōri wa su-kan. [0]
8	this kind of oil-thick food Cont like-Neg
9	(I don't like this kind of oily food)
10 G:	(taking the dish away) Ara sō desu ka. Suimasen-deshi-ta. [+]
11	oh that way Cop(Pol) Q excuse me-Pol-Past

12		(Oh, is that right? [Well] sorry [then])
13 F:		(watching his mother wash the dishes noisily)
14		Okot-ta? [0]
15		angry-Past
16		(Are you angry?)
17 G:		Betsuni okocchai-ma-sen yo. [+]
18		not particularly angry-Pol-Neg M
19		(I'm not particularly angry) (Ueda 1998: 117)

In this example, Kobo-chan's father starts by positioning himself as in debt to
Kobo-chan's grandmother by expressing gratitude for the meal (line 1).
However, this relational identity is discursively challenged when the father
comments the meal was too oily (in line 7), which the grandmother takes as a
criticism, as evident in her sarcastic apology in line 10 and the way she next
starts noisily doing the dishes. The marked up-shift to addressee honorifics, in
a relationship where plain addressee forms are the unmarked norm, implies
that the grandmother thinks Kobo-chan's father has taken an inappropriate
place relative to her in making this criticism. The father's confusion is evident
from him next asking whether she is angry (in line 14), which indicates that the
father may not have intended to be critical of the grandmother's cooking. The
father thus initially seemed to be attempting to enact an identity where he feels
free to give his opinions (personal identity), but the grandmother understood
his comments as an attempt to enact an identity where he feels free to criticize
her cooking (relational identity). The grandmother also appears at first glance
to be enacting a relational identity where she has a lower status and so 'accepts'
the criticism, but the anger she expresses at the same time indicates her
unhappiness with such an identity. This discursive dispute in regards to their
respective places also gives rise to 'impoliteness' in both the way the
grandmother interprets the father's comment as a criticism, and her hyper-
polite responses in lines 10 and 17, which imply heavy sarcasm. In this
situation, then, a particular relational identity is not interactively achieved,
but rather differences between the identities they attempt to attribute to the
other and the identities they attempt to claim for themselves become apparent.
This discursive dispute as to their respective places also gives rise to
'impoliteness' and seems to cause the grandmother to become angry with
Kobo-chan's father

   In another example, Mary, a high school teacher on a scholarship to improve
her Japanese proficiency is interacting with her advisor, a professor at the
university she is attending. While Mary reported wanting to develop a personal
identity that reflected her perceived status as a professional in her interactions
with the professor, the apparent discomfort shown by the professor during this
interaction indicates she was less than successful (an asterix here indicates
inappropriate choice of vocabulary).

(4) (Mary and her academic supervisor are chatting in his office)

1 Mary:	Kono, anō, kono . . . umm, nani, um . . . institution anō shit-te-imasu, ne.
2	this um this umm what um institution um do-Te-Prog M
3	anō omoshiroi anō international, a, anō kyō gi, anō mō sugu,
4	um interesting um international oh um conference um soon
5	anō, um nari-masu.
6	um um become-Pol
7	(Um, you know it, right? Um, there will be an interesting international
8	conference there soon.)
9 Professor:	A, sō desu ka.
10	oh that way Cop(Pol) Q
11	(Oh, is that so.)
12 Mary:	Hai, anō , ju, jo, ichi, juˉichi gatsu no, su ju ichigatsu no,
13	yes um elev' eleve' eleventh month of elev' eleventh month of
14	anō hajime ni.
15	um begin at
16	(Yes, um, Nov, November, in the beginning of November.)
17 Professor:	A'
18	(Oh)
19 Mary:	Tsuitachi, sō desu. Tsutachi kara, a'
20	first that way Cop(Pol) first from uh
21	(The first, yes, from the first, uh.)
22 Professor:	Shit-te-imasu, shit-te-imasu.
23	know-Te-Prog know-Te-Prog
24	(I know about it. I know about it.)
25 Mary:	A sō desu ka. Ja, anō pre- conference workshop no'
26	Oh that way Cop(Pol) Q well then um pre- conference workshop of
27	hōhō* ga, um, kono, kono, zasshi* ni.
28	directions Nom um this this magazine in
29	(Oh. Well, um, the pre-conference workshop directions* are in this
30	magazine*.)
31 Professor:	Kore desu.
32	this Cop(Pol)
33	(In this.)
34 Mary:	Hai, sō, ja, dōzo. And . . . hai omoshiro deshō.
35	yes that way well then please and yes interesting probably
36	(Yes, well, go ahead. Please [look at it]. And . . . yes, it's interesting
37	isn't it.)
38 Professor:	[Silence] (adapted from Siegal 1996: 370–1)

Mary appears to be attempting to enact a relational identity where she and the professor have a more equal professional relationship by introducing news of a conference to the professor, thereby establishing their mutual research interests. This arose from her explicitly stated wish to enact a personal identity as a professional researcher, complementing her identity as a learner of Japanese, in interactions with her academic advisor. However, in so doing she is potentially 'impolite' since knowing about forthcoming conferences is an expected part of the professor's role as a researcher. Mary also neglects to use appropriate honorifics (for example, when asking whether the professor knows about the conference), which could also be perceived as 'impolite' by the professor. In other words, in attempting to take the place of an equal, Mary could be perceived by the professor as not paying sufficient respect to his place and thereby generating 'impoliteness'. This is suggested by the professor's response in line 22 where he impatiently repeats that he is in fact aware of the conference (shitte imasu, shitte imasu, 'I know about it, I know about it').

She also attempts to establish that they have a mutual interest in the conference near the end of the interaction in line 34 (hai omoshiro desho⁻, 'Yes, it's interesting isn't it'). This is also potentially 'impolite' since she is presuming what the professor might think about the conference which goes beyond the place of a more junior colleague. In other words, while Mary appears to be trying to enact a personal identity as a professional researcher, and a relational identity where she is on equal footing with the professor (at least in relation to research matters), her suggestions about the conference go beyond the place she stands as a research student from his perspective, since he is her advisor, not simply a colleague. The professor's discomfort with her attempts to enact such a place and thereby claim such an identity are suggested by his lack of verbal response in line 38 after Mary assumes they have a shared interest in the conference. While Mary may have indeed wanted to establish a professional identity with the professor, the potential 'impolite' implications arising in this interaction indicate that she was not able to successfully do so. (Haugh 2007: 668–72)

Task 8.10 Applying the concept to teaching
Design a five-minute presentation on Japanese politeness, impoliteness and 'place' that you could give to learners of Japanese. Make sure that you provide clear definitions of the basic concepts, and include one of the excerpts analysed. Consider whether you would want learners to replicate Japanese politeness.

Task 8.11 Trying out research
Write a questionnaire with ten open questions about the relation between role/status, and linguistic expressions that reflect social distance and/or power difference. Focus your questions on the situational context of your choice. Distribute the questionnaire to people from as many different cultural backgrounds as possible. Compare the results.

8.5 FURTHER READING TWO

Schneider, K. (2012), 'Appropriate behaviour across varieties of English', *Journal of Pragmatics*, **44: 1022–37.**

Schneider is of the opinion that we should talk not of politeness but of appropriateness. This article shows that small talk between strangers at a party is governed by diverging norms in different national varieties of English, viz. American English (AmE), Irish English (IrE) and English English (EngE). Schneider analysed how macro-social factors of regional, socio-economic, ethnic, gender and age variation related to norms of appropriate behaviour. His project asked 'How does each macro-social factor contribute to pragmatic variation?' He looked for answers to this question by asking informants to write a dialogue at a party involving themselves and a stranger, and analysing the opening turns.

The first findings were in the area of appropriateness across national varieties (AmE, IrE and EngE). In all three varieties, the following speech acts were used:

• GREETING (GREET)	Hi!
• APPROACH (APPR)	Great party, isn't it?
• DISCLOSE Identity (DISC-ID)	I'm Ashley.
• QUESTION Identity (QUE-ID)	What's your name?
• REMARK Identity (REM-ID)	I don't believe we have met.
• COMPLIMENT Appearance (COMPL-AP)	I really like your top.
• QUESTION Host (QUE-HO)	How do you know the hostess?

There were socio-pragmatic differences across varieties, as Schneider explains:

> GREETINGS occur with approximately the same frequency in all three varieties, while the APPROACH (e.g. Great party, isn't it?) is favoured by speakers of IrE and DISCLOSE Identity (e.g. I'm Ashley.) by speakers of AmE. These two acts play only a minor role in the other two varieties, i.e. in EngE and AmE, and in EngE and IrE respectively.
>
> More specific sociopragmatic differences emerge when focusing on the initial turns at talk, which display variety-preferential opening patterns. More than half of all speakers of EngE (56.7%) start their dialogue with a bare GREETING (e.g. Hi.). By contrast, 60.0% of the speakers of AmE use a GREETING which is followed by giving their name (DISC-ID) and in some cases also an explicit request of the interlocutor's name (QUE-ID) or, alternatively, a phrase marking the social distance between the dialogue partners (REM-ID), as in 'Hi. My name is Danielle.' (What's yours? / I don't believe we have met.) Finally, almost three quarters of the speakers of IrE (73.3%) open their dialogues with a GREETING combined with an APPROACH, e.g. 'Hi! Great party, isn't it?' (cf. Schneider, 2010a for further details).
>
> These diverging preferences in the opening turns reveal different interpretations of the communicative task at hand. Speakers of EngE predominantly focus on the discourse position. For them, opening the

conversation seems to have the highest priority. Hence, they initially use only a
GREETING, as at the beginning of any other conversation. For Americans,
on the other hand, the speaker constellation seems to be salient. While they also
use a GREETING, they are mainly concerned with identities, specifically names.
For them, getting to know a stranger is the task which has priority.
GREETINGS are also employed initially by the speakers of IrE, but they are the
only group who in their opening turns overwhelmingly refer to the occasion, i.e.
the party, which is (overwhelmingly) positively evaluated. (Schneider 2012: 1032)

Schneider then goes on to discuss his findings vis-à-vis appropriateness across social
varieties: age and gender differences in the USA. Here, the speech acts were:

- GREETING (GREET)   Hi!
- DISCLOSE Identity (DISC-ID)   I'm Ashley.
- QUESTION Identity (QUE-ID)   What's your name?
- QUESTION After You (QUE-AU)   How are you doing?

He compared the responses of male and female 13–14 year olds and 18–22 year olds:

Obviously, boys and girls in these two age groups have different notions of
appropriateness. Their views diverge as to how to behave verbally in the same
type of situation, i.e. specifically when opening a conversation with a
complete stranger at a party. Greetings seem to be less important for males
than for females. In both age groups, females prefer proper introductions,
whereas males favour less committing questions such as How are you
doing? or What's up? In this connection, it is worth mentioning that
utterances explicitly marking the situation as a meeting between strangers
and thus motivating an exchange of names, e.g. I don't believe we have met (an
act which occurs only infrequently in this subcorpus), are used exclusively by
female speakers. Hence females also seem to be more formal than males.
Comparing the two age groups reveals further interesting differences. In
the older group, males use more DISC-IDs and females more QUE-AUs than
the males and females in the younger group. Thus, male and female behaviour
become more similar (and more adult) as speakers grow older. Another striking
result is the clear drop in the frequency of QUE-ID, i.e. the act explicitly asking
the addressee's name. This face-threatening act seems immature and driven by
childlike curiosity which ignores the needs of the conversational partner. It is
therefore not surprising that this act is reduced to relative insignificance among
young adults of both sexes. Young adults (like older adults) seem to rely more on
the experience that once speakers say their name their interlocutors feel obliged
to reciprocate. (2012: 1034)

Task 8.12 Applying the concept to teaching

Design a task for a lower intermediate class of 13–14-year-old boys and girls that will ask them to enact the party greeting scenario using the polite formulae that this article describes. Keep in mind that:

- the project had boys greeting boys and girls greeting girls
- the young boys used different functions and forms from the girls

Task 8.13 Trying out research

Ask as many people as possible to write a short dialogue between people who have met at a party, but who are now leaving. Make it clear that you want to hear the last few words that they exchange before departing. Ask them to indicate their gender and age group (under 15, 15–30, 30–45, over 45). Analyse the differences according to gender and age. Present your findings to a group of people and make a note of their questions and feedback.

8.6 SUMMARY

This chapter has introduced you to theories of politeness:

- Brown and Levinson's face-saving model
- Leech's polite conversational maxims model
- Spencer-Oatey's rapport-management model
- Watts's model of appropriateness

It has explored theories of impoliteness:

- Culpeper's anatomy of impoliteness, conventionalised impoliteness formulae and implicational impoliteness
- Watts's politic–non-politic model
- Mills's systematic impoliteness
- Archer's unintentional face damage

It has taken into account different variables:

- Situational context – activity type, formality and size of the imposition
- Interpersonal context – status, gender, age, class, education, familiarity
- Cultural background – face, maxims, indirectness and deference

You have considered applications of the theories to your English classroom

- No need to teach it? Immoral to? Essential to?
- Classroom tasks – role-play, presentations, guessing game

8.7 ADDITIONAL READINGS

The following texts are the classics in this field and all merit close examination:

Bousfield, D., and M. Locher (2008), *Impoliteness in Language: Studies on its Interplay with Power in Theory and Practice*, Berlin: Mouton de Gruyter.

Culpeper, J. (2011), *Impoliteness: Using Language to Cause Offence*, Cambridge: Cambridge University Press.

Leech, G. (1983), *Principles of Pragmatics*, New York: Longman.

Brown, P., and S. Levinson (1987), *Politeness: Some Universals in Language Usage*, Cambridge: Cambridge University Press.

9

CONCLUSION

INTRODUCTION

This volume has introduced you to a series of approaches to understanding and analysing language, with a view to helping you as a teacher of EFL improve your teaching and consider directions that your research could go in. It is hoped that you have been able to relate the issues to your teaching context, and to think about ways to adapt the theories to your practical needs in the classroom.

This chapter revisits the themes of the volume to point to a few of the new directions that are emerging in sociolinguistics and pragmatics research. If you are going to write a Masters dissertation, undertake a PhD or simply begin a new research project, you might like to start by thinking about some of the issues listed in Section 9.1.

The chapter also emphasises current trends and future directions of ELT, related to the approaches to understanding language explored in this volume. If, in your teaching context, you are in a position to develop a new EFL curriculum, build new elements into teaching materials or design a new test, or you simply want to keep up with recent thinking in methodology or look for new ideas in your classroom, you might like to evaluate the ideas listed in Section 9.2.

9.1 NEW DIRECTIONS FOR RESEARCH

In Corpus Linguistics research:

- An important development is the qualitative and functional dimension of CL, which involves information about the context. Researchers are developing ways of labelling the database and tagging the linguistic items in such a way that concordances and KWIC searches bring up the social background of the communicators, the roles and relational dimensions, the functions and intentions, as well other situational factors. This will add a more qualitative strength to CL's quantitative potential.
- Whereas CL used to be considered an approach in itself, it is now considered by many as a tool that can be used in conjunction with pragmatics approaches to data analysis, such as ET, CA, SAT, CP and im/politeness theories. A great deal of research in these areas uses CL.

177

- Research on multimedia corpora is advancing. Some researchers are interested in the frequency and collocation of stress, intonation and tone, and the meaning that they carry. Others are looking at body language (head and hand movement) and how it combines with co-occurring words and clusters. Others trace whole body movement and language, as the communicators go about their daily activities.

In Global Englishes research:

- ELF as an area of study is now established: the ELF conference series began in 2008, and *The Journal of English as a Lingua Franca (JELF)* was founded in 2011.
- It is to be expected that there will be further development to the Vienna-Oxford International Corpus of English (VOICE) including updated versions.
- The recently established Centre for Global Englishes at the University of Southampton produces and disseminates research in the area.
- There are increasing calls for research into GE in assessment, since language tests, such as TOEIC, TOEFL, IELTS and CPE, continue to focus on the NES.

In intercultural pragmatics research:

- At the centre is the issue of norms. There has tended to be an unwritten assumption that a language learner must adapt to the norms of the target culture but these norms are now being questioned. There are numerous English-speaking cultures, and this appears to provide a considerable dilemma to the EFL teacher. In many ways, this issue runs in parallel to that of Global Englishes. There is a clear need for ongoing research into the pragmatic norms of the various English-speaking cultures, whether these are Inner Circle cultures or those of English as a Lingua Franca speakers.
- Research on interlanguage pragmatics is increasingly focusing on individual differences in pragmatic development, and there is also a need for further research into the variation in speed of development between different aspects of L2 pragmatics, including different sociopragmatic and pragmalinguistic elements of the target language.

In context and registers research:

- There is a continuing need for the development of corpora which focus on specific registers, and provide up-to-date data to enable a study of current usage, as existing corpora are always becoming dated.
- There is a clear need for more research into the new electronic registers. In particular, there is a lack of research on the way 'brief' forms of communication such as Twitter, and multimodal forms of communication such as Facebook may be affecting the way language is used. As the spoken–written distinction has been identified as the most fundamental factor in register differences, research is needed into

whether electronic forms of communication tend more towards spoken or written communication, or whether a distinct 'third' form of communication is being developed.

In Exchange Theory and Conversation Analysis research:

- CA is being used more than ET in the analysis of classroom discourse, where it has been combined with CL. CA is also being used to analyse interaction in institutional and workplace settings, and media talk in broadcasting.
- There is a vast ongoing literature on intercultural CA studies that takes into account the fact that variation in the structure of interaction from one culture to another can cause pragmatic misunderstandings.
- CA is being used to examine the structure of internet interaction, for example, written online asynchronous discourse and synchronous chat.

In Speech Act Theory and Cooperative Principle research:

- SAT, CP and Relevance Theory are now used widely in studies that compare Global Englishes or other languages, and that bring in social variables such as gender and age.
- Studies are also examining the speech acts and cooperative maxims of online genres such as chat rooms and discussion forums.

In Politeness Theories research:

- The greatest development in politeness theory is currently impoliteness theory. Debates abound as to whether impoliteness includes intention, whether language can be intrinsically impolite, and whether routinised impoliteness is still impolite. There is a need for further research in this area, especially taking into account social and cultural variables.
- There is a need for research into the borderline between politeness and impoliteness.

9.2 NEW DIRECTIONS FOR ENGLISH LANGUAGE TEACHING

Corpus Linguistics in TESOL:

- More and more EFL teachers now use corpora to inform their teaching of socio-cultural and pragmatic meaning. Corpora can be consulted to find answers to learner questions, as in 'What's the difference between "Howdy" and "Hi"?', as well as to satisfy the teacher's own curiosity, as in 'What is used most in polite requests – "would you mind doing" or "do you mind doing", and is there any difference in usage?'
- There has been an increase in data-driven learning (DDL). Teachers present learners with a selection of concordance lines and help them to discover how words are used and infer the rules for themselves by inductive reasoning. Alternatives have

to be used, to bring variety. For example, learners can be invited to search a whole corpus for words that each one personally has problems with, or a competitive element can be introduced as in 'Who can find first the most usual response to "You look good" in the spoken part of COCA and say whether that response is the same as we use?'

Global Englishes in TESOL:

- EFL classrooms, TESOL teacher-education programmes and tests such as CELTA, DELTA rarely incorporate the findings of research in Global Englishes. Although an increasing number of teacher-education and language-teaching coursebooks include sections or chapters on the spread of English, there continues be a need for GE awareness in the classroom.

English across cultures in TESOL:

- Research around bilingualism and code-switching feeds into the ongoing debate concerning the use of the L1 in the L2 classroom. It is clear that research points to the L1 as a valuable resource for both teachers and learners, and this is something that can itself be a source of negotiation between the teacher and learners in the classroom (that is to say, they can negotiate when to use the L1 and for what purposes).
- There in an increasing awareness of the importance of teaching pragmatics in the second language classroom. Textbooks are slowly catching up with this trend but teachers with access to the worldwide web have almost limitless resources of authentic materials which can be used to raise learners' awareness of cross-cultural pragmatics.
- It has also been shown that the development of L2 pragmatic competence mostly requires explicit intervention on the part of instructors. Increasingly, resources are being developed to assist teachers with instruction in L2 pragmatics.

Context and registers in TESOL:

- The ongoing development of understanding in the linguistic and situational features of registers is clearly paralleled in the development of the fields of English for Academic and Specific Purposes.
- The increased use of corpora in register analysis provides stronger empirical evidence of the features of registers; this in turn is leading to a trend for textbooks based on corpus data. Written texts and spoken dialogues used in textbooks will either be directly taken from authentic materials or carefully adapted from them.
- In terms of pedagogy, language awareness plays a particularly strong role in the case of registers. Differences between registers often lack salience and therefore effective teaching on registers often needs to be explicit rather than implicit. The use of explicit-inductive methods may be particularly important.

In other words, the teacher designs a task using authentic texts which guides learners towards an understanding of the way language is used in the targeted registers.

Exchange Theory and Conversation Analysis in TESOL:

- ET and CA are being used in EFL teacher development. Teachers are encouraged to watch a video-recording of their own teaching, and analyse their interaction. For example, they observe how their learners react to the various types of Initiation that they use (elicit, nominate, check etc.) or what proportion of their Feedback is positive and how the learners behave, and debate whether to change their teaching techniques and how.
- Coursebooks are increasingly making learners aware of the routine structure of interaction, rather than teaching isolated utterances.

Speech Act Theory and the Cooperative Principle in TESOL:

- Most coursebooks now contain unit descriptions containing speech acts, such as 'Asking for directions' and 'Telling the time'. Thanks to the influence of corpus findings, books are including more authentic language, with its elisions, colloquialisms etc., to illustrate speech acts and thus no longer suggest that there is a 1:1 form:function correspondence.
- Teaching materials that contain reference to the cooperative principle are few and far between, possibly because of the culture-specific nature of this theory. There is a need for coursebooks that encourage learners to get away from surface meaning and look for underlying meaning.

Politeness Theories in TESOL:

- Politeness formulae such as 'please' and 'thank you' have always been present in ELT, and now courses and materials increasingly contain polite hedges and mitigating expressions in their lexical syllabus. It is the deeper-level value-laden aspects of politeness that are more difficult to explain and teach in coursebooks because the notion of face and what constitutes politeness varies from culture to culture. Teachers are being encouraged to value their own culture and make cultural comparisons.
- What needs to be debated next is the extent to which the findings about impoliteness should be included in teaching materials, and how.

It should be added that rapid technological developments in language teaching will be influential in our understanding of language and the way that it is taught and learned. Examples of questions worth considering are:

- To what extent does online language learning enhance or jeopardise the teaching of fluency?

- Can the flipped classroom, which delivers instruction online outside the classroom and moves 'homework' into the classroom, enable language learners to understand Global Englishes, the Cooperative Principle, Politeness Theories etc.?
- In what way can EFL teachers exploit social media, such as microblogging, wikis, community of practice sites, social networking sites and virtual social worlds to help with language learning?

Finally, in the Introduction to this volume, we said:

> you will learn how to evaluate TESOL methodology, curriculum, course and materials in terms of cooperation, politeness, conversation structure, ideology, power, varieties, domains and genre. Importantly, you will consider ways of teaching with these issues in mind, and designing tasks and lessons with a sociological and cultural focus.

This achieved, we wish you all the best in your teaching and researching careers.

GLOSSARY

accommodation theory	study of the way speakers adapt their language to accommodate to their interlocutors
act	the small Exchange Theory unit: an act can be an Initiation (I), a Response (R) or a Follow-up (F)
adjacency pair	a unit within Conversation Analysis, which consists of a pair of acts, such as when the speaker makes 'an invitation' and the interlocutor's words constitute 'an acceptance'
annotation	tagging individual words or word clusters to indicate features of the lexis, grammar, functions and interaction
bilingualism	a bilingual speaker has two languages as a linguistic repertoire
cluster tool	Corpus Linguistics tool which displays words that regularly recur in patterns or chunks
code-switching	alternation between two or more languages within the same conversation
coherence	the degree to which a text or unit of discourse 'makes sense' as a whole
cohesion	the way in which grammatical and lexical elements link a text together to make it meaningful
colligation	grammar that usually surrounds the word investigated in a concordance
collocation	words frequently co-occurring with the word investigated in a concordance
community of practice	group of people with a common interest and mutual engagement, sharing knowledge, values and beliefs, and maintaining membership through their linguistic and behavioural social practices
concordance	Corpus Linguistics tool which lists key words in context (KWIC), and shows the collocation and colligation
conversational implicature	a feature of the Cooperative Principle, in which speakers flout the maxims and expect hearers

	to infer the meaning that they imply under the surface meaning of the words
cooperative maxim infringing	when speakers fail to observe the Cooperative Principle because they cannot speak informatively, truthfully, relevantly or clearly, for physical or psychological reasons
cooperative maxim flouting	when speakers expect hearers to infer the meaning that they imply under the surface meaning of the words – this is conversational implicature, a feature of the Cooperative Principle
cooperative maxim opting out	when speakers fail to observe the Cooperative Principle because they cannot speak informatively, truthfully, relevantly or clearly, for political, legal or ethical reasons
cooperative maxim violation	when speakers do not observe the Cooperative Principle maxims and know that the hearer thinks that they *are* observing them
corpora	electronic databases of authentic texts selected according to defined research purposes and stored in computers
corpus design	framework behind a corpus that reflects the designer's rationale and provides a representative sample of a larger population
cross-cultural pragmatics	comparison of the way language is used in different cultural groups
deixis	words or expressions which vary in meaning depending on who uses them, and the time and place in which they are used
direct speech act	speech act in which speakers communicate the literal meaning of the words
EFL	English as a Foreign Language. This book uses this term to cover English as a Second or Additional Language.
ellipsis	when a word or words are not used in an utterance, usually because they are communicatively redundant
ELT	English Language Teaching. This book uses ELT to cover all types of teaching: teaching English for Specific Purposes, English as an Additional Language etc.
exchange	Exchange Theory unit which consists of three moves. A series of exchanges constitute a transaction.
Expanding Circle (EC)	countries, other than the IC and OC, where English has spread as the result of globalisation

Face Threatening Act	an act such as an order, request, offer, promise, disagreement or complaint that threatens positive or negative face
face-saving	a central feature of Politeness Theory which depends on strategies that avoid threats to positive and negative face
felicity conditions	conditions that need to be met in order for speech acts to be carried out successfully
floor-holding devices	words or fillers that stop a new speaker taking the floor from the current speaker
foreigner talk	speaker's use of excessively simplified language when trying to accommodate the hearer
genre	specific linguistic features which are used to structure complete texts
Global Englishes	a paradigm for exploring the worldwide spread of English, including World Englishes and English as a Lingua Franca
illocutionary force	what is done in uttering particular words, the immediate function of the words
indigenised	nativised variety which has been influenced by the local culture and language of the people who speak that variety
indirect speech act	speech act in which speakers communicate a different meaning from the apparent surface meaning
Inner Circle (IC)	English-speakers of the countries which are associated with 'native' varieties, e.g. UK, USA, Canada
intercultural pragmatics	the way language is used in communication between speakers from different contexts, involving communication between a non-native and native speakers, or between non-native speakers using a language as a lingua franca
interlanguage pragmatics	study of the development of pragmatic competence in a second language
interruption	in spoken interaction, the point at which a new speaker's words cause the preceding speaker to stop speaking before they have finished their utterance
keyword lists	Corpus Linguistics tool, comparisons of wordlists from smaller corpora against that of a reference corpus, showing frequency differences
lingua franca	a contact language used between speakers of different mother tongues

linguistic imperialism	the dominance of one language over others; it usually has political and economic implications
locutionary act	the act of saying something, the utterance of words
mock-impoliteness	banter and teasing – an offensive way of being friendly
move	Exchange Theory unit which consists of Initiation (I), Response (R) and Follow-up or Feedback (F) acts. An exchange is made up of several moves.
multilingualism	a multilingual speaker has more than two languages as a linguistic repertoire
nativised	indigenised variety which has been influenced by the local culture and language of the people who speak that variety
negative face	the desire not to be imposed upon or impeded
Outer Circle (OC)	countries which have been colonised by Inner Circle countries, where English has an official status along with the national language
overlap	in spoken interaction, the point at which a new speaker's words run simultaneously with the preceding speaker's
pause	silence within a speaker's spoken utterance or between speakers' turns, usually indicated by a number referring to the number of seconds' silence
performative	speech act that contains a verb that names the function
perlocutionary effect	what is done by uttering particular words, the longer term effect on the hearer
positive face	the desire to be liked or appreciated
pragmalinguistics	the way words and expressions are used in specific contexts and what the words and expressions mean in those contexts
pragmatic transfer	the use of pragmatics from your first language in a second language situation
register	a variety associated with certain situational features
sequence	stretches of language in spoken interaction with a particular function such as pre-sequences, insertion sequences, opening sequences and closing sequences
sociopragmatics	the study of what people do in specific contexts; this typically involves the identification of rules and tendencies of behaviour in specific contexts and cultures

Standard English	the variety of English that has developed into the accepted norm. Standard languages are decided by social, political and cultural factors rather than necessarily linguistic ones.
TESOL	Teaching English to Speakers of Other Languages. This book uses this term to refer to teacher education.
transaction	Exchange Theory unit which consists of a string of exchanges. A series of transactions make up a lesson.
transition relevance place	the point where one turn ends and another starts in spoken interaction
turn-taking	an interactive feature studied in Conversation Analysis: the way that one person finishes what they are saying and cedes the floor to the next person, with normally only one person speaking at a time
variety	a form of language with common features – the categorisation is decided based on region, social class, age, gender etc.
wordlist	Corpus Linguistics tool that lists words in alphabetical or frequency order
World Englishes (WE)	a research paradigm that mainly focuses on investigating varieties that predominantly belong to the Outer Circle

BIBLIOGRAPHY

Adolphs, S. (2008), *Corpus and Context: Investigating Pragmatic Functions in Spoken Language*, Amsterdam: John Benjamins.

Aijmer, K. (2009), *Corpora and Language Teaching*, London: Continuum.

Ali, S. (2009), 'Teaching English as an International Language (EIL) in the Gulf Corporation Council (GCC) countries: the brown man's burden', in F. Sharifian (ed.), *English as an International Language: Prspectives and Pedagogical Issues*, Bristol: Multilingual Matters, pp. 34–57.

Alsagoff, L., S. McKay, G. Hu and W. Renandya (eds) (2012), *Principles and Practices for Teaching English as an International Language*, New York: Routledge.

AntConc, http://www.antlab.sci.waseda.ac.jp/antconc_index.html (accessed 21 January 2013).

Archer, D. (2008), 'Verbal aggression in the historical courtroom: related or synonymous?', in D. Bousfield and M. Locher (eds), *Impoliteness in Language: Studies on its Interplay with Power in Theory and Practice*, Berlin: Mouton de Gruyter.

Aston, G., S. Bernardini and D. Stewart (2004), *Corpora and Language Learners*, London: Continuum.

Auerbach, E. (1993), 'Reexamining English only in the ESL classroom', *TESOL Quarterly*, 27(1): 9–32.

Austin, J. (1962), *How To Do Things With Words*, London: Oxford University Press.

Baik, M., and R. Shim (2002), 'Teaching World Englishes via the Internet', *World Englishes*, 21(3): 427–30.

Baker, C. (2007), *A Parents' and Teachers' Guide to Bilingualism*, Bristol: Multilingual Matters.

The Bank of English, http://www.collins.co.uk/books.aspx?group=153 (accessed 21 January 2013).

Bardovi-Harlig, K. (2001), 'Evaluating the empirical evidence: grounds for instruction in pragmatics?', in K. Rose and G. Kasper (eds), *Pragmatics in Language Teaching*, London: Routledge.

Bardovi-Harlig, K., and Z. Dörnyei (1998), 'Do language learners recognize pragmatic violations? Pragmatic versus grammatical awareness in instructed L2 learning', *TESOL Quarterly*, 32: 233–62.

Bardovi-Harlig, K., and R. Mahan-Taylor (eds) (2003), *Teaching Pragmatics*, Washington, DC: United States Department of State.

Bargiela-Chiappini, F., and D. Kádár (eds) (2011), *Politeness across Cultures*, Basingstoke: Palgrave Macmillan.

Barraja-Rohan, A. (2011), 'Using conversation analysis in the second language classroom to teach interactional competence', *Language Teaching Research*, 15(4): 479–507.

Barron, A. (2003), *Acquisition in Interlanguage Pragmatics: Learning How to Do Things with Words in a Study Context Abroad*, Amsterdam: John Benjamins.

Benjamin, http://www.Benjamin.com/jbp/catalogs/corpus.linguistics.eur.2009.pdf (accessed 21 January 2013).

Bhatia, V. (1993), *Analysing Genre: Language Use in Professional Settings*, London: Longman.

Biber, D. (1988), *Variation across Speech and Writing*, Cambridge: Cambridge University Press.

Biber, D. (2006), *University Language: A Corpus-based Study of Spoken and Written Registers*, Amsterdam: John Benjamins.

Biber, D., and S. Conrad (2009), *Register, Genre, and Style*, Cambridge: Cambridge University Press.

Biber, D., S. Johansson, G. Leech, S. Conrad and E. Finnegan (1999), *Longman Grammar of Spoken and Written English*, London: Longman.

Bodba, S.A. (2010), 'Local networks in the formation and development of West African English', in M. Saxena and T. Omoniyi (eds), *Contending with Globalization in World Englishes*, Bristol: Multilingual Matters.

Bolton, K. (2009), 'Varieties of World Englishes', in B. Kachru, Y. Kachru and C.L. Nelson (eds), *The Handbook of World Englishes*, Malden, MA: Wiley-Blackwell.

Bolton, K., and B. Kachru (2006), *World Englishes: Critical Concepts in Linguistics*, Abingdon: Routledge.

Bonacina, F., and J. Gafaranga (2011), '"Medium of instruction" versus "medium of classroom interaction": language choice in a French complementary school classroom in Scotland', *International Journal of Bilingual Education and Bilingualism*, 14(3): 319–34.

Bousfield, D. (2008), *Impoliteness in Interaction*, Amsterdam: John Benjamins.

Bousfield, D., and M. Locher (2008), *Impoliteness in Language: Studies on its Interplay with Power in Theory and Practice*, Berlin: Mouton de Gruyter.

Bowles, H. (2006), 'Bridging the gap between conversation analysis and ESP – an applied study of the opening sequences of NS and NNS service telephone calls', *English for Specific Purposes*, 25: 332–57.

The British National Corpus Sampler, http://www.natcorp.ox.ac.uk (accessed 21 January 2013).

Brown, J. (1995), *The Elements of Language Curriculum*, Boston: Heinle and Heinle.

Brown, L. (2011), 'Korean honorifics and "revealed", "ignored" and "suppressed" aspects of Korean culture and politeness', in F. Bargiela-Chiappini and D. Kádár (eds), *Politeness across Cultures*, Basingstoke: Palgrave Macmillan.

Brown, P., and S. Levinson (1987), *Politeness: Some Universals in Language Usage*, Cambridge: Cambridge University Press.

Bruthiaux, P. (2003), 'Squaring the circles: issues in modelling English worldwide', *International Journal of Applied Linguistics*, 13(2): 159–78.

The Business Letter Corpus, http://www.someya-net.com/concordancer/index.html (accessed 21 January 2013).

Button, G. (1987), 'Moving out of closings', in G. Button and J. Lee, *Talk and Social Organization*, Bristol: Multilingual Matters.

The Cambridge and Nottingham Corpus of Spoken English (CANCODE), http://www.not tingham.ac.uk/cral/projects/index.aspx (accessed 14 July 2014)

The Cambridge International Corpus (CIC), http://www.englishprofile.org/index.php/corpus (accessed 14 July 2014)

The Cambridge Learner Corpus of ESOL,http://www.cambridge.org/elt/corpus/learner_corpus.htm (accessed 21 January 2013).

Camilleri, A. (1996), 'Language values and identities: code switching in secondary classrooms in Malta', *Linguistics and Education*, 8: 83–103.

Campoy, M., B. Belles-Fortuno and M. Gea-Valor (2010), *Corpus-Based Approaches to English Language Teaching*, London: Continuum.

Canagarajah, A.S. (1999), *Resisting Linguistic Imperialism in English Teaching*, Oxford: Oxford University Press.

Canagarajah, A.S. (2005), 'Introduction', in A.S. Canagarajah (ed.), *Reclaiming the Local in Language Policy and Practice*, Mahwah, NJ: Lawrence Erlbaum.

Canagarajah, A.S. (2011), 'Translanguaging in the classroom: emerging issues for research and pedagogy', *Applied Linguistics Review*, 2: 1–28.

Carter, R., and S. Adolphs (2007), 'Linking the verbal and the visual: new directions for corpus linguistics', in O. Mason and A. Gerbig (eds), *Language in Context: Papers in Honour of Michael Stubbs*, Tubingen: University of Tubingen Press.

Carter, R., and M. McCarthy (1995), 'Grammar and spoken language', *Applied Linguistics*, 16(2): 141–58.

Carter, R., and M. McCarthy (1997), *Exploring Spoken English*, Cambridge: Cambridge University Press.

Carter, R., and M. McCarthy (2006), *Cambridge Grammar of English*, Cambridge: Cambridge University Press.

Celce-Murcia, M., and D. Larsen-Freeman (1999), *The Grammar Book: An ESL/EFL Teacher's Course*, 2nd edn, Boston: Heinle and Heinle.

Celce-Murcia, M., and E. Olshtain (2000), *Discourse and Context in Language Teaching: A Guide for Language Teachers*, Cambridge: Cambridge University Press.

Chapman, S. (2011), *Pragmatics*, Basingstoke: Palgrave Macmillan.

Cheng, W. (2012), *Exploring Corpus Linguistics: Language in Action*, London: Routledge.

Christie, C. (2002), 'Politeness and the linguistic construction of gender in parliament: an analysis of transgressions and apology behavior', *Working Papers on the Web*, 3, http://extra.shu.ac.uk/wpw/politeness/christie.htm (accessed 1 February 2011).

Cobb, T., Lexical Tutor, http://www.lextutor.ca/vp/eng/ (accessed 11 November 2012).

COBUILD, http://www.harpercollins.co.uk/aboutharpercollins/Imprints/collins/Pages/Collins.aspx (accessed 22 January 2013).

Cogo, A. (2009), 'Accommodating difference in ELF conversations: a study of pragmatic strategies', in A. Mauranen and E. Ranta (eds), *English as a Lingua Franca: Studies and Findings*, Newcastle upon Tyne: Cambridge Scholars.

Cogo, A. (2012), 'English as a Lingua Franca: concepts, use and implications', *ELT Journal*, 66(1): 97–105.

Cogo, A., and M. Dewey (2006), 'Efficiency in ELF communication: from pragmatic motives to lexico-grammatical innovation', *Nordic Journal of English Studies*, 5(2): 59–93.

Cogo, A., and M. Dewey (2012), *Analysing English as a Lingua Franca: A Corpus-driven Investigation*, London: Continuum.

ConcApp Concordancer, http://www.edict.com.hk/PUB/concapp/ (accessed 21 January 2013).

Conrad, S., and D. Biber (2001), *Variation in English: Multi-dimensional Studies*, London: Longman.

Cook, G. (1989), *Discourse*, Oxford: Oxford University Press.

Corbett, J. (2003), *An Intercultural Approach to English Language Teaching*, Bristol: Multilingual Matters.

The Corpus of Contemporary American English (COCA),http://www.americancorpus.org/ (accessed 21 January 2013).

Cotterill, J. (2007), '"I think he was kind of shouting or something": uses and abuses of vagueness in the British courtroom', in J. Cutting (ed.), *Vague Language Explored*, Basingstoke: Palgrave Macmillan.

Coulthard, M. (1977), *An Introduction to Discourse Analysis*, London: Longman.

Council of Europe (2012), *Council of Europe Language Education Policy*, http://www.coe.int/t/
dg4/Linguistic/Division_EN.asp (accessed 2 November 2012).

Coupland, N. (1995), 'Accommodation theory', in J. Verscheuren, J.-O. Östman and
J. Blommaert (eds), *Handbook of Pragmatics Manual*, Amsterdam: John Benjamins,
pp. 21–6.

Creese, A., and A.J. Blackledge (2010), 'Translanguaging in the bilingual classroom: a pedagogy for learning and teaching?', *The Modern Language Journal*, 94(1): 103–15.

Creese, A., A.J. Blackledge, T. Barac, A. Bhatt, S. Hamid, L. Wei, V. Lytra, P. Martin, C.J. Wu,
D. Yagcioglu (2011), 'Separate and flexible bilingualism in complementary schools: multiple
language practices in interrelationship', *Journal of Pragmatics*, 43(5): 1196–208.

Cruse, D.A. (2000), *Meaning in Language: An Introduction to Semantics and Pragmatics*, New
York: Oxford University Press.

Crystal, D. (2003), *English as a Global Language*, Cambridge: Cambridge University Press.

Crystal, D. (2006), *Language and the Internet*, 2nd edn, Cambridge: Cambridge University
Press.

Culpeper, J. (1996), 'Towards an anatomy of impoliteness', *Journal of Pragmatics*, 25: 349–67.

Culpeper, J. (2005), 'Impoliteness and entertainment in the television quiz show: The Weakest
Link', *Journal of Politeness Research: Language, Behaviour, Culture*, 1: 35–72.

Culpeper, J. (2008), 'Reflections on impoliteness, relational work and power', in D. Bousfield
and M. Locher (eds), *Impoliteness in Language: Studies on its Interplay with Power in Theory
and Practice*, Berlin: Mouton de Gruyter.

Culpeper, J. (2011), *Impoliteness: Using Language to Cause Offence*, Cambridge: Cambridge
University Press.

Cutting, J. (2000), *Analysing the Language of Discourse Communities*, Oxford: Elsevier Science.

Cutting, J. (2006), 'Spoken grammar: vague language and EAP', in R. Hughes (ed.), *TESOL,
Spoken English, Applied Linguistics and TESOL: Challenges for Theory and Practice*,
Basingstoke: Palgrave Macmillan.

Cutting, J. (ed.) (2007), *Vague Language Explored*, Basingstoke: Palgrave Macmillan.

Cutting, J. (2008a), *Pragmatics and Discourse: A Resource Book for Students*, 2nd edn, London:
Routledge.

Cutting, J. (2008b), 'Stance and relations in written communications of an academic group',
unpublished presentation at Inter-Varietal Applied Corpus Studies (IVACS) Group
Conference, University of Limerick.

Cutting, J. (2009), 'Edinburgh Academic Spoken English (EDASE) Corpus: tutor interaction
with East Asian students', unpublished presentation at the Corpus Linguistics Conference
2009, Lancaster.

Davies, A. (2006), 'The native speaker in applied linguistics', in A. Davies and C. Elder (eds),
The Handbook of Applied Linguistics, Oxford: Blackwell.

Dragon Naturally Speaking, http://www.nuance.co.uk/naturallyspeaking/ (accessed 21
November 2012).

Eelen, G. (2001), *A Critique of Politeness Theories*, Manchester: St Jerome Publishing.

Eggins, S., and D. Slade (1997), *Analysing Casual Conversation*, London: Cassell.

ELAN, http://www.lat-mpi.eu/tools/elan/elan-description (accessed 21 November 2012).

Farr, F. (2002), 'Classroom interrogations – how productive?', *The Teacher Trainer*, 16(1):
19–23.

Ferguson, G. (2003), 'Classroom codeswitching in post-colonial contexts: functions, attitudes
and policies', *AILA Review*, 16(1): 38–51.

Ferguson, G. (2009), 'What next? Towards an agenda for classroom codeswitching research',
International Journal of Bilingual Education and Bilingualism, 12(2): 231–41.

Fordyce, K. (2013), 'The differential effects of explicit and implicit instruction on EFL learn-ers' use of epistemic stance', *Applied Linguistics*, advance online publication, doi: 10.1093/applin/ams076.

Fox, K. (2004), *Watching the English*, London: Hodder and Stoughton.

Galloway, N., and H. Rose (forthcoming 2015), *Introducing Global Englishes*, Abingdon: Routledge.

Garfinkel, H. (1967), *Studies in Ethnomethodology*, Englewood Cliffs, NJ: Prentice-Hall.

Gavioli, L. (2005), *Exploring Corpora for ESP*, London: Continuum.

Giles, H., A. Mulac, J.J. Bradac and P. Johnson (1987), 'Speech accommodation theory: the next decade and beyond', in M. McLaughlin (ed.), *Communication Yearbook*, 10, Newbury Park, CA: Sage, pp. 13–48.

Goffman, E. (1967), *Interaction Ritual: Essays on Face-to-Face Behaviour*, Garden City, NY: Doubleday.

Goffman, E. (1972 [1955]), 'On face-work: an analysis of ritual elements in social interac-tion', in J. Laver and S. Hutcheson (eds), *Communication in Face-to-Face Interaction*, Harmondsworth: Penguin.

Goffman, E. (1981), *Forms of Talk*, Oxford: Basil Blackwell.

Graddol, D. (1997), *The Future of English*, London: The British Council.

Graddol, D. (2006), *English Next*, London: The British Council.

Graddol, D., D. Leith and J. Swann (1996), *English: History, Diversity and Change*, London: Routledge.

Grainger, K. (2011), 'Indirectness in Zimbabwean English: a study of intercultural communi-cation in the UK', in F. Bargiela-Chiappini and D. Kádár (eds), *Politeness across Cultures*, Basingstoke: Palgrave Macmillan.

Grice, H. (1975), 'Logic and conversation', in P. Cole and J. Morgan (eds), *Pragmatics*, Syntax and Semantics, Vol. 3, New York: Academic Press, pp. 41–58.

Groom, C. (2012), 'Non-native attitudes towards teaching English as a lingua franca in Europe', *English Today*, 109(28, 1): 50–7.

Grundy, P. (2000), *Doing Pragmatics*, London: Edward Arnold.

Gu, Y. (2011), 'Modern Chinese politeness revisited', in F. Bargiela-Chiappini and D. Kádár (eds), *Politeness across Cultures*, Basingstoke: Palgrave Macmillan.

Günthner, S. (2000), 'Argumentation and resulting problems in the negotiation of rapport in a German-Chinese conversation', in H. Spencer-Oatey (ed.), *Culturally Speaking: Managing Rapport through Talk across Cultures*, London: Continuum.

Hall, J., and W. Eggington (2000), *The Scoiopolitics of English Language Teaching*, Bristol: Multilingual Matters.

Halliday, M.A.K., and R. Hasan (1976), *Cohesion in English*, London: Longman.

Harris, S. (2001), 'Being politically impolite: extending politeness theory to adversarial political discourse', *Discourse and Society*, 12(4): 451–72.

Hatch, E. (1992), *Discourse and Language Education*, Cambridge: Cambridge University Press.

Haugh, M. (2007), 'Emic conceptualisations of (im)politeness and face in Japanese: impli-cations for the discursive negotiation of second language learner identities', *Journal of Pragmatics*, 39: 657–80.

The HCRC Maptask Corpus, http://hcrc.ed.ac.uk/maptask/interface/ (accessed 21 January 2013).

Hill, T. (1997), 'The development of pragmatic competence in an EFL context', doctoral dis-sertation, Temple University, Japan, *Dissertation Abstracts International*, 58, 3905.

Holliday, A. (2005), *The Struggle to Teach English as an International Language*, Oxford: Oxford University Press.

Holmes, J. (1995), *Men, Women and Politeness*, London: Longman.

The Hong Kong Corpus of Spoken English,http://langbank.engl.polyu.edu.hk/HKCSE/HKCSE.htm (accessed 21 January 2013).

Hornby, N. (1998), *About a Boy*, London: Victor Gollancz.

Houtkoop-Steenstra, H. (1991), 'Opening sequences in Dutch telephone conversations', in D. Boden and D. Zimmerman (eds), *Talk and Social Structure*, Cambridge: Polity Press.

Huang, Y. (2007), *Pragmatics*, Oxford: Oxford University Press.

Hudson, R.A. (1996), *Sociolinguistics*, Cambridge: Cambridge University Press.

Hunt, G. (2010), 'Centrifugal and centripetal forces in the discourse of early years reading sessions', unpublished PhD thesis, University of Edinburgh.

IDEA, International Dialects of English Archive, http://web.ku.edu/~idea (accessed 15 June 2012).

Information on Corpus Building, http://www.corpus.bham.ac.uk/corpus-building.shtml (accessed 23 January 2013).

The International Corpus of English (ICE), http://www.ucl.ac.uk/english-usage/ice/ (accessed 21 January 2013).

Introduction to Corpus Linguistics, http://www.engl.polyu.edu.hk/corpuslinguist/corpus.htm (accessed 23 January 2013).

Jenkins, J. (2000), *The Phonology of English as an International Language: New Models, New Norms, New Goals*, Oxford: Oxford University Press.

Jenkins, J. (2003), *World Englishes: A Resource Book for Students*, London: Routledge.

Jenkins, J. (2006), 'Current perspectives on teaching World Englishes and English as lingua franca', *TESOL Quarterly*, 40(1): 157–81.

Jenkins, J. (2007), *English as a Lingua Franca: Attitude and Identity*, Oxford: Oxford University Press.

Jenkins, J. (2009), *World Englishes: A Resource Book for Students*, 2nd edn, London: Routledge.

Jenkins, J. (2012), 'English as a Lingua Franca from the classroom to the classroom', *ELT Journal*, 66(4): 486–94.

Jenkins, J., A. Cogo and M. Dewey (2011), 'Review of developments in research into English as a Lingua Franca', *Language Teaching*, 44(3): 281–315.

Jeon, E., and T. Kaya (2006), 'Effects of L2 instruction on interlanguage pragmatic development: a meta-analysis', in J.M. Norris and L. Ortega (eds), *Synthesizing Research on Language Learning and Teaching*, Amsterdam: John Benjamins, pp. 165–211.

Johns, T. (1991), '"Should you be persuaded": two samples of data-driven learning materials', *ELR Journal*, 4: 1–16, special issue 'Classroom Concordancing', ed. T. Johns and P. King.

Johnson, K. (1995), *Understanding Communication in Second Language Classrooms*, Cambridge: Cambridge University Press.

Jørgensen, J.N. (2008), 'Polylingual languaging around and among children and adolescents', *International Journal of Multilingualism*, 5: 161–76.

Kachru, B. (1985), 'Standards, codification and sociolinguistic realism: the English language in the outer circle', in R. Quirk and H.G. Widdowson (eds), *English in the World: Teaching and Learning the Language and Literatures*, Cambridge: Cambridge University Press, pp. 11–30.

Kachru, B. (ed.) (1992a), *The Other Tongue: English across Cultures*, Champaign: University of Illinois Press.

Kachru, B. (1992b), 'World Englishes: approaches, issues and resources', *Language Teaching*, 25(1): 1–14.

Kachru, B., and C.L. Nelson (2006), *World Englishes in Asian Contexts*, Hong Kong: Hong Kong University Press.

Kachru, B., and L.E. Smith (2008), *Cultures, Contexts and World Englishes*, New York: Routledge.

Kachru, B., Y. Kachru and C.L. Nelson (eds) (2009), *The Handbook of World Englishes*, Chichester: Wiley-Blackwell.

Kasper, G., and K. Rose (2002), *Pragmatic Development in a Second Language*, Oxford: Blackwell.

Kim, H. (2008), 'The semantic and pragmatic analysis of South Korean and Australian English apologetic speech acts', *Journal of Pragmatics*, 40: 257–78.

Kirkpatrick, A. (2007), *World Englishes: Implications for International Communication and English Language Teaching*, Cambridge: Cambridge University Press.

Kirkpatrick, A. (2011), 'Research into language education at the Research Centre for Language Education and Acquisition in Multilingual Societies (RCLEAMS) at the Hong Kong Institute of Education, China', *Language Teaching*, 44(3): 394–8.

Kirkpatrick, A. (2012), 'English as an Asian Lingua Franca: the "Lingua Franca Approach" and implications for language education policy', *Journal of English as a Lingua Franca*, 1(1): 121–39.

Koutlaki, S.A. (2002), 'Offers and expressions of thanks as face enhancing acts: tæ'arof in Persian', *Journal of Pragmatics*, 34: 1733–56.

Kubota, R. (2001), 'Teaching World Englishes to native speakers of English in the USA', *World Englishes*, 21(1): 47–64.

Kubota, R. (2012), 'Awareness of the politics of EIL: toward border-crossing communication in and beyond English', in A. Matsuda (ed.), *Principles and Practices of Teaching English as an International Language*, Bristol: Multilingual Matters, pp. 55–69.

Lakoff, R. (1972), 'Language in context', *Language*, 48: 907–27.

The Lancaster Corpus of Children's Project Writing,http://www.lancs.ac.uk/fass/projects/lever/index.htm (accessed 21 January 2013).

Lave, J., and E. Wenger (1991), *Situated Learning: Legitimate Peripheral Participation*, Cambridge: Cambridge University Press.

Lee, D., http://devoted.to.corpora (accessed 23 January 2013).

Lee, D., and J. Swales (2006), 'A corpus-based EAP course for NNS doctoral students: moving from available specialized corpora to self-compiled corpora', *English for Specific Purposes*, 25: 56–75.

Leech, G. (1983), *Principles of Pragmatics*, London: Longman.

Leech, G. (2005), 'Politeness: is there an east–west divide?', *Journal of Foreign Languages*, 6, http://www.ling.lancs.ac.uk/geoff/leech2006politeness.pdf (accessed 16 June 2007).

Leech, G. (2008), *Language in Literature: Style and Foregrounding*, Harlow: Pearson Longman.

Leung, C., and B. Street (2012), 'Linking EIL and literacy: theory and practice', in L. Alsagoff, S.L. McKay, G. Hu and W. Renandya (eds), *Principles and Practices for Teaching English as an International Language*, New York: Routledge, pp. 3–6.

Liang, X. (2006), 'Identity and language functions: high school Chinese immigrant students' code-switching dilemmas in ESL classes', *Journal of Language, Identity, and Education*, 5(2): 143–67.

Lin, A.M.Y. (1996), 'Bilingualism or linguistic segregation? Symbolic domination, resistance and code switching in Hong Kong schools', *Linguistics and Education*, 8: 49–84.

Lin, A.M.Y. (2008), 'Code-switching in the classroom: research paradigms and approaches', in Nancy H. Hornberger (ed.), *Encyclopedia of Language and Education*, vol. 10, New York: Springer, pp. 273–86.

Lindström, A. (1994), 'Identification and recognition in Swedish telephone conversation openings', *Language in Society*, 23: 231–52.

Liu, D. (2008), 'Linking adverbials: an across-register corpus study and its implications', *International Journal of Corpus Linguistics*, 13(4): 491–518.

Locher, M.A., and R.J. Watts (2008), 'Politeness theory and relational work', *Journal of Politeness Research*, 1(1): 9–33.

Macaro, E. (2001), 'Analysing teachers' codeswitching in foreign language classrooms', *The Modern Language Journal*, 85(4): 531–48.

Mair, C. (ed.) (2003), *The Politics of English as a World Language*, Amsterdam: Rodopi.

Martin, P.W. (2003), 'Interactions and inter-relationships around text: practices and positionings in a multilingual classroom in Brunei', *International Journal of Bilingual Education and Bilingualism*, 6(3/4): 185–201.

Martin-Jones, M., and M. Saxena (2003), 'Bilingual resources and "funds of knowledge" for teaching and learning in multi-ethnic classrooms in Britain', *International Journal of Bilingual Education and Bilingualism*, 6(3/4): 267–82.

Matsuda, A. (2002), 'Representation of users and uses of English in beginning Japanese textbooks', *JALT Journal*, 24(2): 182–200.

Matsuda, A. (2003), 'Incorporating World Englishes in teaching English as an international language', *TESOL Quarterly*, 37(4): 719–29.

Matsuda, A. (2012), *Principles and Practices of Teaching English as an International Language*, Bristol: Multilingual Matters.

Mauranen, A. (2003), 'The corpus of English as lingua franca in academic settings', *TESOL Quarterly*, 37(3): 513–27.

McArthur, T. (1987), 'The English languages?', *English Today*, 11(3): 12–13.

McArthur, T. (1998), *The English Languages*, Cambridge: Cambridge University Press.

McCarthy, M. (1991), *Discourse Analysis for Language Teachers*, Cambridge: Cambridge University Press.

McCarthy, M. (2003), '"Talking back": small interactional response tokens in everyday conversation', *Research on Language and Social Interaction*, 36(1): 33–63.

McCarthy, M., J. McCarten and H. Sandiford (2005), *Touchstone 1–4: From Corpus to Course Book*, Cambridge: Cambridge University Press.

McEnery, T., and A. Wilson (1996), *Corpus Linguistics*, Edinburgh: Edinburgh University Press.

McEnery, T., R. Xiao and Y. Tono (2006), *Corpus-based Language Studies: An Advanced Resource Book*, London and New York: Routledge.

McKay, S.L. (2002), *Teaching English as an International Language: Rethinking Goals and Approaches*, Oxford: Oxford University Press.

Meierkord, C. (1996), *Englisch als Medium der interkulturellen Kommunikation. Untersuchungen zum non-native-/non-native speaker – Diskurs*, Frankfurt am Main: Lang.

Mey, J. (1994), *Pragmatics. An Introduction*, Oxford: Blackwell.

The Michigan Corpus of Academic Spoken English (MICASE),http://micase.elicorpora.info/ (accessed 21 January 2013).

Mills, S. (2003), *Gender and Politeness*, Cambridge: Cambridge University Press.

Modiano, M. (1999a), 'International English in the global village', *English Today*, 15(2): 22–34.

Modiano, M. (1999b), 'Standard English(es) and educational practices for the world's lingua franca', *English Today*, 15(4): 3–13.

Modiano, M. (2009), 'EIL, native-speakerism and the failure of European ELT', in F. Sharifian (ed.), *English as an International Language: Perspectives and Pedagogical Issues*, Bristol: Multilingual Matters, pp. 58–77.

MonoConc Pro (2000), http://www.athel.com/mono.html (accessed 24 January 2013).

Moussu, L., and E. Llurda (2008), 'Non-native English-speaking English language teachers: history and research', *Language Teaching*, 41(3): 315–48.

Mufwene, S. (2001), *The Ecology of Language Evolution*, Cambridge: Cambridge University Press.

Mufwene, S., J.R. Rickford, G. Bailey and J. Baugh (1998), *African-American English: Structure, History and Use*, London: Routledge.

Mullany, L. (2011), 'Im/politeness, rapport management and workplace culture: truckers performing masculinities on Canadian ice-roads', in F. Bargiela-Chiappini and D. Kádár (eds), *Politeness across Cultures*, Basingstoke: Palgrave Macmillan.

Mullany, L., and P. Stockwell (2010), *Introducing English Language: A Resource Book for Students*, Oxford: Routledge.

Murphy, B. (2009), '"She's a fucking ticket": the pragmatics of FUCK in Irish English – an age and gender perspective', *Corpora*, 4(1): 85–106.

Muysken, P. (2000), *Bilingual Speech: A Typology of Code-Mixing*, Cambridge: Cambridge University Press.

Nunn, R. (2003), 'Intercultural communication and Grice's Principle', *Asian EFL Journal*, 5(1), http://asian-efl-journal.com/journal-2003/ (accessed 14 July 2014).

Nvivo, http://www.qsrinternational.com/products_nvivo.aspx (accessed 5 December 2012).

Ochs, E., E.A. Schegloff and S.A. Thompson (1996), *Interaction and Grammar*, Cambridge: Cambridge University Press.

O'Driscoll, J. (2007), 'Brown and Levinsons' face – how it can and can't help us to understand interaction across cultures', *Intercultural Pragmatics*, 4(4): 463–92.

O'Keeffe, A., B. Clancy and S. Adolphs (2011), *Introducing Pragmatics in Use*, London: Routledge.

O'Keeffe, A., M. McCarthy and R. Carter (2007), *From Corpus to Classroom: Language Use and Language Teaching*, Cambridge: Cambridge University Press.

Online concordance, http://corpus.byu.edu/bnc/ (accessed 21 January 2013).

The Oxford Text Archive, http://ota.ahds.ac.uk (accessed 21 January 2013).

Paltridge, B. (2012), *Discourse Analysis*, London: Bloomsbury Academic.

Pennycook, A. (1998), *English and the Discourses of Colonialism*, London: Routledge.

Pennycook, A. (2001), *Critical Applied Linguistics: A Critical Introduction*, Mahwah, NJ: Lawrence Erlbaum Associates.

Pennycook, A. (2009), 'Plurilithic Englishes: towards a 3D model', in K. Murata and J. Jenkins (eds), *Global Englishes in Asian Contexts: Current and Future Debates*, Basingstoke: Palgrave Macmillan, pp. 194–207.

Phillipson, R. (1992), *Linguistic Imperialism*, Oxford: Oxford University Press.

Phillipson, R. (2002), 'Global English and local language policies', in A. Kirkpatrick (ed.), *Englishes in Asia: Communication, Identity, Power and Education*, Melbourne: Language Australia, pp. 7–28.

Phillipson, R. (2003), 'Point-counterpoint: "World English" or "World Englishes"? On negating polyphony and multicanonicity of Englishes. Perspective 2. Review of Brutt-Griffler: *World English: A study of its development*', *World Englishes*, 22(3): 324–6.

Phillipson, R. (2008), 'Lingua franca or lingua frankensteinia? English in European integration and globalization', *World Englishes*, 27(2): 250–67.

Phillipson, R. (2009a), 'Disciplines of English and disciplining by English', *The Asian EFL Journal Quarterly*, 11(4): 8–28.

Phillipson, R. (2009b), 'The tension between linguistic diversity and dominant English', in A. Mohanty, M. Panda, R. Phillipson and T. Skutnabb-Kangas (eds), *Social Justice through Multilingual Education*, Bristol: Multilingual Matters, pp. 85–102.

Prodromou, L. (2006), 'A reader responds to J. Jenkins's "Current perspectives on Teaching World Englishes and English as a Lingua Franca"', *TESOL Quarterly*, 41(2): 409–13.

Quirk, R., S. Greenbaum, G. Leech and J. Svartvik (1985), *A Comprehensive Grammar of the English Language*, London: Longman.

Rashka, C., P. Sercombe and H. Chi-Ling (2009), 'Conflicts and tensions in codeswitching in a Taiwanese EFL classroom', *International Journal of Bilingual Education and Bilingualism*, 12(2): 157–71.

Reppen, R. (2009), 'Internet and corpus-based English instruction', presentation at the ETAROC 18th International Symposium, Taiwan, http://doflal.niu.edu.tw/download. php?filename=210_378c496f.docanddir=newsandtitle=%E6%BC%94%E8%AC%9B%E8% AD%B0%E7%A8%8B (accessed 13 November 2012).

Reppen, R. (2010), *Using Corpora in the Language Classroom*, Cambridge: Cambridge University Press.

Richards, J.C. (2001), *Curriculum Development in Language Education*, Cambridge: Cambridge University Press.

Ronald, J., C. Rinnert, K. Fordyce and T. Knight (2012), *Pragtivities: Bringing Pragmatics to Second Language Classrooms*, Tokyo: JALT Pragmatics SIG.

Rowling, J.K. (1997), *Harry Potter and the Philosopher's Stone*, London: Bloomsbury.

Ruiz, R. (1984), 'Orientations in language planning', *NABE Journal*, 8: 15–34.

Sacks, H. (1992), *Lectures on Conversation, Volumes I and II*, Oxford: Blackwell.

Sailaja, P. (2009), *Indian English*, Edinburgh: Edinburgh University Press.

Sara, http://sara.natcorp.ox.ac.uk/lookup.html accessed 21 January 2013).

Saraceni, M. (2008), 'English as a lingua franca: between form and function', *English Today*, 24(2): 20–6.

Saxena, M., and T. Omoniyi (2010), *Contending with Globalization in World Englishes*, Bristol: Multilingual Matters.

Schauer, G. (2009), *Interlanguage Pragmatic Development: The Study Abroad Context*, London: Continuum

Schegloff, E.A. (1972), 'Sequencing in conversational openings', in J. Gumperz and D. Hymes (eds), *Directions in Sociolinguistics: The Ethnography of Communication*, New York: Holt, Rinehart and Winston, pp. 346–80.

Schneider, K. (2012), 'Appropriate behaviour across varieties of English', *Journal of Pragmatics*, 44: 1022–37.

Schulz, R. (2008), 'Focus on form in the foreign language classroom: students' and teachers' views on error correction and the role of grammar', *Foreign Language Annals*, 29(3): 343–64.

The Scottish Corpus of Texts and Speech (SCOTS Project), http://www.scottishcorpus.ac.uk/ (accessed 21 June 2014).

Searle, J. (1969), *Speech Acts*, Cambridge: Cambridge University Press.

Searle, J. (1976), 'A classification of illocutionary acts', *Language in Society*, 5: 1–23.

Seedhouse, P. (2004), *The Interactional Architecture of the Language Classroom*, Oxford: Blackwell.

Seidlhofer, B. (2001), 'Closing a conceptual gap: the case for a description of English as a lingua franca', *International Journal of Applied Linguistics*, 11: 133–58.

Seidlhofer, B. (2003), *Controversies in Applied Linguistics*, Oxford: Oxford University Press.

Seidlhofer, B. (2004), 'Research perspectives on teaching English as a lingua franca', *Annual Review of Applied Linguistics*, 24: 209–39.

Seidlhofer, B. (2007), 'English as a lingua franca and communities of practice', in S. Volk-Birke and J. Lippert (eds), *Anglistentag 2006 Halle Proceedings*, Trier: Wissenschaftlicher Verlag Trier, pp. 307–18.

Seidlhofer, B. (2009), 'Common ground and different realities: world Englishes and English as a lingua franca', *World Englishes*, 28(2): 236–45.

Seidlhofer, B. (2011), *Understanding English as a Lingua Franca*, Oxford: Oxford University Press.

Sharifian, F. (ed.) (2009), *English as an International Language: Perspectives and Pedagogical Issues*, Bristol: Multilingual Matters

Sifakis, N., and A. Sougari (2003), 'Facing the globalisation challenge in the realm of English Language Teaching', *Language and Education*, 17(1): 59–71.

Sifianou, M. (2011), 'On the concept of face and politeness', in F. Bargiela-Chiappini and D. Kádár (eds), *Politeness across Cultures*, Basingstoke: Palgrave Macmillan, pp. 42–58.

Sinclair. J. (2004), *How to Use Corpora in Language Teaching*, London: Continuum.

Sinclair, J., and M. Coulthard (1975), *Towards an Analysis of Discourse*, Oxford: Oxford University Press.

Soars, J., and L. Soars (1986), *Headway Intermediate Student's Book*, Oxford: Oxford University Press.

Sowden, C. (2012), 'ELF on a mushroom: the overnight growth in English as a Lingua Franca', *ELT Journal*, 66(1): 89–96.

Spada, N. (2011), 'Beyond form-focused instruction: reflections on past, present and future research', *Language Teaching*, 44(2): 225–36.

Spada, N., and Y. Tomita (2010), 'Interactions between type of instruction and type of language feature: a meta-analysis', *Language Learning*, 60: 263–308.

The Speech Accent Archive, http://accent.gmu.edu/ (accessed 14 June 2012).

Speechware, http://www.speechware.be/ (accessed 23 January 2013).

Spencer-Oatey, H. (2000), *Culturally Speaking: Culture, Communication and Politeness Theory*, London: Continuum.

Spencer-Oatey, H. (2008), 'Introduction', in H. Spencer-Oatey (ed.), *Culturally Speaking: Culture, Communication and Politeness Theory*, 2nd edn, London: Continuum.

Sperber, D., and D. Wilson (1986), *Relevance: Communication and Cognition*, Cambridge, MA: MIT Press.

Strevens, P. (1980), *Teaching English as an International Language*, Oxford: Pergamon.

Stubbs, M. (1983), *Discourse Analysis*, Oxford: Blackwell.

Swales, J. (2004), *Research Genres: Exploration and Applications*, Cambridge: Cambridge University Press.

Taguchi, N. (2012), *Context, Individual Differences and Pragmatic Competence*, Bristol: Multilingual Matters.

Takahashi, S. (2001), 'The role of input enhancement in developing pragmatic competence', in K. Rose and G. Kasper (eds), *Pragmatics in Language Teaching*, Cambridge: Cambridge University Press.

Tanaka, K. (1997), 'Developing pragmatic competence: a learners-as-researchers approach', *TESOL Journal*, 6(3): 14–18.

Tanaka, N., H. Spencer-Oatey and E. Cray (2008), 'Apologies in Japanese and English', in H. Spencer-Oatey (ed.), *Culturally Speaking: Culture, Communication and Politeness Theory*, London: Continuum.

Terkourafi, M. (2008), 'Toward a unified theory of politeness, impoliteness, and rudeness', in D. Bousfield and M. Locher (eds), *Impoliteness in Language: Studies on its Interplay with Power in Theory and Practice*, Berlin: Mouton de Gruyter, pp. 45–74.

Text World, http://textworld.com/ (accessed 21 January 2013).

Thomas, J. (1983), 'Cross-cultural pragmatic failure', *Applied Linguistics*, 4: 91–112.

Thomas, J. (1995), *Meaning in Interaction*, London: Longman.

Tono, Y. (2008), 'TaLC in action: recent innovations in corpus-based English Language Teaching in Japan', presentation at the 8th Teaching & Language Corpora Conference, Lisbon, Portugal, 3–6 July.

Transana, http://www.transana.org/ (accessed 19 January 2013).

Tsui, A. (1994), *English Conversation*, Oxford: Oxford University Press.

Ukosakul, M., (2005), 'The significance of "face" and politeness in social interaction as revealed through Thai "face" idioms', in R.T. Lakoff and S. Ide (eds), *Broadening the Horizon of Linguistic Politeness*, Amsterdam: John Benjamins, pp. 117–25.

Üstünel, E., and P. Seedhouse (2005), 'Why that, in that language, right now? Code-switching and pedagogical focus', *International Journal of Applied Linguistics*, 15(3): 302–25.

The Vienna–Oxford International Corpus of English (VOICE), http://www.univie.ac.at/voice/ accessed 14 February 2013).

Waldvogel, J. (2005), 'The role, status and style of workplace email: a study of two New Zealand workplaces', unpublished doctoral dissertation, School of Linguistics and Applied Language Studies, Victoria University of Wellington, New Zealand.

Waldvogel, J. (2007), 'Greetings and closings in workplace e-mail', *Journal of Computer-Mediated Communication*, 12: 456–77.

Walsh, S. (2006), *Investigating Classroom Discourse*, London: Routledge.

Walsh, S. (2011), *Exploring Classroom Discourse*, London: Routledge.

Watts, R. (2003), *Politeness*, Cambridge: Cambridge University Press.

Watts, R. (2005), 'Linguistic politeness research: Quo vadis?', in R. Watts, S. Ide and K. Ehlich (eds), *Politeness in Language: Studies in its History, Theory and Practice*, 2nd edn, Berlin: Mouton de Gruyter.

Webcorp, http://www.webcorp.org.uk (accessed 13 January 2013).

Wei, L. (ed.) (2000), *The Bilingualism Reader*, London and New York: Routledge.

Wei, L., and L. Milroy (1995), 'Conversational code-switching in a Chinese community in Britain: a sequential analysis', *Journal of Pragmatics*, 23(3): 281–99.

Wenger, E. (1998), *Communities of Practice: Learning, Meaning, and Identity*, Cambridge: Cambridge University Press.

Widdowson, H. (1994), 'The ownership of English', *TESOL Quarterly*, 28(2): 377–89.

Widdowson, H. (1997), 'EIL, ESL and EFL: global issues and local interests', *World Englishes*, 16(1): 135–46.

Wierzbicka, A. (2003), *Cross-cultural Pragmatics: The Semantics of Human Interaction*, 2nd edn, Berlin: Mouton de Gruyter.

Wilson, D., and D. Sperber (2004), 'Relevance theory', in L.R. Horn and G. Ward (eds), *The Handbook of Pragmatics*, Oxford: Blackwell, pp. 607–32.

WMatrix (2007), http://ucrel.lancs.ac.uk/wmatrix/ (accessed 21 October 2012).

WordSmith (2004), http://www.lexically.net/downloads/version4/ (accessed 21 October 2012).

Yano, Y. (2001), 'World Englishes in 2000 and beyond', *World Englishes*, 20(2): 119–31.

Yano, Y. (2009), 'The future of English: beyond the Kachruvian Three Circle Model?', in K. Murata and J. Jenkins (eds), *Global Englishes in Asian Contexts: Current and Future Debates*, Basingstoke: Palgrave Macmillan, pp. 208–25.

Ylänne, V. (2008), 'Communication accommodation theory', in H. Spencer-Oatey (ed.), *Culturally Speaking: Culture, Communication and Politeness Theory*, 2nd edn, London: Continuum, pp. 164–86.

Yule, G. (1996), *Pragmatics*, Oxford: Oxford University Press.

Žegarac, V., and M. Pennington (2008), 'Pragmatic Transfer', in H. Spencer-Oatey (ed.), *Culturally Speaking: Culture, Communication and Politeness Theory*, 2nd edn, London: Continuum.

INDEX

bold = glossary definition; *t* = table; *f* = figure

Printed and bound by CPI Group (UK) Ltd, Croydon, CR0 4YY

18/03/2025

01834111-0012